# Sport Coaching with Diverse Populations

Sports coaches apply their skills in a wider variety of contexts, and with a more diverse range of athletes and participants, than ever before. This book introduces the professional competencies and knowledge needed to build successful working relationships across the different communities and groups with which coaches operate.

The book offers important insight for coaches who work with specific populations including different age groups; black, Asian and minority ethnic (BAME) people; those of different gender or sexual orientation; individuals with disabilities or illness; the socio-economically disadvantaged; and refugees. Drawing on real-world case studies, such as coaching girls in combat sports and coaching cardiac rehab patients, and adopting a critical approach to values, philosophy and pedagogic process, this book argues that understanding the recipient of coaching and their particular needs is as important as content knowledge.

With contributions from leading coaching researchers and practitioners, this is important reading for developing coaches, students on sports courses and other individuals involved in the sport pedagogy domain who seek to gain a better understanding of the demands of meeting the specific needs of people in the coaching process.

**James Wallis** is Principal Lecturer in Sport, Coaching and Exercise Science at the University of Brighton, UK, as well as Visiting Lecturer at the German Sports University, Germany. His main teaching and research interests are in the design and delivery of youth sport programmes. He has extensive applied experience in coaching and coach education in performance and sport for development contexts. He has most recently contributed to the development of coaching programmes in professional cricket and Freestyle BMX.

**John Lambert** is First Team Scout at a football club in the English Premier League. He was previously Principal Lecturer in Sport Coaching and Physical Education at the University of Brighton, UK, and Visiting Lecturer at the German Sport University, Germany. He is a UEFA A licence coach and worked for ten years as a coach educator and researcher on a major international sport for development programme.

# Routledge Research in Sports Coaching

The *Routledge Research in Sports Coaching* series provides a platform for leading experts and emerging academics in this important discipline to present ground-breaking work on the history, theory, practice and contemporary issues of sports coaching. The series sets a new benchmark for research in sports coaching, and offers a valuable contribution to the wider sphere of sports studies.

Available in this series:

**Leadership in Sports Coaching**
A social identity approach
*Paul Cummins, Ian O'Boyle and Tony Cassidy*

**Learning to Mentor in Sports Coaching**
A Design Thinking Approach
*Edited by Fiona C. Chambers*

**Care in Sport Coaching**
Pedagogical Cases
*Edited by Colum Cronin and Kathleen Armour*

**Professional Advances in Sport Coaching**
Research and Practice
*Edited by Richard Thelwell and Matt Dicks*

**Athlete Learning in Elite Sport**
A Cultural Framework
*Edited by Natalie Barker-Ruchti*

**Sport Coaching with Diverse Populations**
Theory and Practice
*Edited by James Wallis and John Lambert*

For more information about this series, please visit: https://www.routledge.com/Routledge-Research-in-Sports-Coaching/book-series/RRSC

# Sport Coaching with Diverse Populations
Theory and Practice

Edited by James Wallis and John Lambert

LONDON AND NEW YORK

First published 2021
by Routledge
2 Park Square, Milton Park, Abingdon, Oxon OX14 4RN

and by Routledge
52 Vanderbilt Avenue, New York, NY 10017

*Routledge is an imprint of the Taylor & Francis Group, an informa business*

© 2021 selection and editorial matter, James Wallis and John Lambert; individual chapters, the contributors

The right of James Wallis and John Lambert to be identified as the authors of the editorial material, and of the authors for their individual chapters, has been asserted in accordance with sections 77 and 78 of the Copyright, Designs and Patents Act 1988.

All rights reserved. No part of this book may be reprinted or reproduced or utilised in any form or by any electronic, mechanical, or other means, now known or hereafter invented, including photocopying and recording, or in any information storage or retrieval system, without permission in writing from the publishers.

*Trademark notice*: Product or corporate names may be trademarks or registered trademarks, and are used only for identification and explanation without intent to infringe.

*British Library Cataloguing-in-Publication Data*
A catalogue record for this book is available from the British Library

*Library of Congress Cataloging-in-Publication Data*
A catalog record has been requested for this book

ISBN: 978-0-367-42746-7 (hbk)
ISBN: 978-0-367-85479-9 (ebk)

Typeset in Goudy
by Deanta Global Publishing Services, Chennai, India

# Contents

| | |
|---|---|
| *List of figures* | vii |
| *List of tables* | viii |
| *List of contributors* | ix |
| *Acknowledgements* | xi |
| | |
| **Introduction**<br>JAMES WALLIS | 1 |
| | |
| 1  **Coaching for youth performance: Challenging tradition through understanding and applying non-linear approaches to skill development**<br>JAMES WALLIS AND TIM VAN NOORT | 5 |
| | |
| 2  **Coaching children and youth: Building physical foundations**<br>FLORIS PIETZSCH AND JAMES WALLIS | 24 |
| | |
| 3  **Understanding the sport values of young people and recognising the implications for their coaches: Sport for kids not kids for sport**<br>JOHN LAMBERT | 38 |
| | |
| 4  **Coaching female combat athletes: Creating positive environments for women and girls**<br>CATHERINE PHIPPS, ANASTASIA KHOMUTOVA AND ALEX CHANNON | 47 |
| | |
| 5  **Sport coaching in a disadvantaged community: A case study of Freestyle BMX**<br>BEN GOULD AND CARLOTTA GIUSSANI | 60 |
| | |
| 6  **A structural shift in voluntary work with refugees: A case study of sports clubs in Germany**<br>SEBASTIAN BRAUN, KATRIN ALBERT, MAREIKE ALSCHER AND STEFAN HANSEN | 72 |

vi  *Contents*

7  **The importance of sport in engaging refugees: 'It's only a game?'**     85
MARK DOIDGE

8  **Addressing the under-representation of BAME coaches:
An examination of the EFL mandatory code of coach
recruitment in professional football club youth academies**     100
STEVEN BRADBURY AND DOMINIC CONRICODE

9  **Coaching and teaching LGBT youth**     113
GILLIAN TEIDEMAN AND GRAHAM SPACEY

10  **Disability sport coaching: 'You just coach the athlete not the
disability'**     131
CHRIS CUSHION, TABO HUNTLEY AND ROBERT TOWNSEND

11  **Coaching athletes with intellectual disabilities: Same thing
but different?**     142
NATALIE J. CAMPBELL AND JON STONEBRIDGE

12  **The role of physical activity in cancer rehabilitation**     160
LOUISA BEALE AND JAN SHEWARD

13  **Decreasing the fear of falling in older adults: The use of
Adapted Utilitarian Judo**     175
ÓSCAR DEL CASTILLO ANDRÉS, LUIS TORONJO HORNILLO,
MARÍA TERESA TORONJO HORNILLO AND MARÍA DEL CARMEN CAMPOS MESA

14  **Physical activity and ageing: Keep moving!**     187
PETER WATT AND JANUS GUDLAUGSSON

**Concluding thoughts and future considerations**     201
JAMES WALLIS AND JOHN LAMBERT

*Index*     209

# Figures

| | | |
|---|---|---:|
| 1.1 | The Rainbow Coaching System two-dimensional pitch map | 12 |
| 3.1 | The relative importance of values in youth sport. *Source: Adapted from Whitehead, 2011* | 42 |
| 9.1 | Students' perceptions of homophobic name-calling among peers, adapted from Athanases and Comar (2008, p. 20) | 126 |
| 12.1 | Key stages of the cancer care pathway where physical activity has potential benefit (adapted from Stevinson et al., 2017) | 162 |
| 12.2 | Impact of physical activity on dimensions of quality of life in cancer survivors (adapted from Burke et al., 2017) | 163 |
| 13.1 | Typology of the falls | 178 |
| 13.2 | Consequences of the falls | 178 |
| 13.3 | Scores obtained in the FES-I before and after the intervention according to levels of fear of falling | 182 |
| 14.1 | Range of outcomes of an intervention program, including both the behaviour of being physically active and more physiologic outcomes | 192 |
| 14.2 | Behaviour performance, adapted from Bandura (2004) | 193 |

# Tables

| | | |
|---|---|---|
| 2.1 | Summary recommendations | 33 |
| 3.1 | Frequency of spontaneous expression of sport values | 40 |
| 12.1 | CU Fitter™ programme exclusion criteria | 169 |
| 13.1 | Description of the sample according to fall history and incidents | 177 |
| 13.2 | Structure and contents of the Adapted Utilitarian Judo lessons | 179 |
| 13.3 | FEES-I pre-post intervention scores and values by variables analysed and complete group | 181 |

# Contributors

**Katrin Albert** – Research associate at the Department of Sport Science, Humboldt-Universität zu Berlin, Germany

**Mareike Alscher** – Associate researcher Maecenata Institute, Berlin, Germany

**Louisa Beale** – Principal Lecturer in Sport and Exercise Science, University of Brighton, UK

**Steven Bradbury** – Lecturer in Sport, Equality and Diversity, School of Sport, Exercise and Health Sciences, Loughborough University, UK

**Sebastian Braun** – Professor for Sport Sociology, Department of Sport Science at the Humboldt-Universität zu Berlin, Germany

**Natalie Campbell** – Senior Lecturer in Sport & Exercise Sciences, University of Gloucestershire, UK

**María del Carmen Campos Mesa** – Full-Time Professor, Department of Physical Education and Sports, University of Seville, Spain

**Óscar del Castillo Andrés** – Full-Time Professor, Department of Physical Education and Sports, University of Seville, Spain

**Alex Channon** – Senior Lecturer in Physical Education and Sport Studies, University of Brighton, UK

**Dominic Conricode** – Doctoral Researcher, School of Sport, Exercise and Health Sciences, Loughborough University, UK

**Chris Cushion** – Professor of Coaching and Pedagogy, School of Sport, Exercise and Health Sciences, Loughborough University, UK

**Mark Doidge** – Senior Research Fellow, University of Brighton, UK

**Carlotta Giussani** – International Sport Consultant, Europe

**Ben Gould** – Senior Lecturer in Education, University of Brighton, UK

**Janus Gudlaugsson** – Sport and Health Scientist, Iceland

x  *Contributors*

**Stefan Hansen** – Research associate at the Department of Sport Science, Humboldt-Universität zu Berlin, Germany

**Tabo Huntley** – Senior Lecturer in Sport Coaching, Liverpool John Moores University, UK

**Anastasiya Khomutova** – Senior Lecturer in Physical Education and Sport Studies, University of Brighton, UK

**Catherine Phipps** – Lecturer in Sport Education and Development, Solent University, UK

**Floris Pietzsch** – Senior Lecturer in Sport, Coaching and Exercise Science, University of Brighton, UK

**Jan Sheward** – Founder and trustee of Cancer United, UK

**Graham Spacey** – Consultant in Sport for Development and Peace, inFocus Consultancy and Olympic Study Centre, University of Johannesburg

**Jon Stonebridge** – Round the World Challenge Project Manager, The Royal Mencap Society, UK and Loughborough Special Olympics basketball coach, UK

**Gillian Teideman** – Principal Lecturer in Physical Education, University of Brighton, UK

**Luis Toronjo Hornillo** – Member of the Physical Education, health and sport research group, University of Seville, Spain

**María Teresa Toronjo Hornillo** – Education Scientific Commissioner, European Judo Union

**Robert Townsend** – Lecturer in Sport Coaching and Pedagogy, University of Waikato, New Zealand

**Tim van Noort** – Professional cricket coach, UK

**Peter Watt** – Associate Professor, University of Brighton, UK

# Acknowledgements

To Dr Jean Whitehead, who encouraged, inspired and mentored me in the early years of my academic career. She has been, and remains, a true critical friend (John).

First, to the contributors for their willingness to provide such rich content able to embody and exemplify the central principles of the book. Second, to all those in the coaching and coach education community who 'get it' and are committed to evolving what we know and what we do (James).

# Introduction

*James Wallis*

There are three compelling reasons why this book was conceived. First, our experience has shown us that many coaches struggle to recognise the diversity of the groups with which they work and therefore fail to adapt their coaching according to the needs of the recipients. Coaches commonly use words such as athlete-centred, holistic or age-appropriate as part of their vernacular but are rarely given practical guidance on how these concepts are realised or brought to life. Second, there is an ongoing frustration that 'content knowledge' continues to dominate coach education content, its prioritisation based on the misguided belief that coaching proficiency is dependent on knowledge of the sport above all else. Our third motivation was based on our awareness of increasing numbers of coaches, coach educators and academics who excel in their work within specific contexts, with specific populations, creating fertile environments and overcoming diverse challenges to enhance engagement, learning or performance. We have assembled a selection of these expert practitioners to author chapters offering an insight into their work. In *Becoming a Sports Coach* (Wallis and Lambert, 2016), we wanted to highlight the three questions of 'why, how and what' of coaching. The objective of this book is to support the growing awareness of 'who' in the work of coaches.

In addition, this book aims to:

- Support coaches working with diverse populations and in a wide range of contexts
- Provide theoretical underpinning and applied examples of specific contexts through case studies
- Accentuate a need for coaches to recognise the importance of acquiring knowledge of their context and of their participants
- Challenge coaches to be reflective within and upon their work by reviewing their practice relative to the specific needs and aspirations of their participants

### New landscape, new knowledge?

The prioritisation of content or sports knowledge in traditional coach education pathways has been well reported. Coach education programmes traditionally

## 2 James Wallis

have shown scant regard for the need to adapt practice according to the context within which they work There has been a gradual evolution in the sports coaching world which has seen it begin to encompass broad discussion of pedagogic process as well as piece-meal inclusion of the demands of coaching contexts and populations. It is clear that the sports coaching landscape is changing dramatically. Not only is coaching increasingly a point of focus for academic research, but also there has been a transformation in the nature of the coaching workforce. It is the continued drive towards professionalisation and its implications for coach knowledge that is arguably catalysing most significant change. Most recently, in the United Kingdom, the Chartered Institute for the Management of Sport and Physical Activity (CIMSPA) released its first sets of professional standards within the sport and physical activity sector. Included in this are sets of standards for a coach, a coaching assistant, coaching in high-performance sport, a strength and conditioning trainer and a graduate strength and conditioning coach. Specific competencies relating to the knowledge and skills of coaching specific populations are explicitly highlighted within each standard. In addition, there are 'population specialism' standards for practitioners aspiring to work with children of differing ages, people with long-term conditions, inactive people or antenatal and postnatal clients. Each specialism highlights awareness of the need for a stronger emphasis on participant knowledge in coach education, accreditation and development. In part, this evolved position has emerged from a definition of coaching set out by Sport England in the Coaching Plan for England 2017–2021 as:

> Improving a person's experience of sport and physical activity by providing specialised support and guidance aligned to individual needs and aspirations. (Sport England, 2016: p. 4)

When aligning these more recent industry-led, vocational influences on the demands and expectations of contemporary coaching and coach education, it is also useful to be reminded of the position of leading academics on what constitutes effective or expert coaching practice. Cote and Gilbert's integrative definition of coaching effectiveness makes explicit reference to person and context:

> professional, interpersonal and intrapersonal knowledge to improve athletes' competence, confidence, connection and character in specific coaching contexts. (2009, p. 316)

Whilst recognising that not all who we coach are athletes or wish to be treated as athletes, this definition captures the multi-faceted demands on coaches, as well as the obligations on coach educators.

Diverse populations have also been an increasing point of focus in the sports research and scholarly communities. Individual populations have been the subject of texts that, like this book, aim to increase knowledge, highlight good practice and inspire reflective thought. In their *Handbook of Youth Sport* (2016,

p. 1), Green and Smith talk of a growth of interest in youth sport in 'fields' such as education, health, sport development and policy, as well as in 'disciplines' such as sociology, psychology and medicine. Youth sport is comparatively well served in the scholarly world.

A second appropriate example is that of Kohe and Peters' *High Performance Disability Sport Coaching* (2017), a text which draws together a very impressive range of authors and examples of varied practice in the field. Within this text, the editors refer to the work of Martin and Whelan (2014) on 'Effective Practices of Coaching Disability Sport.' In this review, the authors raise numerous themes pertinent to effective practice in disability sport coaching, some of which are unique and relative within disability sport, but some of which could be extended to all coaching regardless of population or context. For example, the lack of specific coach education, the tension that exists when the coach puts the sport before the person, learning population-specific skills 'on the hoof' and nurturing a strong coach–athlete relationship. The world of 'disability sport' itself is difficult to define and set parameters for, indeed some would prefer to ignore the difference between 'able and 'disabled' and instead view all sports participants on a 'continuum of difference' (Howe, 2017). The domain has drawn scholarly attention which has subsequently boosted understanding and awareness.

The purpose of citing these two examples is to highlight the increasing awareness of diversity in sports coaching and the continued need to cater to specific needs, interests and aspirations. As seen here, texts aligned to specific populations have emerged in recent years which signpost coaches to enhanced knowledge on how to maximise their effectiveness. In-depth knowledge of participants is required and should be seen on at least an equal footing with the more traditional content knowledge often prioritised by coaches. The distinctiveness of this book, however, is the provision of academic and applied case studies across a wide range of populations, providing the reader with initial insight and support from which to base further, more focused research.

## The organisation of the book

A new coaching landscape requires a new view of the knowledge required for coaches and coach educators to recognise and enhance the advancing the status, esteem and role of coaching. More importantly, coaches require knowledge that will provide positive impacts on all participants regardless of individual needs or circumstance. It is some of the uniqueness of diverse groups that this book attempts to highlight.

This book attempts to highlight current thinking and practice across a diverse range of populations. Each chapter follows a common thread by drawing together academics and practitioners to communicate their specialist 'niche' in the ever-widening landscape of sports coaching. Chapters include reference to key theoretical positions relative to specific populations and contexts, before presenting case study examples of impactful practice. It was a logical decision for us to order chapters chronologically, broadly through the life-course. The first three chapters attend to three key, contemporary issues in the coaching of children in sport; the use of non-linear approaches, physical training and a timely review of the sport values held by young people drawing on the seminal work of Martin Lee. With the growing concern for children's long-term retention and health through and within sports, these chapters challenge readers to continue to strive to build positive foundations for lifelong engagement in sport and physical activity. Following on are diverse chapters sharing insights into; women in combat sports, LGBT youth, sports in disadvantaged communities, assimilation of refugees into community settings in the United Kingdom and Germany and an examination of the English Football League's mandatory code for the recruitment of black, Asian and minority ethnic (BAME) coaches.

Two chapters focus on disability coaching. The first is a broad overview of some of the discourses on the social construction of disability in sport and coaching; the second is an insight into coaching athletes with intellectual disability, an area that is one of the least represented in scholarly publications yet very recently beginning to gather greater attention. Chapter 12 is a timely chapter on the efficacy of sport and physical activity for the long-term health and well-being of individuals undergoing or recovering from cancer treatment reflecting a growing interest in that area. Very recent recommendations and ground-breaking practice are discussed through the case study of CU Fitter, a specialist training environment for individuals at different stages of diagnosis, treatment and recovery from cancer. Considering the ageing demographic in all industrialised societies, the final two chapters discuss theory and case study practice in promoting and delivering positive activity habits for elderly populations.

Whilst the uniqueness of each person and each context is a persistent message throughout this book, there are common themes and principles that emerge as applicable across populations and contexts. The book concludes with a summary that highlights consistent themes that run through the book, accentuating the need for coaches to continue to work towards placing the person at the centre of their thinking and practice.

## References

Cote, J., and Gilbert, W. (2009). 'An integrative definition of coaching effectiveness and expertise.' *Journal of Sport Science & Coaching*, 4 (3), 307–323.

Green, K., and Smith, A. (2016). *Routledge handbook of youth sport*. London: Routledge.

Howe, D. (2017). 'Coaching in the flagship paralympic sport.' In: Kohe, G.Z., and Peters, D. M., eds. *High performance disability sport coaching*. London: Routledge.

Kohe, G.Z., and Peters, D.M. (2017). *High performance disability sport coaching*. London: Routledge.

Martin, J., and Whalen, L. (2014). 'Effective practices of coaching disability sport.' *European Journal of Adapted Physical Activity*, 7 (2), 13–23.

Sport England (2016). *Coaching in an active nation: The coaching plan for England 2017–21*. London: Sport England.

Wallis, J., and Lambert, J. (2016). *Becoming a sports coach*. London: Routledge.

# 1 Coaching for youth performance

## Challenging tradition through understanding and applying non-linear approaches to skill development

*James Wallis and Tim van Noort*

## Introduction

Maximising youth sport participation and performance has always been a central concern within the field of sport pedagogy, but in recent years it has assumed increasing importance within the academic domains of skill acquisition, sport psychology, strength and conditioning, physiology and medicine. The first three chapters of this book cover a selection of youth coaching themes that are of current interest in both academic and applied contexts. Whilst this chapter intends to advance coach understanding of the development of sport-specific and game skills, the next chapter will present a detailed analysis of current views and practice in functional physical training of youth performers. The third chapter in the sequence on coaching youth populations offers an overview of previous research into values and motives that can sustain involvement in sport and physical activity.

## Coaching for youth performance

Since the pioneering work of Bunker and Thorpe (1982) on Teaching Games for Understanding (TGfU), there has been greater interest in pedagogic approaches in youth sport that are considered to be more dynamic, open and non-linear. Traditional approaches to developing sport performance in youth populations have tended to prioritise the isolation and targeting of key technical skills through coaching interventions that often divorce the performer from the environment. The aim of this first chapter is to review and then apply some contemporary approaches to the coaching of sport skills in youth populations. The review elaborates on intertwined pedagogic processes that are broadly termed 'non-linear' or 'ecological' approaches, before drawing on some examples of current practice in a youth cricket performance setting in the United Kingdom. The chapter begins with an overview of traditional approaches to the coaching of youth performers, attempting to answer two key questions to assist understanding of the current landscape.

## Traditional approaches to developing youth performance

### *Where do they come from?*

It is difficult to pinpoint the specific evolutionary processes that have informed some of the most enduring traditional beliefs and practices in youth sport coaching. Most current explanations of contemporary practice tend to draw on the framework of occupational socialisation, originally used to explain PE teacher practice (Lawson, 1983, 1986). Mapping the experiences of PE teachers from a trainee, through a newly qualified teacher, to an experienced (socialised) teacher is also a useful trajectory to try to understand the pathways and practice of sport coaches. Lawson proposed three hypotheses that could explain how PE teacher pedagogic choices were shaped by socialisation. Each hypothesis is considered below from the perspective of sport coach education and development.

First, acculturation through personal experiences in sport and PE has been viewed as a significant impacting factor on PE teacher intentions for future practice (Lawson, 1983; Lortie, 1975). New recruits to the teaching profession adopt a custodial approach (Moy et al., 2016) to their work, choosing to re-cycle and re-use the same pedagogies that they experienced themselves, most often based on what they perceive to have 'worked' for them. Further research has contended that unless new recruits are critically challenged on their beliefs, which are based on anecdotes of their own experiences, the impact of training and CPD may be minimal (Curtner-Smith, 2007; Moy et al., 2016). It is suggested here that similar inhibitory beliefs can commonly impact the value of coaching programmes, particularly when considering the coaching behaviours imposed on youth performers. The use of personal biography and emulation of traditional approaches, as opposed to embracing more contemporary, evidence-based pedagogies, is an on-going challenge to the PE profession and one which requires continued effort to address in sport coaching where there is, at best, a 'time-lag' between research findings and applied coaching practice (Farrow et al., 2008; Ford et al., 2010; Ross et al., 2018).

The perception that the label of 'expert' coach must be underpinned by experience as a high-status athlete has been commonly reported across diverse coaching contexts (Erickson, Côté and Fraser-Thomas, 2007; Nash and Sproule, 2009). This perception has become a 'normalised assumption amongst the sporting discourse of many international contexts' (Blackett, Evans and Piggott, 2018, p. 2). The acceleration of former players into senior coaching positions, often in the absence of opportunities to gain experience of alternative pedagogical models, lack of awareness of the centrality of wider knowledge bases aside from sport knowledge (e.g. holistic knowledge of youth performers) and lack of appreciation of the relativism of coaching, is not conducive to the success of youth coaching programmes. This single, expedient linear view of youth coach development may be damaging and does not reflect reality. By contrast, as a coaching career unfolds, it has been seen that the perceived importance or value of a personal sporting career has become less significant for a coach (Nash and Sproule, 2011).

Lawson's second hypothesis of the origin of socialisation in teacher training is based on the structure and content of formalised teacher education programmes. In the coaching domain, formal coach education through National Governing Body accredited awards, or 'badges,' have been the dominant pathway into coaching roles. Running parallel to this convention has been the expansion of diverse university-based degree level programmes. It is not the intention here to

*Coaching for youth performance*   7

debate the relative merits or limitations of either pathway but to encourage readers to critically self-reflect on the dominant perspectives and content received in their coach education experiences. Characteristics of coaching effectiveness and expertise have been difficult to define despite burgeoning academic interest in the field. Côté and Gilbert (2009, p. 316) offer the following definition:

> The consistent application of integrated professional, interpersonal, and intrapersonal knowledge to improve athletes' competence, confidence, connection and character in specific coaching contexts.

For coaches aspiring to achieve 'effective' or 'expert' status, it should be viewed as a requirement to interrogate the relative contributions of their formal coach education pathway to the achievement of each dimension of this definition. For example, contributions to *professional knowledge* should not be exclusive to sport content knowledge (technical, tactical 'drills') but extend to building understanding of the specific needs of participants, their learning preferences and the pedagogic processes that are most likely to enhance retention and performance. Contributions to *interpersonal knowledge* should include a reference to the specific and holistic needs of youth performers as being distinct to adult populations. Contributions should also include a reference to the objectives of the coaching context, whether youth performance, participation, health or the development of positive social behaviour.

Lawson's third and final hypothesis concerns the workplace culture and specific work context of the teacher. In the coaching domain this form of socialisation may occur through pressure exerted to practice in a particular way, adopting certain approaches and through imitation of senior figures. Cushion and Jones (2014, p. 277) present the major function in coaching as 'the imparting of enduring values and an ideology that guides behaviour in accordance with given expectations' resulting in beliefs and practice becoming uncritically accepted into daily routines as part of a 'hidden curriculum' of coaching and coach education. When embedded in a specific context, it is suggested that coaches adopt the prevailing routines, approaches and accepted norms of that context in order to 'fit-in' and to be perceived to be practising 'correctly.' Work by Blackett et al. (2018) investigated the recruitment of rugby and football academy coaches into senior positions. Findings suggested a deliberate approach to recruitment that prioritised the identification of current senior players who currently embodied the club's values. The findings support the contention that socialised practice is considered an asset, even a pre-requisite, to coaching in academy settings where existing values, beliefs and systems could be unquestionably sustained. Traditional conceptions of coaching become strengthened and legitimised by new coaches who conform to contextual norms, which in turn are implicitly communicated to players. This is a cycle that is on-going in sport. Such recruitment processes, whether conscious or subconscious, run the risk of proliferating existing traditions and threaten to limit the evolution of practice, which can keep pace with research, evidence and new approaches in the field of youth sport (Cushion and Jones, 2014).

## What are traditional approaches in youth sport coaching, and what are their limitations?

When adopting a pedagogic approach, it is recommended that coaches understand the underpinning theoretical framework that can account for learning and how it takes place. Moving beyond having the knowledge of *what* to coach is the growing contemporary expectation that coaches will also be able to articulate the *how* and *why* of their coaching decisions (Wallis and Lambert, 2016). A lack of a rationale for the choice of their pedagogical approach may suggest a coach's acceptance of contextual norms in keeping with the principles of socialisation outlined above. Uncritical adoption of coaching practice may inhibit participation and performance. The following four paragraphs communicate some of the most common approaches in youth sport coaching, with their (evidence-based) limitations included.

### Reproductive coaching

The development and popularisation of a Spectrum of Teaching Styles (Mosston, 1966) was an important landmark in the understanding of alternative pedagogic approaches to the teaching of PE and sport. The spectrum is still a popular vehicle in teacher and coach education. Teacher-centred, closed or reproductive modes of delivery, such as command and practice styles, reside on one end of the spectrum affording limited learner decision-making. Moving along the spectrum, modes of delivery become gradually more open, constructive and learner-centred. The coach guides as opposed to controls the shape and direction of the learning environment offering autonomy, freedom and responsibility to the learners. Reproductive or coach-centred coaching styles are still dominant in the practice of teachers and sport coaches despite significant limitations to the enjoyment, motivation and performance of youth performers. Reasons cited for this dominance are most often based on convenience, simplicity and the often tenuous claims of health and safety requirements. The choice of teaching or coaching style should be based on how participants will best learn the objectives assigned to the session; in this way coaching becomes learner-centred as opposed to coach-centred.

### Technocratic coaching

Traditional session structure may flow from a preparation phase (a decontextualised, physical warm-up) before progressing to a technical phase (decontextualised drills with the intention of learning a specific, isolated movement, concept or technique), ending with a game phase (conditioned game which engineers reproduction of practised technique in a 'game' setting.) The technical phase is most often associated with the development of desirable, even required, movement patterns in pursuit of an 'ideal' or 'correct' technique in decontextualised, mechanical and repetitive drill-based settings (Chow et al., 2009). Recognising the limitations of such an ecologically invalid, one-size-fits-all approach is a key first step in bringing sport coaching in line with modern thinking in pedagogic science. Contemporary approaches to coaching reject the existence of single, imposed, 'text-book' movement patterns for sport performance in favour of personalised, exploratory and creative solutions based on some of the non-linear concepts further discussed in this chapter.

### Deliberate practice

The term was first used following on from Ericsson et al.'s proposition that a minimum of 10,000 hours or ten years of directed, purposeful practice was needed for performers to achieve expert performance in their field (Ericson, Krampe and Tesch-Romer, 1993). The original research involved retrospective estimations of the practice hours that contributed to expertise in diverse fields of human performance including concert violinists and master chess players. This theory was further advanced in popular science texts such as Outliers (Gladwell, 2008) and, even more erroneously applied to learning in sport by Syed (2010) where misapplication and popularisation run the risk of unsuitable, dangerous and even unethical practice being adopted by unskilled and under informed personnel. The provision of a simple, linear equation to the achievement of expert performance through high volumes of repetitive and intense practice, which Erickson himself acknowledged as not intrinsically motivating or enjoyable, are at odds with more contemporary thinking on the development of youth sport performance. The deliberate practice 'rule' has been heavily challenged in psychology (Macnamara et al., 2014) and in sport pedagogy domains (Vierimaa, Erickson and Côté, 2016).

### Early specialisation

Most criticisms of the deliberate practice perspective on youth sport development centre around debates on early specialisation. Defined as 'intensive year-round training in a single sport at the exclusion of other sports' (Jayanthi et al., 2013, p. 251), early specialisation demands, early commitment to one sport, focused high-intensity training and early exposure to competitive contexts (Baker et al., 2009).

Traditional approaches to maximising youth performance may have embraced the 'the more, the earlier, the better' philosophy of training based on the questionable belief that high junior performance will lead to high senior performance. One is not reliant upon the other (Brouwers, Bosscher and Sotiriadou, 2012). Indeed evidence has consistently reported maladaptive outcomes to the specialisation approach, which have been shown to expose performers to a significant risk of withdrawal from sport due to injury, burnout or limited progress (Gould et al., 1996; Baker, 2003, Côté and Abernathy, 2012). A higher proportion of time in play-based activities and in performing in other sports, that is a more diversified approach to youth sport development,

10    *James Wallis and Tim van Noort*

are considered more beneficial and supportive to long-term retention in sport and subsequent health and performance. Whilst this section does not intend to undermine the importance of well-designed, balanced and constructive practice, it must be set against a suitable understanding of developmental trajectories of youth performers, balanced with intrinsically motivating play and work within the physical, social and economic constraints of youth performers. The rest of this chapter aims to contribute to the literature in the sport coaching domain, which seeks to support the continued understanding and application of contemporary coaching approaches in youth sport.

## Progressive approaches to developing youth performance

Having presented a traditional picture of how coaches of youth performers have commonly operated, the intention for the remainder of this chapter is to present definition, discussion and application of a selection of coaching processes that may broadly fall under the banners of holistic and non-linear approaches. This section will include theoretical insight into facets of non-linear coaching approaches and will be supplemented by applied examples of practice from one professional cricket context. In bringing theory to life we hope to continue to encourage coaches to challenge the 'what, how and why' of their coaching in order to continue to strive to enhance the impact of their work (Wallis and Lambert, 2016). The examples cited here are a selection of content ideas which have been selected to exemplify specific non-linear processes. Readers are welcome to 'consume' the applied ideas presented here. It is hoped, however, that readers are motivated to employ the theoretical principles presented to 'construct' their own distinctive and creative content. The examples cited may also act as reassurance and legitimacy to some readers who intuitively utilise non-linear methods.

The concept of *holistic coaching* is used here to draw attention to the development of the whole person in coaching interventions where the 'person' is recognised as being comprised of biological, emotional, cognitive and behavioural characteristics (Bronfenbrenner, 1977). Whilst traditional perspectives on youth sport coaching focus on the decontextualised transfer of technical and tactical knowledge, through volumes of repetitive practice, a holistic approach takes a broader, individualised and constructivist approach to the learning of sport skills.

The applicability of non-linear pedagogies in youth sport is of particular importance in youth sport settings due to the nonlinearity of the developing child. Whether from biological, emotional or cognitive perspectives the child-youth maturation process poses significant questions, demands and challenges to youth sport. Knowledge of adolescent motivation theory is often lacking in 'professional' youth sport contexts and in NGB coaching pathways. Whilst there is greater awareness of the severe limitations of using mere chronology in organising and selecting in youth sport, the implications of huge variation in biological maturity, as much as ±2 years at 14 years of age, are rarely understood or considered in youth sport performance settings (Capranica and Millard-Stafford, 2011). In addition, there is a limited understanding of the heightened sensitivity of the young body and brain to more open and divergent coaching approaches. For example, most recent thinking in neuroscience universally accepts the plasticity of the child's brain and the way it is shaped by the environment (Schwartz and Begley, 2002). In response, numerous studies have advocated that creativity should be cultivated in early life, ideally before adolescence, after which brain development slows and is less susceptible to environmental influences (Milgram, 1990; Memmert, 2010). The message to coaches to create open and divergent learning designs through environments, which closely replicate the performance setting, is clear and is addressed in the following section.

The concepts of non-linear pedagogy exemplified in the following sections integrate the whole performer within the training environment as opposed to isolate, separate or 'reduce' the performer and the sport into disaggregated, unrelated entities. They reposition coaching interventions as developing the performer *in* the sport as opposed to imposing the sport *on* the performer.

### Non-linear pedagogy

Non-linear pedagogy is a pedagogical framework through which coaches and teachers can design interventions that more closely represent the complexity of sport by recognising the inter-connectedness and interaction of the learner, the environment and the coach (Chow et al., 2016)[1]. Broadly based on guiding principles of ecological psychology and dynamical systems theory, non-linear pedagogy has the potential to bring together contemporary knowledge from research in motor learning and skill acquisition with the applied needs of teachers and coaches. The separation of 'theory' and 'practice,' or the 'academic' and 'applied' are unhelpful in advancing the effectiveness of coaching for youth performance (Lyle, 2018). Non-linear pedagogy is therefore proposed as a suitable framework within which positive skill development in youth performers can operate, which is built on strong theoretical foundations. In short, it has the potential to bring academic and applied communities together. The following sections outline four selected principles of non-linear pedagogy. Embedded in each section are applied examples from a youth sport setting where non-linear pedagogy is seen as a core philosophy in coach practice.

### The Rainbow Coaching System (RCS)

The RCS is a simple piece of hardware that divides the environment into different coloured zones (see Figure 1.1). Cricket RCS divides a cricket pitch into two planes, namely line and length. Length is the area between the two sets of stumps, the line is based around the three stumps and the space either side. In cricket, the stumps are a consistent focal point, so we use these as the primary reference point. Using the RCS as further reference points, the closest line and length to the stumps are coloured white. The colour sequence that follows is green, red, yellow, blue and orange. Length is split into zones measured in metres from the stumps, whereas the line is split into much smaller zones either side

| O | B | Y | RED | GREEN | WHITE | GREEN | RED | Y | B | O |
|---|---|---|---|---|---|---|---|---|---|---|
|   |   |   | 6 5 4 | 3 2 1 | 0 0 0 | 1 2 3 | 4 5 6 |   |   |   |

| STUMPS | | | | | | | | | | |
|---|---|---|---|---|---|---|---|---|---|---|
| **WHITE** | | | | | | | | | | |
| **GREEN** | | | | | | | | | | |
| **RED** | | | | | | | | | | |
| **YELLOW** | | | | | | | | | | |
| **BLUE** | | | | | | | | | | |
| **ORANGE** | | | | | | | | | | |

*Figure 1.1* The Rainbow Coaching System two-dimensional pitch map.

of the stumps. This provides a two-dimensional cross-reference tool for every delivery; for example 'white/white' is the fullest delivery on the stumps and 'orange/orange' is the shortest widest delivery from the stumps. The environment then offers coaches and players limitless opportunity to work in different zones, which are consistent reference points in relation to the stumps. It is common for cricket coaches to use meaningless jargon such as 'back of a length,' 'good length,' 'full length.' All of these terms change dramatically according to the relative heights of bowler and batter, the age of the ball, the pitch conditions. The RCS provides a consistent reference tool to simplify language and to generate more meaningful and supportive training experiences.

## (Re)connecting the performer and the environment

The connection between performer and environment is a central pillar to ecological, non-linear coaching perspectives where performance is dependent on the affordances of the environment and subsequent responses to the environment (Gibson, 1979). An affordance is a relational property between the performer and their environment where the performer draws information from their surroundings on which to base movement responses. Chow et al. (2016) point out that affordances should not be considered 'entities' but as functional features of the environment, which offer opportunities for action which will also be dependent on an individual's perceptions of personal performance attributes. Affordances therefore possess both objective (such as pace of the ball, nature of the playing surface, position of opponents) and subjective features (such as skill level, strength, speed of performer) (Gibson, 1979). In this way the pairing of the objective and subjective affordances in a sport context interact to produce individualised responses to situations and stimuli. For example, a cricket ball delivered in the 'yellow length' at 60 mph to a 13-year-old cricketer yet to have their growth spurt will have the same objective affordances but different subjective affordances to a post-pubescent 13-year-old facing the same delivery from the same bowler on the same surface. Other subjective affordances in this example may also include reaction time, agility, hand-eye coordination, as well as multiple psycho-social factors such as confidence and previous experience of playing the short ball.

Traditional coaching approaches often rely upon assumptions of simple linear learning theories based broadly on information processing. Such approaches are often behaviourist in nature and attempt to strengthen a bond between stimulus (e.g. a ball and its movement properties) and a single required response (e.g. a cover drive in cricket). Non-linear, ecological approaches reject the existence of a required response but rather a never-ending range of possible variations in response based on the distinct affordances of every novel situation. In other words, it involves a shift from stimulus–response to stimulus–responses. The non-linear position draws on the principle of functional variability in constructing movement solutions where performers are encouraged to adopt subtle differences in responses depending on on-going changes to environmental demands and

14  *James Wallis and Tim van Noort*

their 'new' affordances. For example, a 'green' delivery outside off-stump may give the affordance of hitting a cover drive until changes to the pace of bowler, age of the ball, pitch conditions, fielder positions or match situation require variation in responses. Whilst the same shot may be appropriate, subtle changes to movement sequence to time the ball, or head, foot and wrist position to hit the ball wide of fielders may be more suitable responses than the 'correct' response of hitting a technically perfect text-book cover drive. Similarly, subjective affordances in this example may include fatigue or knowledge of previous performance or increased emotional arousal due to match situation or scoreboard pressure! Far from skilled performers demonstrating highly consistent movement patterns it has been shown that expert performers possess greater variability in movements than less skilled performers (Davids et al., 2006) giving them greater capacity to produce different responses to similar stimuli depending on situation and context, for example playing cricket in the early season, in different continents, or in T20 or longer format matches.

Whilst we do not reject the absolute centrality of technical guidance to success of junior sports performance, we do urge coaches to exercise significant caution in the provision of 'correct' movement response, often 'grooved' in repetitious coaching contexts which divorce the player from the diverse affordances of the performance environment. In cricket batting, for example, there may be two or three non-negotiable technical requirements to elicit success that players must demonstrate, for example hitting from a stable base and moving their head to the ball. Evidence of positive coaching should therefore be viewed as changes to performer ability in perceiving and responding to environmental affordances. The following examples connect youth cricket players with features of the performance environment.

### Applied examples in cricket

*The '6-ball challenge' requires the batter to hit a ball with the same properties of line, length, speed and deviation to six differing field positions, for example 55 mph 'yellows' on off-stump. There are no further constraints on the batter other than finding six movement sequences which connect with the ball. Advancement can come with gradually changing the properties of the ball, starting with adding a further colour for one of the six balls.*

*Clock face is a game which requires the batter to hit as many numbers on the clock face as they can in a set number of deliveries. Deliveries of the same line, length and speed, for example '60 mph away swinging greens,' can be provided in blocks of four before a different delivery is announced to the batter.*

*Three-cone rotation is a game where the batter receives six balls of the same property. After each shot a cone is placed as a virtual fielder to take away that scoring option. The bowler/fielder has three cones to place after the first three shots. After each subsequent shot the cone is moved to close off that scoring zone, thus opening up another scoring zone. The game can be adapted with greater variance in type of delivery and with the number of cones used to represent fielders.*

## Coupling perception and action (information and movement)

Having presented the centrality of opportunities for movement, or *affordances*, it is equally important to appreciate the importance of creating learning environments which develop performer ability to draw on relevant information on which to base movements. The coupling of perception and action (or information and movement) is a reciprocal process where information informs movement which then becomes a further source of information, 'we perceive in order to move, but we must also move in order to perceive' (Gibson, 1979, p. 233). Performers draw sensory information from internal (e.g. proprioceptive, kinaesthetic) and external (e.g. visual, audial) sources where each movement significantly impacts on further information. Ecological approaches to coaching require perception and action to be closely coupled in training environments in order to make training functional and representative. Of particular importance are the means with which coaches are able to support young athletes' perception of key information and subsequent organisation of movement responses through maintaining a high degree of fidelity between sources of information and appropriate responses (Gibson, 1979). It is common to witness research on 'immersive training' environments which utilise uncoupled responses such as verbal, button pressing or touch screen responses to visual information. Whilst their results have often been used to support the anticipatory processes and decision-making in lab-based settings, their value to the natural performance setting is less assured as information is not representative and perception – action couplings are absent (Ranganathan and Carlton, 2007).

The use of ball projection machines, for example 'bowling' machines in cricket, has been criticised as being unrepresentative and not allowing batters to learn to utilise key information from a bowler's action (Muller, Abernathy and Farrow, 2006; Pinder et al., 2011). Drawing on subtle differences in body shape, grip, run-up and point of release is considered crucial in the development of expert performance (Pinder et al., 2011). Indeed evidence has shown that the time required to perceive, prepare and move often exceeds the time available for the ball to travel to the batter (Singer, 2000). This evidence alone is sufficient to cast doubt over the efficacy of using projection machines as they cannot provide the vital anticipatory, pre-release information, which are features of successful performance at higher speeds. Equally limiting is the training of the batter to attune to information that is not a feature of the performance setting that leads to poor perception-action couplings.

Despite these issues, the use of ball projection machines should be maintained as an important constituent part of well-balanced practice designs (Muller and Abernethy, 2012; Pinder et al., 2011). Alongside benefits of reducing the workload of bowlers and the potential to propel a ball with reliable and consistent speed, direction and deviation, well-managed use of ball projection machines permeated with 'live' performance may provide opportunities to benefit from the best of both information sources. Visual information from ball flight alone can be part of viable learning design (Ranganathan and Carlton, 2007; Land and

McLeod, 2000) as visual information from ball flight is the most salient information on display to the batter (Muller and Abernethy, 2012). This may be of particular significance to coaches of junior performers where reducing available sources of information, or honing attention to particular information (in this case ball flight alone) may enhance performance, whilst still observing the centrality of keeping a close couple of information and movements. Simplifying batting by reducing the speed or deviation of the ball, or by providing known information prior to delivery, such as known line or length of the ball may allow batters to attune more exclusively to specific information and the building of functional responses. A further benefit may be batters becoming highly attuned to moving based on ball flight information alone, which is then augmented when information from a live performance is also available. This may be particularly evident for youth performers, where lower speeds are commonly used, and in sports such as cricket, where players need to be highly attuned to ball flight due to deviation of the ball pre- and post contact with the ground. As a result, some of the examples provided below recommend the use of ball projection machines, in unison with live performance. This balance, if information is effectively displayed and highlighted through such suitable practice designs, will enhance batters' ability to attune to properties of both bowler and ball.

### Applied examples in cricket

*At the most basic level, the RCS is a reference tool for batters and bowlers to develop their understanding of length and line. Coupling perception and action according to the information presented from the bowler or feeder and from the flight path of the ball is instrumental in successful batting. From a bowling perspective, being able to plan, execute and evaluate the line and length they are trying to bowl, and are actually bowling, is equally instrumental to successful performance.*

*Batters may start with 'specific rainbow' where they receive a block of deliveries, perhaps as many as 50, that look the same. Most often this will be 'greens' on off-stump at low speed. The batter can attune to the properties of the feed and the flight of the ball. A second block, another 50, will be a very different length, perhaps 'yellow.' The information on display from the feed and ball flight is very different in each block and the batter can be attuned and helped to move accordingly.*

*Laddering is used to move the feed gradually along the rainbow. The batter is now looking for more subtle changes in the information on display. They may receive several balls on one colour before the feed is moved to another 'rung' of the ladder. Input is given to help the batter move in accordance with their own affordances. There is no 'you must move back to a yellow' and 'must come forward to a green.' The batter is finding their own affordances but must demonstrate the two or three non-negotiable technical features of all successful batting.*

*Random rainbow is a more advanced perception-action challenge where deliveries arrive at varying lengths and eventually at random lines, speeds and deviations. The degree of challenge can be set according to the level of the players.*

*Bowlers are at the genesis of every cricket 'moment' and as a result often have less time pressure on their perception-action couplings. The following are examples of the use of the RCS in coaching bowlers to better understand and execute their planned delivery.*

Bowlers pre-plan a colour (length) to bowl and then evaluate the length they actually hit. In this way the bowler is perceiving what ball they wish to deliver and organising their movements to achieve this outcome. Throughout their bowling action they are continuing to draw on perceptions of their body in time and space to elicit 'feel' for their action and the desired delivery. They are then challenged to call the colour they hit and whether it marries up with their intention. In this way bowlers are perceiving-acting-perceiving in trying to execute their plan.

Having built an understanding of length the context can be manipulated to further challenge perception-action processes. For example the intended colour can be dictated by a verbal cue as they pass the umpire in their run-up, or more ecologically valid would be to require the bowler to respond to a colour cue such as a cone being held up by a wicket keeper, or by having the batter moving their stance as the bowler approaches.

A much more advanced perception-action demand on the bowler would be to require them to close their eyes at the point of delivery and a few steps into their follow-through. To hone the perception of 'feel' the bowler can be tested to state the length they 'felt' they bowled.

## Manipulating constraints

The popular constraints-led approach (CLA) to teaching sport skills is an eco-logical coaching approach based on how the performer perceives and responds to their environment. Newell (1986) categorised constraints within three distinct groups as either derived from features of the performer, the environment or the task. Success in sport requires the individual to construct movement responses to unique interactions of constraints; coaching should provide representative training opportunities which manipulate constraints allowing performers to prac-tice functional movement solutions. Central to this approach is the recognition of the individual nature of learning based on each person's unique interactions and perceptions of the environment and the ever-changing, dynamic relation-ship that the performer has with their environment further rendering traditional stimulus–response (behaviourist) approaches as inadequate for the learning of sport skills.

Specific to junior sport settings, performer constraints refer to features or char-acteristics of the performer. This has significant implications for coaches of junior athletes given the rapid and holistic changes in physical, emotional and cognitive

18  *James Wallis and Tim van Noort*

development. For example, with the rapid change to relative limb length or to increases in power, speed or reach junior cricketer may develop different affordances when batting, which enables them to hit over a fielder where previously this would have resulted in being caught out. Similarly, increased height and strength will afford a bowler the opportunity to bowl a shorter delivery (a 'yellow' or a 'blue'). Unique performer constraints change quickly in junior sport due to growth and maturation; hence performers should be encouraged to develop their own methods and solutions to movement problems throughout their adolescent years, as opposed to one 'correct response' as per traditional technocratic coaching would espouse. Coaches must also be sympathetic to dramatic changes to performer constraints and the challenges that junior athletes have in maintaining skill levels during periods of rapid growth.

Environmental constraints derive from physical features of the sport context, as well as social and cultural factors that influence performance. The culture of junior sport environments (as outlined earlier in this chapter), or the philosophical approach of the coach, is a socio-cultural example which may be key constraints to the development of junior performance. Further cultural constraints may be the prioritisation of resources, the historic significance of a sport to a culture and even the political or ideological value placed on success in sport. Environmental constraints may include weather and subsequent heat, light and humidity. Athletes may also need to attune to performing at altitude and the resulting different affordances of projectiles. Further features of the physical environment pertinent to sport coaching may be the playing surface where, for example in cricket, properties of the pitch vary across locations, but can also vary in one batting innings.

Of most applied significance to the everyday planning and interventions of coaches are task constraints. Open to coaches are a myriad of adaptations to task constraints which guide and support performers to find solutions to movement problems. For example, coaches may manipulate size of equipment, pitch sizes, team overloads or game conditions in order to create an environment from which performers can derive information and construct individual responses (Renshaw et al., 2009). Manipulating task constraints changes the affordances open to the performer, their unique relationship with the environment and the possible strategies in achieving the required goal. Varying task constraints encourages players to explore different solutions to changes in the environment generating more diverse and creative solutions. Awareness and skilled use of task, performer and environmental constraints can build highly representative, functional (and fun) session content for junior performers.

### Applied examples in cricket

*The inter-connectedness of the features of non-linear processes is highlighted here in that the examples cited under 'connecting the performer with the environment' and 'perception-action coupling' can also be considered under the broad banner of manipulating constraints. A further example of each type of constraint is outlined below.*

*Coaching for youth performance*  19

*Setting hypothetical field placings and match scenarios are common task constraints, most often used in net practice in the last six deliveries where a set number is required by the batter. At this point both batter and bowler(s) inject renewed energy, thought and emotion into the session. Scenarios and specific task constraints should be designed to create learning opportunities specific to player needs. For example, pairing opening batters against opening bowlers who are using a new ball. Batters are tasked with leaving the ball as often as possible in the first 36 balls. Bowlers are tasked with forcing the batters to play a shot, this maximising the use of the new ball. By changing the age of the ball, or the match situation, both batters and bowlers are challenged to adapt to meet the new demands.*

*Successful performer constraints should take into account the whole player. In this respect, manipulating the physical demand of a task in order to fatigue the players is a legitimate performer constraint. For example, repeated sprints, or alternative appropriate physical task, embedded into a net practice session. Creating cognitive or emotional load are also legitimate performer constraints. How the player's technique holds up under these constraints is a key indicator of coaching needs and ultimately player development.*

*Environmental constraints, as outlined in the section above, are often less controllable and less in the gift of the coach. They often blur into task and performer constraints. Within cricket the natural environment contains potent factors which significantly influence how the game is played. Weather and pitch conditions will dramatically change the behaviour of the ball and can change over periods of play. Coaching which can utilise real-time environmental changes, or at least mimic conditions by changing the ball, moving from grass to differing artificial surfaces or altering light and noise in training settings may all be considered valid attempts at manipulating environmental constraints.*

## Balancing stability and instability

With little or no manipulation of constraints, performers are not required to reorganise movements. In such a scenario there is little variability of practice or movement afforded; such interventions are considered to offer the learner a high degree of stability in learning tasks. Striking a balance between stability and instability is an important and delicate consideration. On the one hand is the need to create a positive psychological platform for learning predicated on high perceived competence feeding intrinsic motivation. This can be achieved through generating high success through repetition in stable learning environments. Reducing decisions, closing affordances and limiting movement possibilities with the intention of generating instant success are appealing and often necessary coaching decisions. This may be particularly important in the developmental and introductory phases of junior sport where stable relationships between perception and action may be more important, at least initially (Land and McLeod, 2000).

However, as suggested in previous sections of this chapter on traditional approaches, the dangers of losing creativity in youth performers by closing off affordances through controlling coaching behaviours are concerns of the overuse

## 20  *James Wallis and Tim van Noort*

of stable coaching approaches. Therefore, creating well-considered and gradual instability is an important feature of coaching for long-term development, despite the likelihood that immediate performance outcomes may diminish (Renshaw et al., 2009). Whilst a completely open, 'free' coaching environment, with no specified information from coach to performer, is not appropriate, a gradual manipulation of constraints as performers develop mastery of prior tasks affords the benefits of the constructivist, non-linear approach whilst also protecting against any negative psycho-social impacts such as loss of confidence or motivation.

### Applied examples in cricket

*Within cricket there are multiple ways in which coaches can offer the relative psychological safety of high stability. A batter mastering the technical basics of hitting the ball with a straight bat may have the stability of having prior knowledge of the speed, line and length of delivery. Gradually introducing instability by reducing what is known by the batter pre-delivery, the coach is creating a more open task where information gathering, processing and movement are under greater pressure. Similarly, from a bowling perspective, a bowler mastering the technical principle of alignment in order to enhance consistency may be better served with high stability, at least initially. Previous sections exemplifying the use of the RCS in association with principles of non-linear pedagogy all need to be planned and delivered with an awareness of appropriate levels of stability to protect confidence but also generate learning. Gradual reduction in stability creates a more valid and fertile training environment, finding a suitable balance for each player is essential.*

## Concluding thoughts

This chapter has attempted to outline the limitations of traditional thinking in the coaching of sport skills to youth performers and to instead advocate non-linear approaches in coaching designs. Early models of coaching technical and tactical understanding in sport, such as TGfU, evolved as a response to early academic and practitioner attempts to promote more functional, enjoyable and situated learning for children in physical education and game contexts. The non-linear approaches outlined here offer a theoretical basis to coaching interventions, which (re)connect the performer with their environment in ways which have the potential to generate creative and diverse affordances to movement problems that are inherent in every sport. The significance and value of such approaches to the learning of youth performers cannot be over-emphasised based on the nonlinearity of their developing minds and bodies and the reported limitations of traditional, reductionist coaching.

Embedded in the second half of this chapter are numerous examples of the application of non-linear approaches to the coaching of cricket by an intuitive 'expert' practitioner who has long practised through a non-linear and constraints-based lens but was inhibited in his early career by socialised cultural traditions in structure, content and delivery in cricket coaching. Presenting evidence-based, theoretical and applied insights to an alternative philosophy for cricket coaching responds to the 'how and what' of junior coaching. It is time for cricket to address the 'who' of junior cricket coaching by re-prioritising the knowledge required for coaches to be successful in delivering youth programmes.

## Note

1 For a comprehensive overview of non-linear pedagogy for sport and physical education, see Chow, Davids, Button and Renshaw, 2016.

## References

Baker, J. (2003). 'Early specialization in youth sport: A requirement for adult expertise.' *High Ability Studies*, 14 (1), 85–94.

Baker, J., Cobley, S., and Fraser-Thomas, J. (2009). 'What do we know about early sport specialization? Not much!' *High Ability Studies*, 20 (1), 77–89.

Blackett, A., Evans, A., and Piggott, D. (2018). '"They have to toes the line": A Foucauldian analysis of the socialization of former elite athletes into academy coaching roles.' *Sport Coaching Review*, 8, 2–20.

Bronfenbrenner, U. (1977). 'Toward an experimental ecology of human development.' *American Psychologist*, 32 (7), 513–531.

Brouwers, J., De Bosscher, V., and Sotiriadou, P. (2012). 'An examination of the importance of performances in youth and junior competition as an indicator of later success in tennis.' *Sport Management Review*, 15 (4), 461–475.

Bunker, D., and Thorpe, R. (1982). 'A model for the teaching of games in the secondary school.' *Bulletin of Physical Education*, 10, 9–16.

Capranica, L., and Millard-Stafford, L. (2011). 'Youth specialisation: How to manage competition and training.' *International Journal of Sports Physiology and Performance*, 6 (4), 572–579.

Chow, J.-Y., Davids, K., Button, C., Renshaw, I., Shuttleworth, R., and Uehara, L. (2009). 'Non-linear pedagogy: Implications for teaching games for understanding.' In: Hopper, T., Butler, J., and Storey, B., eds. *TGFU simply good pedagogy: Understanding a complex challenge*. Ottawa: Ottawa Physical Health Education Association, 122–135.

Chow, J.-Y., Davids, K., Button, C., and Renshaw, I. (2016). *Non-linear pedagogy in skill acquisition: An introduction*. London: Routledge.

Côté, J., and Gilbert, W. (2009). 'An integrative definition of coaching effectiveness and expertise.' *Journal of Sport Science & Coaching*, 4 (3), 307–323.

Côté, J., and Abernethy, B. (2012). 'A developmental approach to sport expertise.' In: Murphy, S., ed. *The Oxford handbook of sport and performance psychology*. New York: Oxford University Press, 435–447.

Curtner-Smith, M.D. (2007). 'The impact of critically oriented physical education teacher education on pre-service classroom teachers.' *Journal of Teaching in Physical Education*, 26 (1), 35–56.

Cushion, C., and Jones, R.L. (2014). 'A Bourdieusian analysis of cultural reproduction: Socialisation and the "hidden curriculum" in professional football.' *Sport, Education and Society*, 19 (3), 276–298.

Davids, K., Bennett, S.J., and Newell, K. (2006). *Movement system variability*. Champaign, IL: Human Kinetics.

Ericcson, K.A., and Tesch-Romer, C. (1993). 'The role of deliberate practice in the acquisition of expert performance.' *Psychological Review*, 100 (3), 363–406.

Erickson, K., Côté, J., and Fraser-Thomas, J. (2007). 'Sport experiences, milestones, and educational activities associated with high-performance coaches' development.' *The Sport Psychologist*, 21 (3), 302–316.

Farrow, D., Baker, J., and McMahon, C. (2008). *Developing sports expertise: Researchers and coaches put theory into practice.* London: Routledge.

Ford, P.R., Yates, I., and Williams, M. (2010). 'An analysis of practice activities and instructional behaviours used by youth soccer coaches during practice: Exploring the link between science and application.' *Journal of Sport Sciences*, 28 (5), 483–495.

Gibson, J. (1979). *The ecological approach to visual perception.* Boston, MA: Houghton Mifflin.

Gladwell, M. (2008). *Outliers: the story of success.* New York: Little, Brown and Company.

Gould, D., Tuffey, S., Udry, E., and Loehr, J. (1996). 'Burnout in competitive junior tennis players: I. A quantitative psychological assessment.' *The Sport Psychologist*, 10 (4), 322–340.

Jayanthi, N., Pinkham, C., Dugas, L., Patrick, B., and Labella, C. (2013). 'Sports specialization in young athletes: Evidence-based recommendations.' *Sports Health*, 5 (3), 251–257.

Land, M., and McLeod, P. (2000). 'From eye movements to actions: How batsmen hit the ball.' *Nature Neuroscience*, 3 (12), 1340–1345.

Lawson, H.A. (1983). 'Towards a model of teacher socialisation in Physical Education: The subjective warrant, recruitment and teacher education (Part 1).' *Journal of Teaching in Physical Education*, 2 (3), 3–16.

Lawson, H.A. (1986). 'Occupational socialisation and the design of teacher education programmes.' *Journal of Teaching in Physical Education*, 5 (2), 107–116.

Lortie, D. (1975). *Schoolteacher: A sociological study.* Chicago: University of Chicago Press.

Lyle, J. (2018). 'The transferability of sport coaching research: A critical commentary.' *Quest*, 70 (4), 1–19.

Macnamara, B., Hambrick, D., and Oswald, F. (2014). 'Deliberate practice and performance in music, games, sports, education, and professions: A meta-analysis.' *Psychological Science*, 25 (8), 1608–1618.

Memmert, D. (2010). 'Creativity, expertise and attention: Exploring their development and their relationships.' *Journal of Sport Sciences*, 29 (1), 93–104.

Milgram, R.M. (1990). 'Creativity: An idea whose time has come and gone.' In M.A. Runco and R.S. Albert, eds. *Theory of creativity.* Newbury Park, CA: Sage, 215–233.

Mosston, M. (1966). *Teaching physical education.* Columbus, OH: Merrill.

Moy, B., Renshaw, I., Davids, K., and Brymer, E. (2016). 'Overcoming acculturation: Physical education recruits' experiences of an alternative pedagogical approach to games teaching.' *Physical Education and Sport Pedagogy*, 21 (4), 386–404.

Muller, S., Abernethy, B., and Farrow, D. (2006). 'How do world-class cricket batsmen anticipate a bowler's intention?' *The Quarterly Journal of Experimental Psychology*, 59 (12), 2126–2186.

Muller, S., and Abernethy, B. (2012). 'Expert anticipatory skill in striking sports: A review and a model.' *Research Quarterly for Exercise and Sport*, 83 (2), 175–187.

Nash, C., and Sproule, J. (2009). 'Career development of sport coaches.' *International Journal of Sports Science and Coaching*, 2, 105–108.

Nash, C., and Sproule, J. (2011). 'Insights into experiences: Reflections of an expert and novice coach.' *International Journal of Sports Science and Coaching*, 6 (1), 149–161.

Newell, K.M. (1986). 'Constraints on the development of coordination.' In Wade, M., and Whiting, T., eds. *Motor development in children: aspects of coordination and control*. Dordrecht: Martinus Nijhoff, 341–360.

Pinder, R.A., Davids, K.W., Renshaw, I., and Araujo, D. (2011). 'Representative learning design and functionality of research and practice in sport.' *Journal of Sport and Exercise Psychology*, 33 (1), 146–155.

Pinder, R., Renshaw, I., Davids, K., and Kerherve, H. (2011). 'Principles for the use of ball projection machines in elite and developmental sport programmes.' *Sports Med*, 41 (10), 793–800.

Ranganathan, R., and Carlton, L. (2007). 'Perception-action coupling and anticipatory performance in baseball batting.' *Journal of Motor Behaviour*, 39 (5), 369–380.

Renshaw, I., Davids, K., Shuttleworth, R., and Chow, J.-Y. (2009). 'Insights from ecological psychology and dynamical systems theory can underpin a philosophy of coaching.' *International Journal of Sport Psychology*, 40 (4), 540–602.

Ross, E., Gupta, L., and Sanders, L. (2018). 'When research leads to learning, but not action in high performance sport.' *Progress in Brain Research*, 240, 201–217.

Schwartz, J., and Begley, S. (2002). *The mind and the brain: Neuroplasticity and the power of mental force*. New York: HarperCollins.

Singer, R.N. (2000). 'Performance and human factors: Considerations about cognition and attention for self-paced and externally-paced events.' *Ergonomics*, 43 (10), 1661–1680.

Syed, M. (2010). *Bounce: How champions are made*. London: Routledge.

Vierimaa, M., Erickson, K., and Côté, J. (2016). 'The elements of talent development in youth sport.' In: Green, K., and Smith, A., eds. *Routledge handbook of youth sport, 464-475*. London: Routledge.

Wallis, J., and Lambert, J. (2016). *Becoming a sports coach*. London: Routledge.

# 2 Coaching children and youth
## Building physical foundations

*Floris Pietzsch and James Wallis*

## Introduction

The entry years into adolescence in the child's journey into sport are critical to their long-term participation and performance. This is a crucial period in shaping what follows, and yet understanding and application of appropriate process in this most influential of phases is often hindered by myths, misconceptions and limitations of traditional and out-dated approaches. This chapter sets out to present a brief overview of some of the key contemporary issues in the development of early foundations for children in sport before reviewing some established models of youth sport development, with the greatest emphasis being placed on the formative years of involvement in organised sport. Particular attention is given to discussion of areas of growing importance in recent years; the activity status, physical training and conditioning of youth performers. The chapter concludes with recommendations for the design of functional, supportive and beneficial activity programmes for pre-pubescent performers.

## Physical foundations

Physical inactivity is increasingly becoming a worldwide epidemic. The World Health Organisation (WHO) now recognises physical inactivity as the fourth-biggest leading cause of attributable global mortality (WHO, 2010). Many children in the United Kingdom do not meet the physical activity recommendations of at least 60 minutes of moderate- to vigorous-intensity physical activity per day, and it has been suggested that as much as 67% of boys and 79% of girls aged between 4 and 15 years old do not achieve adequate physical activity to aid health (Standage et al., 2014). Physical inactivity is one of the main causes of the growing worldwide obesity epidemic. A comprehensive review of literature as part of the 'Global Burden of Disease Study' was conducted, which provided an insight into the obesity changes in adults and children between 1980 and 2013 worldwide. The study reported a substantial increase (47% change) in children and adolescents between 1980 and 2013 with 23.8% of boys and 22.6% of girls being classed as overweight or obese in 2013 worldwide, with most prevalence in developed countries. In the United Kingdom, these figures are higher, with 26.1% of boys and 29.2% of girls below 20 years of age being classed as

Coaching children and youth 25

overweight or obese (Ng et al., 2014). The economic cost of inactivity is continuing to increase. According to one governmental publication the estimated extra costs of sustaining the inactive Britons both directly and indirectly amount to a total of £20 billion a year (HM Government and Mayor of London, 2014) with a further £8 billion required by 2020 (UK active KIDS, 2015, 2018).

Our view about the age at which physical activity declines has tended to be somewhat subjective, and many health education practitioners and policy makers assumed that physical activity declined during the adolescent years. However, there has been little tangible evidence to substantiate this. Many of the studies attempting to identify changes in physical activity during the adolescent years lacked the use of accurate physical activity measurement devices, such as accelerometers, which are now more accessible (Farooq et al., 2018). There is now growing evidence that the age in which physical activity declines is around the age of six to seven years old (Farooq et al., 2018). Interestingly, there is evidence that the decline in physical activity is linked to motor skill competence (also known as motor proficiency, motor performance, fundamental motor skill, motor ability or motor coordination). High motor skill competence in childhood is thought to have a significant influence on many long-term health, fitness and physical activity outcomes in later life (Lubans et al., 2010). Growing evidence seems to suggest that solid foundations for lifelong health and performance appear to be established in the formative years (Telama et al., 2005), with basic movement competence a central determinant (Jaakkola et al., 2016).

A seminal work by Gallahue, Ozmun and Goodway (2012) set out to identify a substantive list of fundamental movements, divided into three broad categories:

- Stability, or balance, for example bending, twisting, swaying, reaching
- Locomotive, or movement, for example running, dodging, hopping, jumping, skipping
- Manipulative, or object control skills, for example, throwing, striking, kicking, catching

These movements, he contended, could be considered the building blocks of future movement competence and eventually sports performance. His work extended to qualitative analyses of children's movements which could be classified as in the initial, elementary or mature stages of development.

Importantly, children do not simply learn functional movement skills naturally or by chance and neither is this simply linked to maturation status (Freitas et al., 2015). That is to say that physical maturation is not linked to motor coordination development in a linear fashion, and it has been described as 'age related but not age determined' (Robinson et al., 2015, p. 1274). In fact, many children do not fully develop their motor skill capabilities until they approach adulthood and it is suggested that this contributes largely to the drop off in physical activity (Stodden et al., 2014). Lopes and colleagues (2011) tracked physical activity with children aged six for three years and showed that children who were classed as high motor skill capable registered the highest amounts of total physical activity but interestingly also maintained high levels of physical activity up to the age of nine years.

Conversely, those children who were classed as being moderate or low motor skill capable saw a significant reduction in total physical activity over a three-year period. It would suggest that those with high amounts of fundamental motor skill competencies sustain activity levels. It appears that there is a clear positive relationship between motor competence and physical activity across childhood, and that this is also closely linked to both cardiorespiratory endurance and muscular strength development and that motor competence is a precursor to weight status and subcutaneous fat levels (Henrique et al., 2018). That is to say that low motor capability is a significant factor in physical inactivity during the childhood years and plays a large role in health. It therefore appears important that research and intervention turn their attention to the earlier years in childhood.

## The practitioner problem

It is important to highlight that this key moment in childhood physical development coincides with primary school education that is not without problems in relation to the delivery of physical education. Primary school educators have consistently reported a lack of confidence in delivering physical activity classes, received a limited amount of initial teacher training in the subject and sparse opportunity for continual professional development (Griggs, 2012; Smith, 2015; Howells and Meehan, 2019). Physical education within primary schools has also been reported as less important by senior school staff and managers (Griggs, 2012), which has led to inadequate planning, insufficient curriculum time and limited resources. There are also significant retention issues within the profession, with 33% of primary school teachers leaving the profession within the first five years and during 2017 more individuals left the profession than actually joined (House of Commons briefing paper, 2019). Given this context, it is not surprising that many senior school managers have turned to out-sourcing elements of the primary PE curriculum to sport coaching franchises, with the aim of offering greater competence and economic viability.

Smith (2015, p. 876) highlights that introducing external sports coaches does not come without problems. Educators have expressed concerns over their lack of teaching qualifications and a desire to 'prioritize sporting objectives over educational goals associated with the process of teaching and pupil learning.' Coaches are often newly qualified, have obtained just one National Governing Body short course award and are relatively inexperienced. It has been suggested that they struggle with class management and lack the pedagogical understanding surrounding youth education development (Smith, 2015). It is clear that, within the United Kingdom, at least, there tend to be limited numbers of suitable, qualified physical activity professionals targeting fundamental movement in youth populations. The awareness and knowledge that this is such a key developmental period for lifelong activity further highlights the need for urgent attention in this regard. The next section aims to support the understanding of positive physical training before moving onto theoretical models of long-term athlete development which can guide practice.

## Physical training of youth populations

Understanding of physical activity and health in youth populations has developed considerably over the past 40 years. Despite advancements, youth obesity is at an all-time high whilst also many youth athletes are becoming over specialised in one sport, regularly injured and exhibiting chronic musculoskeletal dysfunctions (DiFiori et al., 2014; Myer et al., 2015). Perhaps this is a result of early misunderstandings from public health organisations or simply due to a lack of clear empirical evidence that was available at the time or more likely a combination of multiple factors including some previously mentioned. One clear area for confusion and controversy surrounds the guidance on resistance training in youth populations.

Early studies into the benefits of resistance training for children initially showed mixed results (Vrijens, 1978; Docherty et al., 1987) with only some indication that preadolescent boys may benefit. Concerns that resistance training may stunt growth and increase the likelihood of injuries are also common due to historical beliefs. A very early study by Kato and Ishiko (1964), who researched the impacts of heavy labour on Japanese children's stature, is possibly to blame for early misunderstandings as they suggested that a child's stature was negatively affected by exercise. By 1985, however, the National Strength and Conditioning Association (NSCA) wrote their first position statement on the subject and concluded that 'strength training might begin at any age' (NSCA, 1985, p. 28) and was already well practised in Eastern bloc countries. The NSCA later extended this further by stating that 'weight bearing physical activity is essential for normal bone formation and growth' (Faigenbaum et al., 2009, p. 66). Gunter et al. (2008) reported the benefits of resistance training in child populations where eight-year-olds showed significant improvements in bone mineral content after a seven-month jumping exercise programme. Furthermore, recent evidence on diverse benefits have also been reported such as; muscular strength beyond expected maturation markers (Behringer et al., 2010; Faigenbaum et al., 2011), improved body composition (Schranz et al., 2013), motor skill proficiency (Behringer et al., 2011; Cattuzzo et al., 2016), improved insulin sensitivity in overweight adolescents (Shaibi et al., 2006), improved motor skill development (Duncan et al., 2017), reduced incidence of injury (Faigenbaum et al., 2009) as well as improved cardiac function and mental health (Faigenbaum et al., 2011; Faigenbaum et al., 2013). Such evidence has led to position statements and recommendations from multiple organisations such as the World Health Organisation (WHO, 2010), the United Kingdom Strength and Conditioning Association (Lloyd et al., 2012), National Strength and Conditioning Association (Faigenbaum et al., 2009; Lloyd et al., 2016) and the International Olympic Committee (Bergeron et al., 2015).

Whilst views on pre-pubescent strength and resistance have changed steadily over time, there is now a comprehensive body of evidence that there are significant multiple benefits to be gained.

## Developmental models in children's sport

### Early insights

Some of the earliest insights into the design and delivery of organised youth sport include the seminal work in 1978 of Rainer Martens' Joy and Sadness of Children's Sport. Central to Martens's account were observations of the predominant attitudes, behaviours and structures that evolved out of unprecedented growth of interest in youth sport, most significantly the exponential growth of Little League Baseball. Having been 'corporatised' in the mid-1950s, Martens claims Little League lost its innocence and central objective to 'keep kids in sports and out of courts,' in favour of capital and economic gain. He attempted to answer five 'formidable questions' that are summed up below:

1. *Are sports good for our children's physical and psychological health?*
2. *Is there too much pressure to win?*
3. *Will the demise of children's sports be parents who vicariously live their athletic yesteryears through their young athletes?*
4. *Are young athletes over-coached by under-qualified adults?*
5. *Is there any fun left in kids' sports?*

(Martens, 1978, p. 18)

Moving forward 20 years and these questions remain as pertinent as ever in narratives surrounding children's sport. Concepts such as early specialisation, deliberate play, burnout, talent identification and motivational climate are all clearly recognisable in this early work but without specific label. The expansion of youth sport programmes, along with their marketability and commercial potential, had influenced the skills and knowledge bases of adult 'coaches' and administrators which created an environment where children were commonly viewed as mini-adults and could be trained as such.

The response from the sport research community in recent years has been to advance an argument for a more holistic understanding of children's growth and development in order to support evidence-based interventions to enhance sport and physical activity outcomes. Central to this have been attempts to construct developmental models which present pathways from the point of entry to adult performance and attempt to capture the holistic complexity of sport development. Two of the most widely recognised and applied models are briefly outlined below.

### Long-Term Athlete Development

Originally conceived from physical and motor skill development perspectives, the Long-Term Athlete Development (LTAD) model has been adopted by a wide range of national and international sporting bodies as a way of structuring training and programming based on maturation (or stage) instead of chronology (age) (Balyi and Hamilton, 2004). The LTAD model offers simple and coherent recommendations and is inherently athlete-centred by virtue of its emphasis on the onset of the adolescent growth-spurt through monitoring of peak height and peak weight velocity. The proposed pathway to adult performance is observant of gender differences in maturation and is divided into linear stages of FUNdamentals (6–9 years), learning to train (B – 9–12, G – 9–11), training to train (B – 12–16, G – 11–15), training to compete (B – 16–18, G – 15–17) and, finally, training to win (B – 18+, G – 17+). It is widely held that the LTAD framework significantly accelerated the understanding of children in sport and led to multiple further iterations of and adaptations to the central premise of the model. Subsequent models were mainly catalysed by critical reflection on its major assumptions. The most commonly challenged assumption was the existence of 'windows of opportunity' in childhood and adolescence within which children are suggested to be more sensitive to training-induced physical gains (Ford et al., 2011). The lack of empirical and longitudinal evidence to support the programming of specific physical training emphases through the developmental years was likewise subjected to widespread critique (Lloyd and Oliver, 2012). These issues, along with their applied implications, are further explored in the final sections of this chapter.

## Developmental Model of Sport Participation

Whilst sharing some structural and chronological similarities with LTAD, the first iteration was the Developmental Model of Sport Participation (DMSP), which proposed a single linear pathway divided into three stages labelled the sampling years (6–12), the specialising years (12–15) and the investment years (post 16) (Côté and Fraser-Thomas, 2007). The model is grounded in psycho-social and skill development domains whereby each stage recommends a narrowing of the range of sports along with a shift in balance from predominantly intrinsically motivating *play-based activity* to a greater volume of *deliberate practice* post-adolescence. Cognisant of differing motives in youth sport performance, the DMSP was later adapted by Côté and Fraser-Thomas (2007) to accommodate three differing trajectories resulting in three differing potential adult athlete outcomes:

- *Recreational participation in sport and physical activity* influenced by high amounts of deliberate play, high involvement in several sports and focus on health, fitness and enjoyment
- *Elite performance* through narrowing of sports and a gradual shift from deliberate play to deliberate practice through the specialising and investment years resulting in high enjoyment and high physical health
- *Elite performance through early specialisation* on one sport from entry to adult and high emphasis on deliberate practice over deliberate play resulting in low enjoyment and low physical health

Recognising the likelihood of changes to children's participation motives born out of personal or social preference or physical development is a further strength of the DMSP as performers can shift trajectories to accommodate their needs and motives as they mature.

## 30 *Floris Pietzsch and James Wallis*

The rest of this chapter now moves to outline key theoretical positions on evidence-based functional movement programmes for pre-pubescent performers. Given this emphasis, the following sections are framed by further adaptations of the LTAD framework, the Youth Physical Development Model (Lloyd and Oliver, 2012) and the Composite Youth Development Model (Lloyd et al., 2015).

### Positive youth physical development

Along with the recognition that physical inactivity experienced in youth populations is a growing problem, there are also concerns of over-specialisation of children into single sports. Early specialisation can be defined as sport training that requires high-intensity, year-round focus in one particular sport and revolves around a high volume of deliberate practice aimed towards performance sport (Waldron et al., 2019). It has previously been shown that children who specialise early generally undertake inappropriate volumes, intensities and frequencies of training and experience lengthy competitive periods which lead to a greater risk to injury and psychological burnout (Baker et al., 2009; Myer et al., 2015; Waldron et al., 2019). Policy and practice which continue to emphasise early specialisation in youth sport seems to have increased in recent years (Waldron et al., 2019) with many National Governing Bodies continuing to extend junior age group competitive structures, ranking systems and talent identification geared towards a more performance orientation in the misguided belief that there is a positive linear relationship between hours invested, success in junior competition and eventual achievement in elite adult sport.

An alternative view on early specialisation is in diversification or sampling, which actively encourages young children to participate in a breath of physical activities and in doing so may facilitate a transfer of fundamental motor skills between sports (Baker et al., 2009). It also allows greater interaction with a wider social network, typically involve more hours of play rather than focused practice and at least partially negates the risk of burnout, drop out or injuries, as depicted in the DMSP (Côté and Fraser-Thomas, 2007). Importantly, it has been demonstrated that the diversification route does not hinder the development of performance sport, especially for sports where expertise occurs after maturation (Côté and Vierimaa, 2014; Baker et al., 2009). Indeed, research by Bridge and Toms (2013) has shown that there is 'an increased likelihood of achieving a higher standard of competition when individuals participate in three competitive sports during the specialising years of the DMSP model' (p. 95). In this respect, Gullich (2014) reviewed time spent in organised training and non-organised play in both field hockey and other sports through childhood, adolescence and adulthood in Olympic medal-winning hockey players and those players who were only able to achieve the national level. The national-class hockey players did not spend any less time in hockey training when compared to the Olympic medal winners but did spend less time in other sporting activities at a younger age. The Olympic medal winners played more organised and unorganised sports across multiple sports and specialised later in their life (the average age of specialisation was

9.4 years and 15 years, respectively). Therefore, one might question whether it is ethical, or indeed necessary, to structure youth sport through a specialisation lens, instead of opening the door to a much wider range of sports through play and exposure to diverse fundamental movement education.

### The Youth Physical Development Model and the Composite Youth Development Model

Most recently the work by Lloyd and colleagues (Lloyd and Oliver, 2012; Lloyd et al., 2015) has led to an international agreement that long-term athlete development should indeed encapsulate all youth physical development rather than exclusively for young athletes. The Youth Physical Development Model (YPDM), conceived in 2012 and adapted in 2015 and amended and renamed the Composite Youth Development model (CYDM), is an up-to-date, well-rounded and generally accepted model that includes a more holistic and inclusive approach to youth physical development whilst also including the important aspects of the LTAD model with regard to key moments of physical development (Lloyd et al., 2015). Notably, it is now recognised that all components of fitness are trainable at all ages and stages of maturation; however the magnitude of adaptations may be greater within key areas of the maturation process. The CYDM now also includes a psycho-social development, which holds a key aim to 'ensure the child or adolescent remains motivated for lifetime engagement with sports and physical activity' (Lloyd et al., 2015, p. 1445).

## Applications to practice

Diverse athletic motor skill competencies (AMSC), suggested by Moody et al. (2013), which underpin the concepts of fundamental movement skills, aim to improve overall athletic motor skill competency whilst also preparing children for more advanced training at a later stage. The AMSC model suggests that all children should be aiming to develop physical competency across a wide spectrum of physical skills and capabilities. These competencies target key physical qualities including:

- Lower body bilateral and unilateral
- Acceleration/deceleration/reacceleration
- Throwing/catching/grasping
- Jumping/landing/rebounding mechanics
- Anti-rotation/core bracing
- Upper body pushing and upper body pulling

For the 'lower body bilateral' component, the movement of the squat is typically used to exemplify this physical competency. The bodyweight squat has previously been used as a means of screening athletes and assessing their movement pattern (Myer et al., 2014). One simple exercise can help identify whether an individual exhibits muscle imbalances, lacks a range of motion, performs the movement with incorrect muscle firing or exhibits thoracic stiffness. Should an individual have the capabilities to carry out a successful squat, then they have the capability to perform the exercise with numerous training progressions in mind. This may initially result in repetitions of the movement to determine whether the quality of the movement continues and if so may therefore progress to additional external resistance training or a more technically demanding variation of the movement. What is crucial here is that movement competence precedes progression or addition of further resistance. Should the individual not be able to demonstrate competence in the squat, then the practitioner is encouraged to determine what the limiting factors might be. Common limiters may be varied such as the range of motion limitations in pelvic complex, poor coordination, misalignment or muscle imbalances (Myer et al., 2014). The practitioner should not progress this individual through a squat pattern until such factors have been identified and rectified. The individual earns the right to progression based on their ability to competently carry out the movement. In this respect, progressions in exercise streams should be linked to physical competency capabilities rather than chronological age and therefore help determine when a child is ready to undertake more advanced resistance training. It is quite possible that a child may actually exhibit greater physical competencies due to good coaching and training when compared to an adult who may exhibit a number of dysfunctions. Movement competence is not linear or age-dependent.

Of contemporary importance to strength and conditioning coaching is the need to generate learning tasks, environments and designs which are fun, are engaging and offer opportunities for exploratory movement (Lloyd et al., 2020). This is only limited by coach creativity in the design of activities that can target athletic movement skill competencies, embedded into sport-specific games and practices. Examples of this could be in the form of obstacle courses or physical challenges, which may involve partner assistance and usually involve bodyweight gymnastic type movements until further progression is warranted. A central concern in all activity is the demonstration and execution of movement competence but of equal importance is to create an environment which affords autonomy and a clear sense of relatability to the child's preferred sport. The YPDM and the CYDM place significant emphasis on fundamental movement skills before progressing to sport-specific skills. It is this design of sport-specific practice which embeds movement competence that moves physical conditioning of youth athletes into a modern era where pedagogic and psycho-social coaching tools are beginning to become recognised and applied.

Although classic exercise prescription using sets, repetitions and intensities have previously been shown to improve strength and competence (Faigenbaum et al., 2011), these may not necessarily be the most effective or appropriate method of coaching in very young children. The AMSC should form the basis of all physical movement and should help practitioners to prescribe and target key exercises to develop these physical traits. Lloyd and colleagues (2020) have suggested that interventions lasting as little as 20 minutes, with tasks using 2–4 sets and 6–12 repetitions two to three times per week can have positive adaptations in motor skill competency. It is common for children to possess a varying

*Table 2.1* Summary recommendations

| | |
|---|---|
| General Principles (Children) | • 60 minutes of moderate to vigorous activity per day is recommended for all children, which should include integrative neuromuscular training<br>• Muscular strength and the development of fundamental movement skills should form the foundations for all children. This should include a wide array of athletic motor skill competencies which should be individualised<br>• Young children (< 7 years) should be encouraged to engage in more fun related activities, which are less structured and target the development of physical competencies. Additional resistance training may be appropriate when significant achievement in a wide array of physical competencies is obtained. This should be gauged on physical competency ability rather than chronological age<br>• Diversification should be encouraged through a variety of physical activities which need not be sport focused but aimed towards supporting the development of a wide spectrum of motor skills<br>• Early specialisation and any notion of accruing 10,000 hours of deliberate practice should be avoided<br>• Youth physical activity should incorporate an appropriate balance between deliberate practice and deliberate play<br>• Athletic development should not be limited to just young athletes but rather to all children<br>• Youth sport success should be defined as the development of the whole athlete and the person as the core focus which shapes lifelong engagement with physical activity, as opposed to short-term sporting competition success<br>• Physical education within primary schools requires significant help and support to enable society to achieve success in youth populations. Practitioners should be suitably qualified and skilled in delivering age-appropriate physical activity classes. Teacher training and coach education should include both the academic content knowledge but also pedagogic skills to deliver physical education to youth populations |
| General Principles (Adolescence) | • Children who engage in competitive sports should also follow a periodised physical preparation conditioning programme to help avoid the development of muscular imbalance and help reduce the risks of injury<br>• Physical programming should continue to develop upon the AMSC pathways with a view that the initial high quality of movement can then be progressed further with more advanced training methodologies<br>• Maturation status, either through the assessment of peak height velocity or percentage of parental height, should be monitored to allow a more accurate identification of biological age. This in turn may aid the training prescription and understanding of the individual's physical capabilities<br>• As children develop through adolescence, the balance between play and deliberate practice can change in favour of more deliberate practice. The same can be true of increases in training and competition but never at the expense of the well-being of the individual<br>• Training and competition should be closely monitored for signs of overtraining, burnout or potential risk to injury. Rest and recovery and a period of transition or off-season should form part of the calendar year |

## 34 Floris Pietzsch and James Wallis

degree of capability across the AMSC, which will require the coach to develop the ability to differentiate the tasks across the group of participants. Typical progressions seen in adult populations of increasing resistance or velocity may also not be immediately appropriate. Instead, coaches should focus on the fluidity and coordination of movements and ensure consistent quality of movement is achieved before increases in intensity or progression are considered. The ultimate aim would be for all AMSC to be achieved to a consistently high standard.

A clear and important factor within youth physical development is that it requires a high degree of specialist knowledge from both strength and conditioning, and pedagogic perspectives. Incomplete knowledge may explain current worrying trends in developing lifelong activity, athletic competence and more injury-free youth performers. The aim of this chapter was to highlight and explain why this may be the case and begin to offer some practical solutions and answers for future educators and practitioners. Children need to engage in moderate to vigorous activity on a daily basis which should be fun and engaging whilst also offering a suitable challenge. The development of fundamental movement skills which aim to develop AMSC can be positively associated with improvements in fitness, physical activity and a reduction in injury; obesity; and other health-related factors. The CYDM (Lloyd, 2015) is the latest model for youth long-term development and encompasses a multitude of important factors such as maturation, key windows of training adaptation, psycho-social development and long-term athlete development. To conclude this chapter, Table 2.1 summarises some of the most important messages when planning and delivering physical training to children and adolescents.

## References

Baker, J., Cobley, S., and Fraser-Thomas, J. (2009). 'What do we know about early sport specialization? Not much.' *High Ability Studies*, 20 (1), 77–89.

Balyi, I., and Hamilton, A. (2004). *Long-term athlete development: Trainability in childhood and adolescence: Windows of opportunity, optimal trainability*. Victoria: National Coaching Institute British Columbia and Advanced Training and Performance Ltd.

Behringer, M., Vom Heede, A., Yue, Z., and Mester, J. (2010). 'Effects of resistance training in children and adolescents: A meta-analysis.' *Pediatrics*, 126 (5), 1199–1210.

Behringer, M., Heede, A.V., Matthews, M., and Mester, J. (2011). 'Effects of strength training on motor performance skills in children and adolescents: A meta-analysis.' *Pediatric Exercise Science*, 23 (2), 186–206.

Bergeron, M.F., Mountjoy, M., Armstrong, N., Chia, M., Cote, J., Emery, C.A., Faigenbaum, A., Hall, G., Kriemler, S., Leglise, M., Malina, R.M., Pensgaard, A.M., Sanchez, A., Soligard, T., Sundgot-Borgen, J., van Mechelen, W., Weissensteiner, J.R., and Engebretsen, L. (2015). 'International Olympic Committee consensus statement on youth athletic development.' *British Journal of Sports Medicine*, 49 (13), 843–851.

Bridge, M.W., and Toms, M.R. (2013). 'The specialising or sampling debate: A retrospective analysis of adolescent sports participation in the UK.' *Journal of Sports Sciences*, 31 (1), 87–96.

Côté, J., and Fraser-Thomas, J. (2007). 'Play, practice, and athlete development'. In: D. Farrow, J. Baker, and C. Macmahon, eds. *Developing sport expertise: Lessons from theory and practice*. New York: Routledge, 17–28.

Côté, J., and Vierimaa, M. (2014). 'The developmental model of sport participation: 15 years after its first conceptualization.' *Science and Sports*, 29, S63–S69.

Cattuzzo, M.T., and dos Santos Henrique, R., Ré, A.H.N., de Oliveira, I.S., Melo, B.M., de Sousa Moura, M., de Araújo, R.C., andStodden, D. (2016). 'Motor competence and health related physical fitness in youth: A systematic review.' *Journal of Science and Medicine in Sport*, 19 (2), 123–129.

Difiori, J.P., Benjamin, H.J., Brenner, J., Gregory, A., Jayanthi, N., Landry, G.L., and Luke, A. (2014). 'Overuse injuries and burnout in youth sports: A position statement from the American Medical Society for Sports Medicine.' *Clinical Journal of Sport Medicine*, 24 (1), 3–20.

Docherty, D., Wenger, H.A., Collis, M.L., and Quinney, H.A. (1987). 'The effects of variable speed resistance training on strength development in prepubertal boys.' *Journal of Human Movement Studies*, 13, 377–282.

Duncan, M.J., Eyre, E.L.J., and Oxford, S.W. (2017). 'The effects of 10 weeks integrated neuromuscular training on fundamental movement skills and physical self-efficacy in 6–7 year old children.' *Journal of Strength and Conditioning Research*, 22, 3348–3356.

Faigenbaum, A.D., Kraemer, W.J., Blimkie, C.J.R., Jeffreys, I., Micheli, L.J., Nitka, M., and Rowland, T.W. (2009). 'Youth resistance training: Updated position statement paper from the national strength and conditioning association.' *Journal of Strength and Conditioning Research*, 23 (5), Suppl 5, 5, 560–579.

Faigenbaum, A.D., Farrell, A., Fabiano, M., Radler, T., Naclerio, F., Ratamess, N.A., Kang, J., and Myer, G.D. (2011). 'Effects of integrative neuromuscular training on fitness performance in children.' *Pediatric Exercise Science*, 23 (4), 573–584.

Faigenbaum, A.D., Lloyd, R.S., and Myer, G.D. (2013). 'Youth resistance training: Past practices, new perspectives, and future directions.' *Pediatric Exercise Science*, 25 (4), 591–604.

Farooq, M.A., Parkinson, K.N., Adamson, A.J., Pearce, M.S., Reilly, J.K., Hughes, A.R., Janssen, X., Basterfield, L., and Reilly, J.J. (2018). 'Timing of the decline in physical activity in childhood and adolescence: Gateshead Millennium Cohort Study.' *British Journal of Sports Medicine*, 52 (15), 1002–1012.

Ford, P., De Ste Croix, M., Lloyd, R., Meyers, R., Moosavi, M., Oliver, J., Till, K., and Williams, C. (2011). 'The long-term athlete development model: Physiological evidence and application.' *Journal of Sport Sciences*, 29 (4), 389–402.

Freitas, D.L., Lausen, B., Maia, J.A., Lefevre, J., Gouveia, É.R., Thomis, M., and Malina, R.M. (2015). 'Skeletal maturation, fundamental motor skills and motor coordination in children 7–10 years.' *Journal of Sports Sciences*, 33 (9), 924–993.

Galahue, D., Ozmun, L., and Goodway, J. (2012). *Understanding motor development: Infants, children, adolescents, adults.* New York: McGraw-Hill.

Griggs, G. (2012). 'Standing on the touchline of chaos: Explaining the development of the use of sports coaches in UK primary schools with the aid of complexity theory.' *Education 3-13*, 40 (3), 259–269.

Güllich, A. (2014). 'Many roads lead to Rome - developmental paths to Olympic gold in men's field hockey.' *European Journal of Sport Science*, 14 (8), 763–771.

Gunter, K., Baxter-Jones, A.D.G., Mirwald, R.L., Almstedt, H., Fuchs, R.K., Durski, S., and Snow, C. (2008). 'Impact exercise increases BMC during growth: An 8-year longitudinal study.' *Journal of Bone and Mineral Research*, 23 (7), 986–993.

Henrique, R.S., Bustamante, A.V., Freitas, D.L., Tani, G., Katzmarzyk, P.T., and Maia, J.A. (2018). 'Tracking of gross motor coordination in Portuguese children.' *Journal of Sports Sciences*, 36 (2), 220–228.

House of Commons Library (2019). 'Teacher recruitment and retention in England'. Briefing paper, February, no. 7222. www.parliament.uk (accessed March 2019).

## 36 Floris Pietzsch and James Wallis

Howells, K., and Meehan, C. (2019). 'Walking the talk? Teachers' and early years' practitioners' perceptions and confidence in delivering the UK Physical Activity Guidelines within the curriculum for young children.' *Early Child Development and Care*, 189 (1), 31–42.

HM Government and Mayor of London (2014). 'Moving more, living more, the physical activity Olympic and Paralympic legacy for the nation.' https://www.gov.uk/government/uploads/system/uploads/attachment_data/file/279657/moving_living_more_inspired_2012.pdf. Accessed 6th January 2020.

Jaakkola, T., Yli-Piipari, S., Huotari, P., Watt, A., and Liukkonen, J. (2016). 'Fundamental movement skills and physical fitness as predictors of physical activity: A 6-year follow-up study.' *Scandinavian Journal of Medicine and Science in Sports*, 26 (1), 74–81.

Kato, S., and Ishiko, T. (1964). 'Obstructed growth of children's growth due to excessive labour in remote corners'. *Proceedings of International Congress of Sports Sciences*, Tokyo, Japanese Union of Sports Sciences.

Lloyd, R., Faigenbaum, A., Myer, G., Stone, M.H., Oliver, J.L., Jeffreys, I., Moody, J., Brewer, C., and Pierce, K. (2012). 'UKSCA position statement: Youth resistance training.' *UK Strength and Conditioning Association*, 26, 26–39.

Lloyd, R.S., and Oliver, J.L. (2012). 'The youth physical development model: A new approach to long-term athletic development.' *Strength and Conditioning Journal*, 34 (3), 61–72.

Lloyd, R.S., Oliver, J.L., Faigenbaum, A.D., Howard, R., De Ste Croix, Mark B.A., Williams, C.A., Best, T.M., Alvar, B.A., Micheli, L.J., Thomas, D.P., Hatfield, D.L., Cronin, J.B., and Myer, G.D. (2015). 'Long-term athletic development, part 1: A pathway for all youth.' *Journal of Strength and Conditioning Research*, 29 (5), 1439–1450.

Lloyd, R.S., Oliver, J.L., Faigenbaum, A.D., Howard, R., De Ste Croix, Mark B.A., Williams, C.A., Best, T.M., Alvar, B.A., Micheli, L.J., Thomas, D.P., Hatfield, D.L., Cronin, J.B., and Myer, G.D. (2015). 'Long-term athletic development, part 2: Barriers to success and potential solutions.' *Journal of Strength and Conditioning Research*, 29 (5), 1451–1464.

Lloyd, R.S., Cronin, J.B., Faigenbaum, A.D., Haff, G.G., Howard, R., Kraemer, W.J., and Oliver, J.L. (2016). 'National strength and conditioning association position statement on long-term athletic development.' *Journal of Strength and Conditioning Research*, 30 (6), 1491–1509.

Lloyd, R.S., and Oliver, J.L. (2020). *Strength and conditioning for young athletes: Science and application* (2nd ed.). Abingdon: Routledge.

Lopes, V.P., Rodrigues, L.P., Maia, J.A.R., and Malina, R.M. (2011). 'Motor coordination as predictor of physical activity in childhood.' *Scandinavian Journal of Medicine and Science in Sports*, 21 (5), 663–669.

Lubans, D.R., Morgan, P.J., Cliff, D.P., Barnett, L.M., and Okely, A.D. (2010). 'Fundamental movement skills in children and adolescents: Review of associated health benefits.' *Sports Medicine*, 40 (12), 1019–1035.

Martens, R. (1978). *The joy and sadness of children's sport*. Champaign, IL: Human Kinetics.

Moody, J.M., Naclerio, F., Green., P., and Lloyd, R.S. (2013). 'Motor skill development in youths'. In: R.S. Lloyd, and J.L. Oliver, eds. *Strength and conditioning for young athletes: Science and applications*. Oxford, UK: Routledge Publishing, 49–65.

Myer, G.D., Kushner, A.M., Brent, J.L., Schoenfeld, B.J., Hugentobler, J., Lloyd, R.S., Vermeil, A., Chu, D.A., Harbin, J., and McGill, S.M. (2014). 'The back squat: a proposed assessment of functional deficits and technical factors that limit performance.' *Strength and Conditioning Journal*, 36 (6), 4–27.

Myer, G.D., Jayanthi, N., Difiori, J.P., Faigenbaum, A.D., Kiefer, A.W., Logerstedt, D., and Micheli, L.J. (2015). 'Sport specialization, part I: Does early sports specialization increase negative outcomes and reduce the opportunity for success in young athletes?' *Sports Health: A Multidisciplinary Approach*, 7 (5), 437–442.

National Strength and Conditioning Association (1985). 'Position paper on prepubescent strength training.' *National Strength and Conditioning Association Journal*, 7 (4), 27–31.

Ng, M., Fleming, T., Robinson, M., Thomson, B., Graetz, N., Margono, C., and Gakidou, E. (2014). 'Global, regional, and national prevalence of overweight and obesity in children and adults during 1980–2013: A systematic analysis for the global burden of disease study 2013.' *The Lancet*, 384 (9945), 766–781.

Robinson, L.E., Stodden, D.F., Barnett, L.M., Lopes, V.P., Logan, S.W., Rodrigues, L.P., and D'Hondt, E. (2015). 'Motor competence and its effect on positive developmental trajectories of health.' *Sports Medicine*, 45 (9), 1273–1284.

Schranz, N., Tomkinson, G., and Olds, T. (2013). 'What is the effect of resistance training on the strength, body composition and psychosocial status of overweight and obese children and adolescents? A systematic review and meta-analysis.' *Sports Medicine*, 43 (9), 893–907.

Shaibi, G., Cruz, M., Ball, G., Weigensberg, M., Salem, G., Crespo, N., and Goran, M. (2006). 'Effects of resistance training on insulin sensitivity in overweight Latino adolescent males.' *Medicine and Science in Sports and Exercise*, 38 (7), 1208–1215.

Smith, A. (2015). 'Primary school physical education and sports coaches: Evidence from a study of school sport partnerships in north-west England.' *Sport, Education and Society*, 20 (7), 872–888.

Standage, M., Standage, M., Wilkie, H.J., Wilkie, H.J., Jago, R., Jago, R., Foster, C., Foster, C., Goad, M.A., Goad, M.A., Cumming, S.P., and Cumming, S.P. (2014). 'Results from England's 2014 report card on physical activity for children and youth.' *Journal of Physical Activity and Health*, 11, Suppl 1, 545–550.

Stodden, D.F., Gao, Z., Goodway, J.D., and Langendorfer, S.J. (2014). 'Dynamic relationships between motor skill competence and health-related fitness in youth.' *Pediatric Exercise Science*, 26 (3), 231–241.

Telama, R., Yang, X., Viikari, J., Välimäki, I., Wanne, O., and Raitakari, O. (2005). 'Physical activity from childhood to adulthood: A 21-year tracking study.' *American Journal of Preventative Medicine*, 28 (3), 267–273.

UKActive kids (2015). 'Generation inactive: An analysis of the UK's childhood inactivity epidemic and tangible solutions to get children moving'. www.ukactive.com (accessed 29/03/2019).

UKActive kids (2018). 'Generation inactive 2: Nothing about us, without us'. www.ukactive.com (accessed 29/03/2019).

Vrijens, J. (1978). 'Muscle strength development in the pre and postpubescent age.' *Medicine and Sport*, 11, 152–158.

Waldron, S., DeFreese, J.D., Register-Mihalik, J., Pietrosimone, B., and Barczak, N. (2019). 'The costs and benefits of early sport specialization: A critical review of literature.' *Quest*, 72 (4) 1–18.

World Health Organisation (2010). *Global recommendations on physical activity for health*. Geneva: WHO Press.

# 3 Understanding the sport values of young people and recognising the implications for their coaches

## Sport for kids not kids for sport

*John Lambert*

### Introduction

Sport is often regarded as possessing inherent qualities, such as 'fairness,' 'trying hard,' 'acceptance of winning and losing' and 'working with others' that shape and influence young people. Whilst recognising the physical, social and moral benefits that sport can bring to the lives of young people, alongside the cultural values that it implicitly promotes, it is important to recognise that the research evidence is nuanced, reporting a dissonance between the values of young people and the value and benefits claimed for sport provision (Devine and Telfer, 2013). Coaches are charged with the responsibility of 'providing' sporting opportunities for the young, and gaining knowledge of which sport values those young people espouse must be central to an understanding of their decision-making processes. It is therefore incumbent on sport providers to seek to develop an awareness of the value priorities of children, who do not think like adults.

This chapter aims to signpost readers to some significant research on the sport values of young people that was led by Martin Lee and colleagues in the 1990s. Martin founded the Institute for the Study of Children in Sport, wrote courses on coaching children for the National Coaching Foundation and produced a book on *Coaching Children in Sport* in 1993. He retired in 2000 after a diagnosis with cancer but he continued to lecture and publish his work on youth sport until his death in 2009. Martin's writing on values was set in the context of his deep concern for the welfare of children in sport and the need for coaches and teachers to see sport and physical education from their perspective.

As a researcher, coach and a sportsman himself, he understood the importance of identifying the values that young people hold in sporting settings and discovering which of these values were the most important to them. He was concerned that children in sport should not be treated like mini-adults and was acutely aware of the increasing prevalence of unethical behaviour in youth sport that is a manifestation of the prevailing attitudes and values that are common to adult professional sport (Lee, 2004b). He was a pioneering thinker who bestowed a legacy that is of value to all those involved in youth sport, including coaches, coach educators, parents and administrators. Once some of his most significant research on values in youth sport is explained and discussed, the chapter will move on to highlight its importance to all those involved in facilitating sport for young people. Some real-life scenarios will then be used to make the main findings from his research applicable to youth coaching and participation contexts, linking theory to practice.

Martin argued that teachers and professionals working with children in sport are important agents of value transmission and change and therefore need to develop a deeper understanding of how sport can offer positive experiences and be used to encourage pro-social values (Lambert, 2013). Values have been defined as 'desirable trans-situational goals, varying in importance, that serve as guiding principles in the life of a person or social entity' (Schwartz, 1994: 5). According to Schwartz (1994), values (a) serve the interests of individuals and groups, (b) motivate action by giving it both direction and intensity, (c) function as standards by which behaviour is evaluated and (d) are learned by individuals from the dominant values of the social groups of which they belong and through their own experiences. If we accept that values underlie behaviour in all situations, then it is important to understand the values that guide the behaviour of children in sport (Lee, 2004a). Once he had secured the necessary funding for his research, Martin set about identifying the sport values that young people hold.

## Identifying the salient sport values that young people *hold*

Rather than make assumptions about the set of values that young athletes may espouse, Martin conducted a study that allowed them to articulate their own sport values. This was achieved by recording the spontaneously expressed values of the population of interest, young people involved in competitive sport.

Lee and Cockman (1995) implemented an inductive procedure that involved using sport-specific moral dilemmas to identify those values that adolescents express spontaneously, thus ensuring ecological validity. Semi-structured interviews were conducted with 87 young male and female soccer and tennis players that ultimately drew 18 salient sport values from the target population. All of the subjects were between 12 and 16 and were involved in competitive sport from high school to international level. The subjects were asked to read hypothetical situations from sport and give possible responses. They were asked to imagine themselves in each scenario and to (a) describe what could be done in each situation, (b) what most people might do and (c) what they themselves would do. This provided a basis for a subsequent conversation about what is important to these young people when participating in their chosen sport. The values are presented in terms of the level of frequency that they were expressed in the interviews (see Table 3.1).

The values listed are sport-specific, as they include sportsmanship and good game (see definitions in Table 3.1) that are absent from general surveys of human values. It also needs to be noted that the list denotes the frequency that these values were expressed in the interviews, which varies significantly from the relative

40  John Lambert

*Table 3.1* Frequency of spontaneous expression of sport values

| Rank | Values | Descriptor |
| --- | --- | --- |
| 1 | Winning | Demonstrating superiority in a contest |
| 2 | Enjoyment | Feelings of satisfaction and pleasure |
| 3 | Sportsmanship | Demonstrating positive behaviour towards opponents and officials. Being a good winner and loser |
| 4 | Caring | Showing concern for others |
| 5 | Fairness | Not allowing an unfair advantage in the contest/ judgement |
| 6 | Contract maintenance | Playing within the spirit of the game, including adhering to laws/rules |
| 7 | Public image | Gaining approval of others. Creating a good impression |
| 8 | Obedience | Avoiding punishment; being dropped, sent off or suspended |
| 9 | Good game | Enjoying the contest regardless of outcome |
| 10 | Companionship | Being with friends with a similar interest in the game |
| 11 | Achievement | Being personally or collectively successful in play, performing to potential |
| 12 | Conscientious | Doing one's best and not letting others down |
| 13 | Team cohesion | Doing something for someone else and for the sake of team performance |
| 14 | Self-actualisation | Experiencing the activity for its own sake and accompanying transcendent feelings |
| 15 | Showing skill | Being able to perform the skills of the game well |
| 16 | Conformity | Conforming to the expectations of the others in the team |
| 17 | Health and fitness | Becoming fit and healthy as a result of the activity, and thus enhancing performance |
| 18 | Tolerance | Being able to get along with others despite interpersonal differences |

*Source: Adapted from Lee, 1997.*

importance of each value in the value systems of the young competitors. The latter was the subject of a later study (Lee, Whitehead and Balchin, 2000), the focus for the next section. In other words, whilst winning was the most talked-about value, it must not be assumed that it was the most important to the young people involved.

### Discovering which sport values are of most *importance* to young people

Values are trans-situational, which indicates that they guide behaviour in all life situations, and they vary in importance implying that they can be ranked in order of importance (Schwartz, 1994). The relative priority that young people give to different values is referred to as their value system. In sport, the desire to win can

Understanding the sport values of young people  41

come into direct conflict with sportsmanship, contract maintenance and other values listed in Table 3.1, leading to values dilemmas and in these circumstances a player's attitudes and behaviour will be guided by the relative importance of each of these values in their personal value system. Martin Lee's interest in examining the value systems of youth athletes provided the impetus for his next stage of research.

Martin and colleagues devised simplified descriptors against each of the 18 previously identified sport values and tested them with 50 sports club members (24 males, 26 females), aged 11–17, in order to ensure that they were understood by the subjects. Following this pilot test, each value descriptor was written in the form of a first-person statement. For example, personal achievement was attached to the descriptor 'I put in the best performance I can,' self-actualisation was described as 'I get a buzz or feel really good when playing' and winning was represented by the caption 'I win or beat others.'

Once suitable descriptors were decided upon, Martin and colleagues used the Youth Sport Value Questionnaire (YSVQ)[1] to find out the relative importance of each of the 18 values with individual participants. The 1,391 young sport competitors (aged 12–16, 47% male, 53% female, all actively involved in competitive sport at varying levels) from schools across the United Kingdom who completed the YSVQ were asked to assess the importance of each of the sport values and this indicated the value systems of each young athlete.

Each participant was asked to give a response against each descriptor in answer to the question, 'When I do sport it is important to me that ...' The range of replies could vary from 'This idea is the opposite of what I believe,' followed by 'This idea is not important to me,' the middle rating being 'This idea is quite important to me,' to 'This idea is extremely important to me' at the other end of the spectrum. The subjects were asked to read a list of phrases representing each of the sport values and then indicate how important each one was to them as an individual. For example, 'I try to be fair,' which represents the value of fairness, was one of the items. A young person may value fairness as being of no particular importance, in which case they would circle the 'not important' option. The phrase 'I get a buzz or feel really good when I am playing' represented the value of enjoyment which they may feel is highly important so would circle the 'extra important' option. The research findings from the YSVQ are presented in Figure 3.1.

Figure 3.1 shows that enjoyment was most important to the young sport competitors, followed by achievement and then a group of socio-moral values consistent with fair play and sportsmanship. Although winning was most frequently referred to and spoken about in the context of moral dilemmas it was the least important to the youngsters when compared to other values in this study. The relative unimportance of winning to adolescent sport competitors will be surprising to some people. Value systems are significant, as it is not enough to know which values youngsters have. We also must know which values are most important because these will dominate when values conflict (Schwartz, 1992).

42  John Lambert

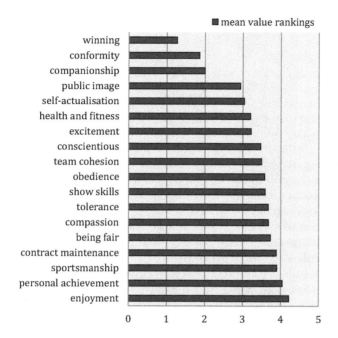

*Figure 3.1* The relative importance of values in youth sport. *Source: Adapted from Whitehead, 2011.*

## What are the implications of the research on young people's sport values for coaches and significant others?

Having ascertained what the sport value priorities of young people are, it is now appropriate to recognise how this research could impact on coaching practice. The following sport-specific scenarios are presented in order to demonstrate how conflict between the values of the coach and the young athlete can manifest itself in a sport setting and the subsequent problems that may occur.

> ### TOM AND ANDY
>
> Tom is 14 years old and plays for his local under-15 football team. His coach is Andy, who happens to be the father of his teammate Jason. Out of a coaching context, Tom gets along fine with Jason and his father and he often visits their house. However, Tom is not enjoying playing and training with his team. For a start, the coaching sessions consist mainly of boring,

*Understanding the sport values of young people* 43

repetitive drills that do not motivate him, or most of his friends for that matter. There is minimal time devoted to playing games. The principal reason that he wants to be there is to play games of football alongside his friends, but his coach is not providing that. They play competitive matches against other teams every Sunday but, instead of the on-pitch time being shared evenly across the squad, the best seven players (according to Andy's judgement), including Jason, get far more playing time than the rest. Tom is one of 'the rest.' Like all of the boys on the touchline, he recognises that some players are better than others and that they have more chance of winning if those kids are on the pitch, but he just wants to play! Andy gets frustrated and annoyed with the team if they lose which puts extra pressure on the players, especially those, like Tom, who are the 'fringe' players. Consequently, they are so nervous when they do play that they neither perform to their potential nor enjoy it. Tom respects the referee's calls on decisions, so Andy's insistence that his players appeal for every decision makes him feel uncomfortable. The result of a match is everything to Andy and even if they play well and lose, the team are told about their shortcomings with no mention of the 'positives.' Tom is becoming disillusioned with football due to the negative experiences that he is subjected to at training and matches and is considering taking up another sport that is more likely to involve less pressure and more fun. Some of the other 'marginalised' players, supported by their parents, are also considering leaving. Nobody has told Andy how these children feel for fear of him taking it as personal criticism.

## SUSIE AND BOB

Bob is the coach at the local tennis club and has been coaching Susie, a 12-year-old girl, since she first arrived at the club with her mother at the age of six. Susie has developed her tennis to the extent that she now represents her county. At the local level she wins nearly all of her matches, but when she plays at representative level her results are disappointing. This frustrates Bob, who is mainly interested in outcome goals and his notion of success is purely framed around winning and losing. Susie tries very hard in every match, is committed to training/coaching sessions and is generally dedicated to her sport. She feels that she is improving in terms of her performance. However, she accepts that most of her opponents at the county level are more talented than her and she is just content to compete against them.

> She enjoys it when she plays at or near to her potential, even if it is not enough to win. Bob does not see it that way. He tries to motivate her by questioning her effort levels and her desire to win, which upsets Susie as she knows that she is doing everything she can to turn the match in her favour. She also feels uneasy when Bob vents his frustration with the officials when line calls do not go in her favour. The situation has come to a head as she is beginning to dread going to county fixtures because she will be likely to be subjected to constant unfair criticism. She feels loyalty to Bob as they have been together six years and she knows that he just wants her to do well, but the situation is unsustainable as her enjoyment is diminishing. She has a difficult choice ahead of her: her options are either to give up tennis, move to another coach or tell Bob that his behaviour is damaging her tennis.

It is likely that one or both of these scenarios resonate with readers, as they are both based on real-life situations that have been encountered by the author both as coach and player. They illustrate how the values of the coach and the young performer can clash. In both cases, it led to a great deal of anguish for the young athlete and a potential breakdown in the coach–athlete relationship. Children are not mini-adults, but the coaches have imposed a set of values from an adult professional sport model on the sport environments that they have facilitated and these values are in direct conflict to the value systems of their young athletes (Bardi and Schwartz, 2013). The coaches make the assumption that the children with whom they work value winning above everything else, whereas enjoyment, fairness, good game, companionship and team cohesion are manifestly more important to them. That is not to say that winning is not important to young people in sport but, as this chapter illustrates, for many of them it is not as important as other values in their personal value system.

In the light of widespread unethical behaviour in adult sport, where there is often a moral conflict between cheating to win and playing fairly, there is a need to minimise the permeation of such behaviour into youth sport (Lee, 1997, Bardi and Schwartz, 2013). The influence of adults, coaches and parents in particular in youth sport can often lead to unethical behaviour from the children as adult values encroach on the playing area. As part of a co-existence project involving Arab and Jewish children in Israel, researchers found that if given autonomy to referee their own games, children are more likely to adhere to the laws and show more sportsmanship (Lambert, 2013). This is consistent with the high relative priority of socio-moral values, such as sportsmanship, contract maintenance and fairness in Lee's research. In both of the above scenarios, the coach, whilst not cheating directly, is trying to gain an unfair advantage by placing extra pressure on the officials. In both cases it has led to embarrassment and anxiety for the young participants concerned, but there is a wider concern that some children may be influenced by the coach enough to adopt such behaviour themselves.

Both of the coaches are well intentioned, but they are unaware of the dissonance created by their methods. Practitioners in the youth coaching domain have difficult decisions to make in terms of practice orientation to match competing demands and assumptions 'for' and 'about' their practice (Devine and Telfer, 2013). They typically feel pressure on them to interpret success in terms of the results that their athletes gain as this is often how others assess their reputation.

If coaches and significant others understood the sport value priorities of young people, then they would be more inclined to adopt a developmental approach which puts emphasis on enjoyment, improvement, collaboration, skill development, fairness and sportsmanship. In turn, this would be more likely to lead to adaptive and cohesive relationships with their young athletes as opposed to value conflict. By meeting the values of young people, coaches are more likely to see improved quality of motivation and sustained participation from their young charges that is ultimately likely to lead to enhanced performance (Duda and Whitehead, 2016).

Alongside his research on children's sport values, Martin worked with coaches in encouraging them to examine their own values in relation to sport and how that impacted on their practice. He encouraged them to interrogate the reasons why they coach children and to look at the values that are important to the club in which they worked (Lee, 1993). This research showed differences in what they value, and consequently how they behave, in life generally as well as in sports settings. Consequently, many of them began to look again at what they believed to be most important. Part of this research was to also facilitate opportunities for coaches to find out what are the most important values to the young people with whom they work.

## Conclusion

As a teacher and a coach, Martin Lee cared about the development and well-being of young athletes, and he was concerned that they should not have an adult sport model imposed on them. His mantra was 'sport for kids' and not 'kids for sport.' He challenged assumptions and conventional wisdom in the field of youth sport. It is hoped that this chapter will bring his work to the wider attention of coaches and coach educators and that it will influence their coaching philosophy and practice as a result. Dr Jean Whitehead, one of his ex-colleagues, has ensured that Martin's academic legacy continues to be accessible to academics in the fields of social psychology and sport science through academic conferences and literature. There is a clear rationale for further research in this area given contemporary problems of sustained engagement in physical activity by young people and the prevalence of unethical behaviour in youth sport (Lee, 2004b). One major challenge is to bridge the evidence–practice divide and raise awareness of Martin's research amongst coach educators and National Governing Bodies (NGBs). Coaches can be very influential in relation to the young people that they work with and therefore have a great responsibility to offer them the most developmentally appropriate experience of sport that they possibly can. The first part of this process should be to understand why children play sport and what is important to them.

## Note

1 For more information on the measurement of values and sport values in general, read Whitehead, J., Telfer, H. and Lambert, J. (2013), *Values in Youth Sport and Physical Education*, London: Routledge.

## References

Bardi, A., and Schwartz, S. (2013). 'How does value structure underlie value conflict? To win fairly or to win at all costs?' In: J. Whitehead, H. Telfer, and J. Lambert, eds. *Values in youth sport and physical education*. London: Routledge, 137–151.

Devine, C., and Telfer, H. (2013). 'Why are sport and physical education valuable? Values, sport and physical education.' In: J. Whitehead, H. Telfer, and J. Lambert, eds. *Values in youth sport and physical education*. London: Routledge, 13–34.

Duda, J.L., and Whitehead, J. (2016). 'Toward quality not quantity in sport motivation.' In: J. Wallis, and J. Lambert, eds. *Becoming a sports coach*. London: Routledge, 110–121.

Lambert, J. (2013). 'How do we teach values through sport? A values-based approach to coaching sport in divided societies.' In: J. Whitehead, H. Telfer, and J. Lambert, eds. *Values in youth sport and physical education*. London: Routledge, 152–165.

Lee, M. (1993). 'Why are you coaching children?' In: M. Lee, ed. *Coaching children in sport: Principles and practice*. London: E. & F.N. Spon, 27–38.

Lee, M., and Cockman, M. (1995). 'Values in children's sport: Spontaneously expressed values among young athletes.' *International Review for the Sociology of Sport*, 30 (3–4), 337–352.

Lee, M. (1997). 'Values foundations of ethical decisions in children's sport.' In: A. Tomlinson, and S. Fleming, eds. *Ethics, sport and leisure: Crises and critiques*. Aachen: Meyer and Meyer, 126–141.

Lee, M., Whitehead, J., and Balchin, N. (2000). 'The measurement of values in youth sport: development of the Youth Sport Values Questionnaire.' *Journal of Sport and Exercise Psychology*, 22 (4), 307–326.

Lee, M. (2004a). 'The importance of values in the coaching process.' In: M. Silva, and R. Malina, eds. *Children and youth in organized sports*. Coimbra: Coimbra University Press, 82–94.

Lee, M. (2004b). 'Values in youth sport and physical education: A conflict of interest?' *The British Journal of Teaching Physical Education*, 35 (1), 6–10.

Schwartz, S. (1992). 'Universals in the content and structure of values: Theoretical advances and empirical tests in 20 countries.' In: M.P. Zanna, ed. *Advances in experimental social psychology*, 25. London: Academic Press, 1–65.

Schwartz, S. (1994). 'Are there universal aspects in the structure and contents of human values?' *Journal of Social Issues*, 50 (4), 19–45.

Whitehead, J. (2011). 'Understanding fair play in youth sport through children's values and attitudes: Some insights of Martin Lee.' *Physical Education Matters*, 6 (1), 23–24, 26–27.

# 4 Coaching female combat athletes

## Creating positive environments for women and girls

*Catherine Phipps, Anastasia Khomutova and Alex Channon*

### Introduction

The aim of this chapter is to illustrate several problems which may be apparent for women and girls practising and competing in combat sports, before offering recommendations for coaches and practitioners to begin to address these concerns. Although the recommendations outlined are based upon issues arising in combat sports particularly, coaches working with women and girls in a range of sports may also find them useful to enhance inclusive practice. The term 'combat sports' encompasses a broad range of different fighting disciplines, with the focus of this chapter being those which are competition-orientated. These are usually institutionally organised activities, including (but not limited to) boxing, Brazilian jiu jitsu (BJJ), judo, karate, kickboxing, mixed-martial arts (MMA) and Muay Thai (Channon and Jennings, 2014). Combat sport environments are somewhat unique in contrast to many sports, in their tendency to operate in gender-integrated settings, where men and women often train and spar together (Carlsson, 2017; Channon, 2014; Maclean, 2016). Although many of these activities are typically considered 'masculine' and are, by and large, numerically dominated by men, some clubs may have a roughly even proportion of men and women members. Recently, the high-profile exposure of women's combat sports through the inclusion of women boxers in the Olympic Games and women mixed-martial artists in the *Ultimate Fighting Championship* early in the 2010s suggests growing public acceptance of, interest in and likely participation in these sports by women.

However, past research on a variety of combat sports has indicated that, despite women's growing presence in the field, gendered hierarchies are often sustained in these mixed environments, and a broad range of problems for women and girls remain present within them. For example, direct discrimination against women from coaches has been found in boxing and kickboxing (Lafferty and McKay, 2004; McNaughton, 2012); sex-differentiated training interactions which position women as inferior to men are apparent in judo (Guérandel and Mennesson, 2007); and men's amateur boxing generally enjoys a higher social status in gyms compared to women's (Tjønndal, 2016). These examples are not exhaustive;

the research literature indicates that a broad range of discriminatory practices towards women and girls are evident in combat sport environments, which we discuss at several points below.

Despite their widespread nature, it is worth stressing that some of these discriminatory practices may not be easy to recognise or readily understood by those involved as 'discrimination' at all. Nevertheless, for women and girls in sport, both tangible and intangible barriers to full and equal participation exist, with 'invisible' male privilege and institutionalised sexism resulting in potentially 'hidden' issues becoming problematic. Thus, this chapter highlights some of the barriers which are tangible and obvious, alongside those which may not be so clear to coaches and practitioners but remain important in the experiences of female combat athletes. If not addressed, these areas of concern may potentially result in lower participation rates, higher drop-out rates and a lack of talent development for women and girls.

Anecdotal evidence – including our own variety of experiences in combat sports – suggests that there are a higher number of male coaches and club owners in comparison to women in this field (Mierzwinski and Phipps, 2015). Indeed, coaching work more broadly is often considered male-dominated and a 'masculine' profession (Kamphoff and Gill, 2013). Accordingly, a lack of women coaches in many combat sports may mean that specific challenges facing women and girls are overlooked, side-lined or ignored, particularly given that men are unlikely to have first-hand experiential knowledge of these problems or wider issues related to sexual discrimination that they represent. Therefore, the ability of women's and girls' male coaches (and training partners) to recognise such problems becomes an important issue to address when considering how to best cater to female combat sports participants.

In this chapter, we attempt to outline three interconnected problems that, based on our joint experiences of participating in, working alongside and researching women's combat sports, we argue to be important for male coaches, in particular, to understand. Although not an exhaustive list, we argue that these are problems which may not be readily apparent to coaches, but are nevertheless crucially important in shaping women's experiences, along with their intentions to either continue participating or drop out of combat sports. These problems are introduced in theoretical terms and then exemplified through the use of fictitious vignettes. We have based these short stories on amalgamations of selected episodes from the first author's experiences of training in a range of combat sports (most recently boxing and Muay Thai) for a total of 20 years; the second author's work as a performance psychologist with female combat athletes over the past three years; and research projects conducted by all three authors spanning the past ten years. While based on factual information and paraphrasing real peoples' stories and quotes, the vignettes are creatively embellished in order to demonstrate the problems under examination in a clear and succinct manner within the confines of this chapter. The vignettes are then followed by suggestions and recommendations for coaches in order to address the outlined concerns.

## 'It's just banter': Considering appropriate language and humour in combat sport environments

This initial section includes a discussion of 'banter,' humour and language in sport settings more broadly, followed by combat sport environments in particular. 'Banter' has been defined by Nichols (2018) as a form of interaction which may be used (particularly by men) to convey sexist and misogynistic ideas, including offensive and abusive language. However, not all 'banter' is exclusionary or discriminatory. According to Rongland and Aggerholm (2013), positive use of humour and 'banter' (which may include jokes, puns, sarcasm, irony and ridicule as well as non-verbal behaviours) can result in an increased level of group cohesion, solidarity, mutual trust and productivity between sportspeople. Such outcomes are often held up as the purpose of banter in sport settings. However, this remains a 'double-edged sword' which, under certain conditions, can also lead to social exclusion, emphasising borders between 'insiders' and 'outsiders' and promoting the superiority of certain groups over others (Ronglan and Aggerholm, 2013).

Consequently, depending on the context, humour and 'banter' may be exclusionary when used at the expense of individuals or particular groups. Indeed, 'sexist' banter and humour (particularly in mixed-gender settings) potentially reinforces ideas that women and girls are 'outsiders' in combat sports, which underpins gender divisions and power hierarchies. Although 'banter' and humour are often used in a casual way, the language may highlight subtle isolation of a section of the community (Willis, 2012; Long, 2000), while reinforcing the belief that women athletes are inferior to men and ought to occupy lower-status positions in sport settings (Jarvie, 2018).

Regarding the dialogue used more broadly in combat sport environments, it is argued gender inequalities and stereotypes can be transmitted and perpetuated through language use. According to Andrés et al. (2014), language is not only a vehicle for communicating ideas, but it also conveys ideologies and power relations in specific contexts. Stereotyped and gender-biased expressions arguably subordinate women and girls, as well as promote their exclusion from 'masculine' activities, mirroring a wider social reality where women are considered inferior (Andrés et al., 2014). For instance, phrases like 'don't throw like a girl' demonstrate gender ideologies and stereotypes in sport settings (Kamphoff and Gill, 2013). In combat sports, phrases like 'punch like a girl' may also be used as an insult, evident in Carlsson's (2017) research on boxing in Scotland, whereby the term was used in a derogatory manner when a boxer of any gender underperformed, or when female boxers complained during training.

These remarks contribute to a culture which is degrading towards women as athletes (Fasting, 2013), reducing them to their gender category rather than respecting them as athletes *per se* (see also Owton, 2015). In addition, this language emphasises men's standards as the model for which everyone should aspire to, reproducing masculinity as the norm and deepening the implication that women are outsiders in this space (Andrés et al., 2014). In turn, perceptions that

## 50 Phipps, Khomutova and Channon

women and girls are less athletic may be perpetuated, potentially impeding them from performing to their true athletic capabilities, a phenomenon known as 'stereotype threat' (Hively and El-Alayli, 2013).

Clearly, gendered language is normalised in society, possibly leading to (unintentional) exclusionary practices within combat sport settings. However, challenging exclusionary and discriminatory language also has the potential to be problematic, particularly as gendered language is often a taken-for-granted, 'normal' feature of sports culture. Thus, confronting coaches (and other practitioners) on their language use may alienate those who consider this a pointless exercise in 'political correctness' (PC), a term which has many negative connotations (Ackroyd and Pilkington, 2007). The criticism of 'political correctness' as having 'gone mad' or 'too far' supports the perspectives of more powerful groups while risking marginalising others, as it discourages them from challenging discriminatory language due to the threat of being categorised as a politically correct kill-joy in a society which generally discredits this label (Ackroyd and Pilkington, 2007). However, this deflection of criticism misses the point; what some may experience as 'just banter' can, in certain respects, have a directly negative impact on somebody else, making them feel as though they do not really belong in the social group that they are trying to be part of.

### Vignette – Stop being so PC!

*Colin, 55, is a kickboxing coach who proudly describes himself as 'old school.' He perceives banter to be a great way of forming relationships with the fighters he coaches, and often drifts between seriousness and joking in his training. He believes that his students enjoy this 'informal' approach; however, the tone of many of his jokes tends to be either implicitly or outright sexist, which his female students (in particular) do not appreciate.*

*During any typical lesson, Colin will make multiple gendered remarks, almost always to his male students, along the lines of comparing them to women and 'schoolgirls' when they fail to meet his expectations; typically, he exhorts them to 'stop hitting like a girl!' Although it is widely understood that Colin does not intend these remarks as indirect insults to the women in the class, the women he trains describe their feelings about these jokes in the following ways:*

*Maria, 17, notices that Colin refers to any sloppy technique executed by the boys as 'schoolgirl-style kung fu'; 'he says, you're not here to learn schoolgirl-style are you? It pisses me off, I'm like, look, I'm right here, you know I am like, literally a schoolgirl, and you're still saying that! It's quite disrespectful.' Shaunee, 22, echoes this: 'he goes, 'right, everybody do press-ups, and girls, do girl-press-ups,' like, on our knees. So what's that mean? We're not part of 'everybody,' like we're different, and we can't do press-ups on our toes because it's too hard? I don't like it, he's a good coach but that's just sexist.'*

*Sara, 30, is one of Colin's older students. She worked up the courage to challenge him about his use of language: 'I told him it made me and the other girls feel uncomfortable that he kept saying this stuff. He said, basically, it's just banter, it's my fault if I got offended. I should get thicker skin, like how can I take punches if I can't deal with him talking about hitting like a girl.' Sara was frustrated that Colin did not even try to see things from her point of view and admitted that she was thinking of moving to another club because he held this attitude.*

*Like Sara, Monique, 42, who had trained with Colin several years previously, also challenged him about his use of language. She ended up leaving his club, to later start her own ladies-only kickboxing classes at a local leisure centre. She says, 'I basically had a bit of a set-to with him. He wouldn't back down, saying like, 'it's just a bit of fun, why do you have to be so uptight? Stop being so PC,' all that sort of thing. He didn't want to accept that his jokes weren't funny to me, that they offended me, so I was like, right, I'm out of here.'*

Recommendations for coaches and practitioners

- Coaches and practitioners in combat sports should engage in reflexive coaching, considering their language use from others' perspectives; could the impact of certain jokes be interpreted differently from their intention? It is also worth considering what is more important – being able to 'have a laugh' in ways which may be perceived and interpreted as sexist, or trying to prevent one's club members from feeling isolated or excluded and potentially quitting.
- Language should promote inclusion and equity; for instance, avoiding gendered terms such as '… like a girl' to describe something as less difficult, effective or valuable than the norm. Coaches should also avoid addressing the whole class as 'boys'/'lads' when women and girls are training, and consider what women may think if they are addressed directly as 'women' while men are described in a gender-neutral way as 'everybody,' or 'the class,' etc.
- As 'banter' and humour are often considered an important aspect of training sessions (and can arguably promote social cohesion and belonging), coaches should aim to foster a climate of inclusive 'banter,' which does not risk marginalising or excluding particular groups.
- These outcomes can be accomplished without having to think too closely about which words one should and should not use. By making the effort to recognise women/girls and men/boys as equals, one's use of inclusive and equitable language should flow naturally from there.

## 'Are you a lesbian?': Assumptions surrounding the sexuality of women and girls in combat sports

Many combat sports are traditionally understood as 'masculine' activities, with an emphasis on strength, power, aggression and physical domination over an opponent. By extension, these activities have historically been considered exclusively male, whereby women may be subject to the 'lesbian label' due to apparent inconsistencies with their choice of activity and gender ideals (Griffin, 2002). In other words, athleticism and understandings of femininity may be regarded as mutually

## 52  Phipps, Khomutova and Channon

exclusive (Kamphoff and Gill, 2013). This is evident within the existing coaching literature; according to Cassidy et al., (2004), stereotypes around sexuality (including the fear of being labelled lesbian) may impact the sports and activities women and girls choose to participate in initially (thereby potentially avoiding 'masculine' sports), as well as their effort and willingness to engage in training programmes if they do become involved. This may be particularly prevalent in those sports which involve the development of muscularity (Cassidy et al., 2004).

Thus, the 'lesbian label' is still common today and used as a tool of sexism to question female athletes' sexuality and femininity, usually when they demonstrate skill and expertise in 'masculine' activities (Travers, 2006). As per the previous section of this chapter, this type of sexism may be passed off as harmless 'banter' which is embedded and normalised in many sporting cultures (Nichols, 2018); however, this perspective fails to recognise the potential negative implications of stereotyping for women and girls in combat sports. Assumptions surrounding the sexuality of women and girls reinforces combat sports as exclusively masculine, potentially discouraging female participation, accentuating the myth that girls and women simply lack interest in 'masculine' sports, which ignores history, ideology and culture which has shaped their experiences and interests (Cooky, 2009). It also potentially places limits on acceptable behaviour and performances for women and girls, for instance regarding physical strength. This has been found in previous research on women in a variety of sports, for instance in football (Engh, 2011).

For those women and girls who do continue their participation in 'masculine' sports, they may feel pressured to emphasise their femininity, often considered interchangeable with heterosexuality (Lenskyj, 2012). Otherwise known as the 'female apologetic,' this process involves the emphasis of typically feminine characteristics, such as long hair, feminine clothing, and the use of make-up to emphasise heterosexual attractiveness (Lenskyj, 2012). It is regarded as a form of 'emphasised femininity' which privileges those who are heterosexually appealing, a coping strategy used by some women in predominantly 'masculine' sports (Engh, 2011). Although the display of femininity by women should not automatically be considered as restrictive and coercive – and can indeed pose a challenge to traditional understandings of gender – women whose femininity involves an over-sexualised image can receive strong criticism in mixed-sex environments (Channon and Phipps, 2017). For instance, stereotypes and assumptions that women are sexually available to their male training partners, and may be predominantly training to meet and sleep with men, threatens the position of women as respected members of their gym (Channon and Jennings, 2014).

Whether women combat athletes are stereotyped as lesbians or viewed by their male training partners primarily as sex objects, in both instances attention has been diverted away from their athletic ability and identity, framing them primarily as sexualised women rather than (fellow) athletes or martial artists. Not only does this risk reducing women to their gender category, but also doing so in a way that treats men's sexual access to them (or not) as the most interesting thing about them.

## Coaching female combat athletes   53

### Vignette – 'The slut of the gym'

*Lena, 33, has been practising BJJ for ten years and has attained the rank of brown belt. She is physically strong, with well-defined muscles, and has short hair. She describes herself as 'a bit of a tomboy' and is happy with this label. However, although she identifies as straight, she is often assumed to be a lesbian by others, which she believes is because of her appearance.*

*At the start of her training in BJJ, she trained at a gym where her ambiguous gender identity and sexuality was often made the butt of jokes by the male coach and her mostly-male, older and senior club mates. Without being 'in' on the joke, she was routinely referred to as someone to watch out for when new female members joined the gym – she was labelled 'the club lesbian' by the coach, who would 'turn' women on the mat 'if they weren't careful.'*

*Lena loved jiu jitsu and didn't know any better than the example set at this club, so she endured the joke at her expense. She felt a pressure to go along with the joke to an extent, even though it made her uncomfortable. However, because she was worried that this could actually put women off from training with her, or from training in BJJ altogether, she openly emphasised the fact that she was dating a man in the club to defuse the joke whenever it was made.*

*However, after this relationship broke up, Lena found it very difficult to stay in the club, since the man she was dating was a senior member who was central to the club's social group. Training together, and with his male friends in a grappling-based martial art, was simply too awkward. She was even asked by the coach to 'give him (her ex) some space' by taking a break from training. At this point, she decided to leave the club. She has seen this same process at other gyms since, noting that 'when relationships break up, it's usually the girl who ends up leaving.'*

*Later, after dating another man at another club she joined afterwards, she became the butt of jokes about her sexuality again. This time, she was openly referred to by her coach as 'the slut of the gym,' because she had had more than one relationship with another jiu jitsu player – her ex was well-known in the local BJJ circles. At one point, an assistant coach even joked that Lena exchanged sexual favours for being taught new techniques, thereby explaining her impressive BJJ skills.*

*Although she knew it was 'just banter,' Lena was humiliated and frustrated by the fact that she could not escape begin sexualised by the men around her. She wanted to be seen as Lena the brown belt – not Lena the lesbian, or Lena the slut. Unsurprisingly, Lena also left this second club.*

### Recommendations for coaches and practitioners

- Avoid publicly discussing or speculating about women's and girls' sexual orientation, as this may serve to perpetuate unhelpful and homophobic myths about women in so-called 'masculine' sports, while also encouraging other club members to view women primarily as sexual objects rather than training partners.
- Similarly, while sexual relationships within combat sports clubs are not uncommon, and coaches may not wish to explicitly discourage this or hide

54  *Phipps, Khomutova and Channon*

it from view, they should be conscious of the impact of consistently referring to women, in particular, with reference to their sexual involvement with others in the club.

- In line with Cassidy et al. (2004), coaches should critically reflect on their own assumptions surrounding women's and girls' sexualities as well as their motivations for training. They should aim to actively consider their own language, avoiding the use of sexist/homophobic terms (which are usually inter-related).
- Coaches should aim to be proactive in creating environments which contest existing stereotypes. This may include challenging others' language use and actions when necessary, to eradicate homophobic and sexualised comments and 'banter,' ensuring an inclusive and safe environment for everyone regardless of their sexuality.

## 'She won't last': Stereotyping women as outsiders and intruders in combat sports

As stated previously, women's participation in combat sports may be increasing (Follo, 2012), but these activities are usually considered 'masculine,' and are typically dominated by men, celebrating power, physical strength, confidence and authority, which are traditionally seen as 'masculine' characteristics (Carlsson, 2017). When women enter such a 'masculine' space, problems may arise from gendered stereotypes and assumptions on the part of others. For instance, some coaches may make presumptions about women's motivations, and it may be assumed that women train only for fitness or self-defence, with no intention of becoming fighters (Jennings, 2015; Lafferty and McKay, 2004; McNaughton, 2012). As such, coaches may invest little effort into women who join their gyms if they presume they are in the 'wrong place' and ultimately 'won't last long,' prioritising men within certain aspects of training, such as sparring, which is an essential element of training for competitive fighting. This was evident in Lafferty and McKay's (2004) research, whereby women boxers had less sparring time, coach instruction and access to key resources in contrast to their male counterparts. This situates combat sports such as boxing as male-dominated activities whereby women may believe they are 'intruding' in a male space by being present; at best, they are only ever second-class citizens of their gyms.

Such an impression can be further entrenched when mixed-sex partner activities, most of all sparring exercises, involve a marked reluctance by men or boys to participate in ways which treat female partners as equals (Channon & Jennings, 2014; McNaughton, 2012; Owton, 2015). According to Guérandel and Mennesson (2007), there is a tendency for male martial artists to relate to their female partners primarily through a 'gender frame' rather than a 'martial arts frame'; that is, they view women and girls *as women and girls*, rather than fellow martial artists. This leads to perceiving sparring (or competitive fighting) encounters with women and girls as 'lose–lose' situations; if they beat or hurt a woman, this is dishonourable and so they lose face as a man, whereas if they are beaten or hurt by a woman, this threatens their masculinity given that they have just 'lost to a girl' (Channon, 2013). Several researchers have argued that when this happens, and men/boys either withdraw all effort from sparring, or put excessive force into their efforts to ensure they 'win,' women and girls are left feeling frustrated and humiliated, and thus are more likely to drop out of clubs, or combat sports altogether.

Therefore, when women and girls do become involved and invested in gyms, tackling the assumption that women don't really belong or fit in is important in order to sustain their participation. Due to societal expectations of appropriate behaviour for women, and the unfamiliar nature of sparring (particularly with men), some women may lack confidence, feel insecure about their ability or intimidated training alongside men. Furthermore, Yap (2016) notes that some women and girls may initially find it difficult to inflict pain on others in a combat sport environment (particularly those women who do initially train for fitness and health reasons) due to the the internalisation of ideas that they should not behave in an aggressive manner. As a consequence, women may have accepted the assumption that combat sports are not really 'for' them, and can be insecure about entering a combat sports gym, being afraid of spoiling everyone else's training or having concerns about being the only woman present (Khomutova, forthcoming). Women can also struggle with the infrastructure in combat sports gyms, which very often lack separate changing rooms or showers for females (Khomutova, forthcoming; Paradis, 2012).

As such, feelings of being out-of-place, not belonging, and so on, are not always the fault of men (or other women) in these environments; they may be a result of internalised gender norms or produced through a lack of available infrastructure. Nevertheless, these are feelings that coaches can and should try to address in order to improve the retention of women in their clubs. With that said, in our experience of researching and participating in this field, coaches do not often take responsibility for doing so. In fact, women and girls are often burdened with the responsibility in this regard; they are very often expected to 'prove' themselves to their male coaches and training partners before receiving the kind of treatment that men and boys tend to receive right away. Moreover, based on their experiences of feeling unwelcome, many women who 'stick it out' eventually assume responsibility for the welfare of other women who join the clubs after them, engaging in a kind of coaching work that more or less amounts to unpaid and unacknowledged labour (Kavoura et al., 2015). For some women, this can distract from their own priorities in training.

## Vignette – 'They're my responsibility'

*Karen, 25, had been thinking about doing boxing for a few years and finally decided to join a boxing club after watching women box at the Olympic Games. When she came to a boxing club for her first session, the male head coach told her, 'We don't have a boxercise class here; you might want to try the leisure centre down the road.'*

Karen explained that she was interested in competitive boxing training and stayed for the session, despite visible scepticism from the coach and the awkwardness of their first encounter. She was not given any advice on training and was asked to train at the edge of the gym space, so the more experienced boxers, who were all men, would have enough room to work.

Despite this, Karen continued to attend regular training sessions for several months. Only after demonstrating her commitment to boxing did the head coach give her more attention and advice related to training. Similarly, the other boxers in the club only started to talk to her and make her feel included in the gym after her skills were visibly improving. Karen explained that when new men joined the club after her, she noticed how they were socially included much faster than she was, and that the coach did not treat them with the same kind of indifference.

About a year after she started, a few younger women joined the club too. Karen says that her coach still doesn't do anything to welcome women in the club, so she tries to help them herself by chatting to them, showing them simple moves and overall mentoring them: 'I want them to feel welcome in the club and to get the attention I didn't have a chance to when I first joined. I'm like the big sister to them. It's quite hard to fit in here with the boys, so I see helping them as my responsibility, really.'

Despite this positive turn, Karen still struggles to get sparring time with male training partners in her weight category, which is necessary since there are no other women at her weight in the gym. She says that it has got too frustrating to keep asking the men at her weight to spar, since nobody goes out of their way to offer, and the coach doesn't ask them to. She has considered leaving the gym for another in order to get better sparring practice but now feels as though she needs to stay for the sake of the other women – even though she is not paid or recognised at all for her role in mentoring them.

Recommendations for coaches and practitioners

- Steps should be taken to encourage participation for all who show an interest in combat sports, including women and girls. Coaches should avoid assuming that women are only interested in fitness-related versions of combat sports, or directing them to other gyms, as this creates an impression that their participation is not normal, valued or desired.
- Gender stereotypes often influence impressions of women's and girls' ability in so-called masculine sports. Coaches should be proactive in questioning their own gendered ideas about the ability of women and girls, avoiding presumptions that they are best suited to training and sparring with each other in every circumstance.
- Greater visibility of women in combat sports may help contest others' stereotyping, as well as inspire women and girls to work harder and achieve more. As such, coaches should actively seek to make female fighters visible, either through discussing professional women's fights, making use of female coaches or assistants, and/or publicly valuing the women in their clubs.
- Although it is wise to see each person as an individual, coaches should remain mindful of possible gender differences between men and women when they first start training. This could mean taking steps to accommodate women's

Coaching female combat athletes 57

and girls' particular needs, effectively 'meeting them where they are' when they start training, as opposed to making assumptions about how long they will last within the gym.

## Summary

In this chapter we have approached the question of coaching women and girls in combat sports via several propositions: firstly, that women and girls are a growing population in various gyms and clubs; secondly, that most combat sports coaches are men; and, thirdly, that many problems facing women and girls may not be immediately obvious to such men. By exploring problems connected to gendered social norms, including issues to do with the perception of what may be unintentionally sexist banter as well as stereotyping and assumptions made by those they train with, we have focused here on some of the social-psychological dimensions of coaching women and girls. This is not to say that problematic issues cannot arise in other areas (such as to do with the physiological demands of managing pregnancy and motherhood, for instance – another problem which male coaches are likely to have very little personal familiarity!). Rather, we chose to focus on these points given their widespread importance to large numbers of women with whom we have conversed, worked and trained in this field, coupled with the fact that the majority of the men we have encountered are often unaware of these as 'problems.' It is our hope that the points made, stories told, and suggestions forwarded in this chapter may help to provoke those working and training in combat sports to consider ways in which they can improve the experiences of women and girls in their clubs.

## References

Ackroyd, J., and Pilkington, A. (2007). 'Keynote: "You're not allowed to say that": Minefields and political correctness.' *Caribbean Quarterly*, 53 (1–2), 49–62.

Andrés, O.C., Granados, S.R., Ramírez, T.G., Mesa, M.C.C., and Motriz, R. C. (2014). 'Gender equity in physical education: The use of language.' *The Journal of Physical Education*, 20 (3), 239–248.

Carlsson, H. (2017). 'Researching boxing bodies in Scotland: Using apprenticeship to study the embodied construction of gender in hyper masculine space.' *Gender, Place and Culture*, 24 (7), 939–953.

Cassidy, T., Jones, R., and Potrac, P. (2004). *Understanding sports coaching: The social, cultural and pedagogical foundations of coaching practice*. Abingdon: Routledge.

Channon, A. (2013). "Do you hit girls?' some striking moments in the career of a male martial artist'. In: Sánchez García, R., and Spencer, D.C., eds. *Fighting scholars: Habitus and ethnographies of martial arts and combat sports*. London: Anthem, 95–110.

Channon, A. (2014). 'Towards the "undoing" of gender in mixed-sex martial arts and combat sports.' *Societies*, 4 (4), 587–605.

Channon, A., and Jennings, G. (2014). 'Exploring embodiment through martial arts and combat sports: A review of empirical research.' *Sport in Society*, 17 (6), 773–789.

Channon, A., and Phipps, C. (2017). 'Pink gloves still give black eyes: Exploring 'alternative' femininity in women's combat sports.' *Martial Arts Studies*, 3 (3), 24–37.

58 *Phipps, Khomutova and Channon*

Cooky, C. (2009). '"Girls just aren't interested": The social construction of interest in girls' sport.' *Sociological Perspectives*, 52 (2), 259–284.

Engh, M.H. (2011). 'Tackling femininity: The heterosexual paradigm and women's soccer in South Africa.' *The International Journal of the History of Sport*, 28 (1), 137–152.

Fasting, K. (2013). 'Dangerous liaisons: harassment and abuse in coaching.' In: Potrac, P., Gilbert, W., and Denison, J., eds. *Routledge handbook of sports coaching*. Oxon: Routledge, 333–344.

Follo, G. (2012). 'A literature review of women and the martial arts: Where are we right now?.' *Sociology Compass*, 6 (9), 707–717.

Griffin, P. (2002). 'Changing the game: Homophobia, sexism and lesbians in sport.' In: Scraton, S., and Flintoff, A., eds. *Gender and sport: a reader*. Oxon: Routledge, 193–208.

Guérandel, C., and Mennesson, C. (2007). 'Gender construction in judo interactions.' *International Review for the Sociology of Sport*, 42 (2), 167–186.

Hively, K., and El-Alayli, A. (2013). '"You throw like a girl:" The effect of stereotype threat on women's athletic performance and gender stereotypes.' *Psychology of Sport and Exercise*, 15 (1), 48–55.

Jarvie, G. (2018). *Sport, culture and society*. Abingdon: Routledge.

Jennings, L.A. (2015). *She's a knockout! A history of women in fighting sports*. London: Rowman and Littlefield.

Kamphoff, C.S., and Gill, D.L. (2013). 'Issues of exclusion and discrimination in the coaching profession.' In: Potrac, P., Gilbert, W., and Denison, J., eds. *Routledge handbook of sports coaching*. Oxon: Routledge, 52–66.

Kavoura, A., Chroni, S., Kokkonen, M., and Ryba, T.V. (2015). 'Women fighters as agents of change: A Brazilian jiu jitsu case study from Finland.' In: Channon, A., and Matthews, C.R., eds. *Global perspectives on women in combat sports: women warriors around the world*. Basingstoke: Palgrave Macmillan, 135–152.

Khomutova, A. (forthcoming). '"Is it okay if I come or will I spoil everyone else's training?": Women's experiences of participating in combat sports.' *Psychology of Sport and Exercise*.

Lafferty, Y., and McKay, J. (2004). '"Suffragettes in satin shorts"? Gender and competitive boxing.' *Qualitative Sociology*, 27 (3), 249–276.

Lenskyj, H.J. (2012). 'Reflections on communication and sport: On heteronormativity and gender identities.' *Communication and Sport*, 1 (1/2), 138–150.

Long, J. (2000). 'No racism here? A preliminary examination of sporting innocence.' *Managing Leisure*, 5 (3), 121–133.

Maclean, C. (2016). 'Friendships worth fighting for: Bonds between women and men karate practitioners as sites for deconstructing gender inequality.' *Sport in Society*, 19 (8–9), 1374–1384.

McNaughton, M.J. (2012). 'Insurrectionary womanliness: Gender and the (boxing) ring.' *The Qualitative Report*, 17 (33), 1–13.

Mierzwinski, M., and Phipps, C. (2015). '"I'm not the type of person who does yoga," Women, 'hard' martial arts and the quest for exciting significance.' In: Channon, A., and Matthews, C.R., eds. *Global perspectives on women in combat sports*. Basingstoke: Palgrave Macmillan, 237–252.

Nichols, K. (2018). 'Moving beyond ideas of laddism: Conceptualising 'mischievous masculinities' as a new way of understanding everyday sexism and gender relations.' *Journal of Gender Studies*, 27 (1), 73–85.

Owton, H. (2015). 'Reinventing the body-self: intense, gendered and heightened sensorial experiences of women's boxing embodiment.' In: Channon, A., and Matthews, C.R., eds. *Global perspectives on women in combat sports: women warriors around the world*. Basingstoke: Palgrave Macmillan, 221–236.

Paradis, E. (2012). 'Boxers, briefs or bras? Bodies, gender and change in the boxing gym.' *Body & Society*, 18 (2), 82–109.

Ronglan, L.T., and Aggerholm, K. (2013). 'Humour and sports coaching: A laughing matter?' In: Potrac, P., Gilbert, W., and Denison, J., eds. *Routledge handbook of sports coaching*. Abingdon: Routledge, 222–234.

Tjønndal, A. (2016). 'The inclusion of women's boxing in the Olympic Games: A qualitative content analysis of gender and power in boxing.' *Qualitative Sociology Review*, 12 (3), 84–99.

Travers, A. (2006). 'Queering sport: Lesbian softball leagues and the transgender challenge.' *International Review for the Sociology of Sport*, 41 (3/4), 431–446.

Willis, P. (2012). 'Witnesses on the periphery: Young lesbian, gay, bisexual and queer employees witnessing homophobic exchanges in Australian workplaces.' *Human Relations*, 65 (12), 1589–1610.

Yap, A. (2016). 'Throwing like a girl: Martial arts and norms of feminine body comportment.' *International Journal of Feminist Approaches to Bioethics*, 9 (2), 92–114.

# 5 Sport coaching in a disadvantaged community

## A case study of Freestyle BMX

*Ben Gould and Carlotta Giussani*

## Introduction

This chapter aims to analyse and present how an indoor skatepark's Freestyle BMX and skateboarding coach education programme (CEP), aimed at encouraging young people from an area of deprivation into BMX Freestyle and skateboarding participation, has grown and flourished in an area of economic and social deprivation in the United Kingdom to become a coaching and performance hub for Freestyle BMX. It aims to do this by highlighting where coaching principles of non-linear pedagogy compliment the nature of BMX Freestyle and skateboarding as sports of expression and creativity to a town, which itself has a historical culture of creativity and expression. By utilising the work of sociologist Pierre Bourdieu, it aims to map the journey of an experienced group of *riders* towards professionalisation as *coaches* involved in the skatepark's coaching provision, as it heads towards its induction into the 'family' of Olympic sports in 2020. The application of Bourdieu's theories of capital to the skatepark's CEP, allows the chapter to show the potential impact of professionalisation on the social development of an area of deprivation. The work of Bourdieu (1988) will also be used to explore the impact of Freestyle BMX's history on its further development towards mainstream culture through his work on 'habitus' and how this history can find alignment within a socially diverse town, such as Hastings. This social exploration aims to highlight that the sport and the social space that it occupies can together operate and develop to reflect each other. Furthermore, through the creation of the CEP, embedded within the fully functioning skatepark for Freestyle BMX and skateboarding, it can impact the sport as a whole as well as the area of deprivation within which the skatepark is located.

## Sport plus or plus sport?

As first and foremost a business enterprise, The Source skatepark operates through The Source BMX Ltd. The parent company was initially founded in 2003 as a retail store for BMX. Today, the Source BMX is an award-winning business recognised as a leading retailer in the BMX and skateboarding markets. In February 2016, the Source BMX launched the Source Park in a renovated former Victorian swimming baths beneath Hastings seafront. The Source Park is currently the largest underground indoor skatepark in the world, and its inception has been a catalyst for BMX Freestyle and skateboarding events from grassroots to world-class level being hosted in the local area. As well as the CEP, the Source Park also includes the Eagles coaching in BMX Freestyle and skateboarding, which aims to encourage local young people into BMX Freestyle and skateboarding by providing a structured, creative and safe environment to learn. Through the Eagles coaching, the Source Park operates as a 'sport-plus' Sport for Development (SfD) programme within the local community as it aims to produce local athletes who can compete professionally on a global scale, whilst they are also able to continue to live and train in the town of Hastings. Alongside this, the CEP allows the Eagles programme to operate a suitable environment within young BMX enthusiasts can learn.

The model of sport as a vehicle for social development is not a new concept. Historically, sport has been used in a wide variety of roles to engage the disengaged, address anti-social behaviour (Sandford et al., 2008), as well as provide elements of larger social regeneration projects (Coalter, 2007a). Sport has been said to facilitate the positive development of social values, life skills and pro-social behaviour (Spaaij and Jeanes, 2013). The relative success of SfD programmes is often determined by their aims and the implementation of particular activities that fulfil those objectives (Harris and Adams, 2016). It is the programme's objectives that determine the focus as either 'sport plus,' where increased participation in a sport can contribute towards social development, or 'plus sport' where social, educational and health programmes use sport as a tool within familiar territory or surroundings to bring people to new experiences (Coalter, 2007b). As Green (2009) highlights, within the plus sport model it may not be the sport itself that holds the key to the social development of its participants, but rather the manner of its implementation (Harris and Adams, 2016). The key difference between the two types of SfD concepts is that 'sport plus' begins with the participation in the sport and can bring about social development, whereas 'plus sport' begins with a social development concept and applies sport to transport the social development message. With the focus on Freestyle BMX and skateboarding at the heart of the programme at the Source Park, it is therefore considered a 'sport-plus' SfD programme, but where the benefits of the programme to the society can still be explored from the position of the participants and coaches. As the Source Park evolves it is likely that the potential of the physical activities for facilitating social development in participants will be further exploited, which may well lead to the 'plus sport' dimension becoming increasingly apparent in its operations.

## Source Coach Education Programme

The two intertwined but distinct coaching programmes, CEP and Eagles, complement one another as the CEP was launched to devise a formalised and recognised coaching pathway for BMX Freestyle and skateboarding in the United Kingdom. Within BMX Freestyle, the absence of any formal National Governing Bodies

(NGBs) has led to the lack of a recognised process for the education or accreditation of coaches, presenting a potential problem to the sustainability of both engagement and improved performance. The CEP intends to develop a coherent coach education course for BMX Freestyle and skateboarding in order to construct a database of well-informed, professional and qualified coaches. Indeed, the CEP aims to anticipate and convert the expected surge of interest in the run-up to the 2020 Olympic Games and beyond into sustained participation by providing qualified and professional coaches operating in suitable facilities.

The initial challenge of the introduction of a structured coaching programme for Freestyle BMX arose from the dichotomy between a 'free-spirited' sport with an absence of any centralised control or governance and the structured coaching regime which some viewed as a perceived threat encroaching on the 'liberated, unshackled DNA' of the sport. Indeed, the notion of coaching as a structured form of training is a new concept in Freestyle BMX, where riders may never have experienced being coached themselves. It was apparent from the outset that the BMX and skate communities would polarise at the prospect of more formal coaching processes. Views ranged from unconditional acceptance and engagement to immediate rejection. The majority remained ambivalent but curious, it is this group who held the key to generating majority support.

Traditional forms of knowledge transfer within Freestyle BMX have come from the informal passing of information and guidance between riders through unstructured forms that range from the sharing of unwritten knowledge on skatepark etiquette to how to progress rider performance. There was therefore a need to adopt a bottom-up approach with consideration paid to the recipients of this coach education pathway and to ensure that the authenticity of the values and heritage of the sport were upheld within the coaching programme. As a result, the course developed in two stages: an initial introduction to coach education with aims to provide the recipients with a generic understanding of coaching, followed by an in-depth and specific course in either the practice of BMX Freestyle or skateboarding coaching. The second stage aimed to maintain the element of creativity and the unstructured nature of the sport itself, in which coaches become active constructors and facilitators of their drills games and coaching content. Hence, the CEP has appropriately responded to challenges presented and developed a coherent coach education course which allows BMX Freestyle and skateboarding to flourish. Simultaneously, it led to the construction of a database of well-informed, professional and qualified coaches in the United Kingdom. Due to the deliberate provision of ownership, agency, individualism and freedom of expression in the design of coaching content, the BMX and skate coaching curriculum was widely embraced by the Source Park fraternity. It was a significant contributor to the breaking of negative perceptions of imposed and centralised coach education that initially inhibited buy-in from some in the BMX and skate communities.

The creative use of non-linear pedagogy as the core philosophy for the development of coaches in the CEP served the needs of the aspiring coaches. Renshaw et al. (2010) describe non-linear pedagogy as being based on 'the constant interactions of individuals and the environment where the learner is placed at the centre of the process as movements and decisions are made based on unique interacting individual, task and environmental constraints' (2010, p. 120). As well as alleviating coaches' initial concerns of imposing a reductionist curriculum which often limits creative thought and individual expression, this approach to practice builds a setting which allows the exchange of skills and knowledge to occur during the coaching process.

## The benefits of non-linear pedagogy

The CEP was built using the core principles of ecological coaching approaches using non-linear pedagogy (Renshaw et al., 2010). Coaches who 'graduate' through the CEP are actively encouraged to design coaching interventions and programme content based on the unique affordances of the rider and the environment, where affordances are the properties of the environment which can be detected as information to support and action, and which is related to an individual's ability to use it (Gibson and Pick, 2000). More specifically, coaches held existing intuitive, unconscious competence in identifying affordances in the environment based on years of spotting opportunities afforded by steps, rails, buildings and other urban structures on which to pull a trick or design a 'line.'[1]' The CEP did not impose content, as to do so would have rejected the relativism of the riders and their surroundings. Each facility, whether purpose-built or not, has infinite possibilities to the rider and skater. Once aware of the non-linear basis for coaching, coaches are blended into the Eagles coaching programme, the in-house BMX and skate lessons for children at the Source.

The Eagles coaching programme aims to provide a structured, creative and safe environment for riders to learn. It offers opportunities for young riders to gain not only technical and equipment knowledge but also self-confidence. Indeed, in contrast with many traditional sports and coaching styles, the Eagles coaching programme embeds the full potential of non-linear pedagogy applied within a sport-setting (Chow et al., 2007). The Eagles programme adopts fun-driven drills which include using different equipment sizes, colours, as well as the use of different areas of the skate park and hypothetical scenarios which importantly raise challenge, intrigue, complexity and intrinsic motivation among participants (Chow et al., 2007). Also, the programme adopts various deliberate play tasks, with the aim of encouraging the participants to adapt and vary their technical skills according to their personal preferences and surrounding environment which promote participants' decision-making skills and facilitate more holistic development (Berry et al., 2008). These coaching styles are multidimensional and aim to not only engender a love for the sport, higher performance and longer active engagement in physical activities but most importantly strongly maintain a connection with the BMX Freestyle and skateboarding sub-culture of unconventionality, uniqueness and creativity (Rieke et al., 2008).

The Eagles coaching programme provides a platform for the coaches, particularly in terms of practically applying the knowledge acquired during the CEP.

Coaches are encouraged to adopt open-ended, discovery, empowering and creative coaching styles – as these promote and ensure a guided and self-paced discovery of the most suitable movements and performance for each participant. Furthermore, coaches are encouraged to continue to actively construct new drills to improve their participants' skills and enjoyment whilst maintaining elements of creativity that are essential to Freestyle BMX. Additionally, through this coaching approach, the coaches not only appear to engender their athletes' love for the sport, but coaches become powerful role models and influential agents in the lives of the participants and also potentially within their local community.

Both the Source CEP and the Eagles coaching programme move beyond the most traditional understanding of coaching and sport provision based on the primary objective of winning, to implement a more holistic and far-reaching comprehension of coaching in terms of enhancing character, personal development, autonomy, decision-making skills, creativity and long-term involvement in the sport. The use of this form of non-linear pedagogy allows participants space to express themselves with freedom and creativity, whilst also improving BMX Freestyle and skateboard skills. The creative nature of Freestyle BMX can be considered a suitable form of expression to a community engrained in artistic culture as well as a town with a strong sporting tradition and a history of producing top sportspeople. This connection between sport and artistic expression aligns with Tomlinson (2004), who outlines that 'sport cannot be understood in isolation, as if it has no connection with other cultural practices and social influences' (2004, p. 163). The geographical positioning and the forms of pedagogy adopted appear to complement the culture of the town and attract new creative talent to the area. An example is Greg Illingworth, the elite BMX rider, who moved to Hastings not only for the BMX 'scene' but also the 'vibe' of the town that he now enjoys residing in (Dolecki and Ramsdell, 2018). The success of the CEP and the Eagles coaching programme is intended to aid the migration of current and future riders to the south coast, which will help further shape the town's future through the exposure of BMX Freestyle and skateboarding's success to the wider society (Navarro, 2006). Having explained the background to the growth of the Source Park, and particularly the CEP, it is now pertinent to analyse the social effect of the project through the conceptual framework of Bourdieu, focussing on the development of social capital.

## Bourdieu, sport and sociology

The CEP aims to impact positively on the lives of the young participants through the coaching pedagogy utilised. Bourdieu's notion of social capital offers a good example of how participants can achieve positively from being part of a social bond through increased 'mutual support, cooperation, trust' which in turn creates exclusive bonds that reinforce group identities (Putnam, 2001, p. 22), whilst being part of the overall Source Park structure. The work of Pierre Bourdieu has been used in many sociological studies of sport to highlight not just the chosen sport but also the behind-the-scenes factors of socialisation (Giulianotti, 2015).

*Sport coaching in a disadvantaged community* 65

This began with work from Bourdieu (1978) and has subsequently been utilised by many academics in the field (Tomlinson, 2004; Fletcher, 2008; Giulianotti, 2015). Additionally, Fletcher (2008) investigated how social class impacts engagement in risk sports. Skinner et al. (2008) suggest that access to sport, through outreach programmes, can enhance the participants' social capital, and Noble and Watkins (2003) highlight the deterministic nature of Bourdieu's theory of habitus and then proceed to contend that habitus allows us to understand class inequality and that choice of sports is particularly important in that contention. It is habitus that is first used in this chapter to explore the context of the skate park within the social setting of Hastings. It then explores the individual examples of the coaches within the park as well as those participating in its coaching programmes. Through the use of habitus, field and capital the aim is to analyse real life examples of the work taking place within the park.

### Habitus

Bourdieu's term habitus does not come with a simple 'definition' of which all are in agreement. Bourdieu makes many attempts to explain the term in more detail to allow further analysis in other areas of academia. Followers of Bourdieu have also made various attempts to succinctly define the term. Navarro (2006) defines habitus as being:

> developed through processes of socialisation and determines a wide range of dispositions that shape individuals in a given society. It is not a 'structure' but a durable set of dispositions that are formed, stored, recorded and exert influence to mould forms of human behaviour.
>
> (2006, p. 16)

This definition suggests that the manner with which we act and the habits we display in our interactions with society evolve out of the interaction of people to or with their society, whilst at the same time not being the responsibility of either the individual or society solely but instead leaving a kind of 'air about the place' (Clark, 1972, p. 182). It has been suggested that this 'air' refers to 'institutional habitus' and one the skate park can and has adopted. McDonough (1997), in Atkinson (2011, p. 333) says these spaces have their 'own habitus – that is to say, its set of dispositions, taken-for-granted expectations and schemes of perception – just like the people who populate it, and this serves to implicitly channel the impact of a cultural group or social class on an individual's behaviour.' The acting out of these 'habits' takes place 'below the level of consciousness and language, beyond the reach of introspective scrutiny or control by the will' (Bourdieu, 1984, p. 466) to form a way of being, acting and performing in certain social situations. With this understanding we are able to apply this to the habitus attached to Freestyle BMX and to the specific habitus displayed by the coaches, which is then subsequently adopted by the participants and forms part of the 'air' of the Source Park.

## Shifting habitus in the development from Rider to Coach

As riders, who have for a long time been part of a sport that has a clear sub-culture attached, the responsibility falls on the athletes to transmit this sub-culture to the next generation. As Rhinehart (2000) suggests, sports such as Freestyle BMX place a huge importance on participant authenticity, sometimes at the expense of skill and ability, and that this authenticity is socially determined and is based around an athlete's 'attitude, style and worldview' (Rhinehart, 2000, p. 512). The subscription of this authenticity can be seen transferring from coach to participant within the Eagles coaching sessions.

Consequently, it is often seen how the young participants begin to replicate the behaviours, actions and body language – arguably also the attitude, style and worldview – of their coaches. Riders and coaches have increasingly learned to alter elements of the sub-culture that may not be appropriate when working within a grass-roots coaching setting. This has led to modes of communication being altered depending on the audience, the understanding of the implementation of logistics and organisational plans that ensure participant safety and the progression and enjoyment of participants as they navigate through the park. Examples such as the use of cones and chalks to control riding speed allows attention to health and safety protocol during the sessions whilst also allowing moves to be more successfully broken into chunks for the benefit of more efficient practice and execution. This has significantly altered the traditional habitus of a skatepark in order to adapt to the business objectives of the skatepark during grass-roots coaching sessions, and it also requires the adoption of a coaching 'persona' from the riders-turn-coaches. The shifting habitus of the skatepark, embodied in the evolved role of *coaches* (former *riders*) was far from a smooth transition as accepted norms had to be challenged, established behaviours and lifestyle choices moderated and a new worldview embraced. This was not universally accepted in the eyes of some members of the community who saw such a shift as too far removed from the traditional heritage of the sport, deciding instead to distance themselves from the evolving coaching programmes at the Source.

Principles such as professional business practice, tend to be in contrast to this sub-culture and as such, it has been a long-term aim to guide the coaching trainees in understanding, appreciating and applying the relevance of notions such as code of conduct and professionalism, planning and structuring of coaching sessions, principles of health and safety as well as ethical practice. This shows a potential clash between a former habitus attached to the Freestyle BMX community and professional business practice. Bourdieu and Wacquant (1992) express that habitus is subject to change through the individual's experiences which go onto modify structures, organisations or institutions, making it an ever-evolving process. As coaches begin the process of professionalisation, the characteristics inevitably then begin to feed down to participants who are attending the skate park and who go on to experience its new form of evolving habitus. The CEP developed at the Source Park represent this new habitus as mainstream coaching principles are merged into the traditionally coach-less, trial and error style that has been the history of Freestyle BMX rider development to date.

## Field

Historically, BMX Freestyle has often been considered and consequently stereotyped as an illegitimate and extreme sport (Honea, 2013). As a sub-culture, BMX falls within the 'Alternative, Extreme or Action' sports which brings with it a lifestyle component in which 'authentic participation requires acceptance into the sport subculture' (Honea, 2013, p. 1253)

This acceptance creates what Bourdieu calls 'field,' which can be likened to a sporting 'field' where rules create structures, which in turn determine the types of people, as well as the types of relationships within that field (Ritzer and Stepnisky, 2017). This subscribing of or to the rules of the field or 'playing the game' is of vital importance for the continuation of the culture of Freestyle BMX's institutional habitus. To embody this habitus, to work within the field and adhere to its 'rules' is what it means to 'be' a Freestyle BMX rider with all the requirements of language, clothing and style that form the Freestyle BMX identity. Operating within this field may result in part to a rejection of 'mainstream' organisations and their 'mainstream' methods (Honea, 2013). This rejection of the mainstream can appear particularly difficult as coaches are being asked to 'professionalise' in ways that can be perceived to work against the sub-culture identity attached to Freestyle BMX and its associated habitus.

The use of language, both verbal and non-verbal, within the skatepark environment can serve as a useful example of this 'field.' The CEP adopted a shared vocabulary to describe the various parts and obstacles in the skatepark, as well as to describe the situations and emotions that the riders experience whilst riding. For example, in terms of verbal language the expressions 'rad' or 'sick' are used to describe a trick/performance that was particularly good and it has been widely appreciated. The coaches are also encouraged to employ terminology to explain the feelings and emotions felt whilst riding, such as 'rad, stoked, pumped and send it!' The acquisition of this terminology is essential to endorse the participants into the wider Freestyle BMX culture as this provide them with the tools to better comprehend the roots and authenticity of this sport.

Within the coaching programmes, trainee coaches have needed to become aware of the importance of the use of appropriate language depending on the participants in front of them and also of the participants' knowledge in terms of skatepark terminology and how to explain it to others. Based on the rider stage of readiness, the coaches will use the appropriate language to ensure the participants will understand the requirements of the practice. In particular, the coaches will introduce the relevant terminology to describe the area of the park and the drill they are asked to perform – often through game-based warm-ups and drills. For example, a participant might be asked to perform two carves on a vert ramp, once going regular and once going goofy. To begin, the coach will be required to explain these key terms in order for the participants to familiarise themselves with the Freestyle BMX terminology. As the participants become more advanced and confident with the terminology of Freestyle BMX, the coaches will begin to increase the use of terminology, referring to more complicated and less commonly utilised obstacles in the skatepark and associated tricks. For example, at

## 68   *Ben Gould and Carlotta Giussani*

this stage a coach might guide a participant during the learning of a line which focuses on improving barspins while dropping in and tailwhips while popping out of the bowl followed by a double peg grind on curved rail. This has not resulted in a complete move away from the most traditional form of communication within a skatepark, but it can be argued that a modified style of communication has been adopted, with young riders appropriately embedding the technical language of Freestyle BMX according to their stage of readiness.

Similarly, in terms of non-verbal language it is also possible to see the use of the fist-bump between the riders and coaches. As a gesture traditionally denoting respect and acceptance, it is utilised in Freestyle BMX as a form of saying 'hello/ goodbye' as well as a symbol to express respect and appreciation. The fist-bump is accepted as a core aspect of the skatepark and Freestyle BMX and remains core to the communication between coach and rider within the Eagles coaching programme. The gesture is used as a symbol to give positive reinforcement and feedback towards someone's good performance or improvement and commitment towards practising a trick. Within the Eagles programme, it is notable that participants begin to emulate the use of the fist-bump autonomously, embedding a key aspect of the identity of the riders, after just a few sessions.

### Fields into capital

Many of the points discussed above involve the coaches interpellating (Althusser, 1971) the culture of mainstream organisations and neoliberal business practices into their own ideologies around Freestyle BMX and skateboarding, which to some riders may sit uncomfortably in their view of the sport's heritage. This evolving field is a necessary one for riders who may wish to sustain a living whilst being around the skatepark and requires them to 'play the game' of business within this field, as well as to fit inside new organisational frameworks such as the International Olympic Committee (IOC). The development of Freestyle BMX culture has not traditionally seen focus on economic capital[2] as a measure of success. This can be seen as a 'clash' with mainstream or 'dominant culture' that largely focuses on the economic capital gained as a measure of success. This then creates activities, which could be seen as 'good taste' or part of 'good culture' as they bring with them an increased likelihood of returning economic capital, and so in turn this form of capital, known as cultural capital, becomes the accepted form of capital to acquire within that society. The juxtaposition for members of the Freestyle BMX community is that their sub-culture identity can become an accepted form of cultural capital, particularly when supported with the ability to produce economic capital from within the sport, but that also requires the acceptance of certain mainstream cultural changes in order for their potential economic capital to increase and the sport's future economic and cultural potential to be fulfilled. This shift towards accepted cultural capital suggests that the majority of the society within which it is placed sees value within the cultural capital of the sport and the uptake of the CEP can be an indicator of how this is viewed socially. This completes the circle from a business perspective as this

*Sport coaching in a disadvantaged community* 69

'value' (Irwin, 2009) is what brings the economic capital required to thrive as a business. When parents are willing to enter into a transaction of their economic capital towards the purchase of cultural capital offered by the skate park coaching programme, then the sport's new habitus suggests a more widely accepted existence within mainstream culture. Through the development of a CEP that is sympathetic to the evolving habitus and field within that sport, it is able to retain the identity of Freestyle BMX whilst also embracing elements of the mainstream culture, which has the potential to enhance the sport and contribute to the on-going regeneration within areas of deprivation.

## Key messages for developing programmes in areas of need

The CEP and Eagles programmes operating at the Source Park are evolving and aiming to ensure Freestyle BMX is best placed for introduction to the Olympics by 2020 and that Hastings can be a focal point for the current and future progression of the sport in the United Kingdom and worldwide. The benefits to an area of social deprivation, whether social, economic, inter personal or educational, hold significant potential to a town in its attempt to continue to thrive. This grass-roots sport-plus SfD project, with its firmly rooted sub-culture as an alternative and extreme sport, has presented its challenges. Key messages or lessons learned for similar community-based projects in areas of social need may include:

- A continued long-term, bottom-up process which aims to ensure that the authenticity of Freestyle BMX would remain core as the CEP further develops and perhaps more congruently co-exists with mainstream culture.
- Flexibility and a willingness to embrace change from stakeholders across the sport. This may result in a changing of the habitus of the sport, as it becomes more 'mainstream' and also requires behavioural changes amongst key stakeholders within the sport in terms of embracing principles that are normally positioned within mainstream culture and that follow the neoliberal business modelling seen in much of the developed world.
- The creation and implementation of the CEP have shown the importance of allowing authentic coaches' voices in the development of coaching programmes to ensure tacit elements of the sub-culture are transferred to the next generation of athletes. This ties participants to their sport and allows them to communicate with other participants around the world.
- Preserved authenticity for the coaches who are the bedrock of future participation and allowing them to act as important role models who are able to promote change in other people by embedding the historical values from which Freestyle BMX was born to the next generation of BMX riders.
- Realistic expectations and aspirations from project planners in the design and development of coach education programmes. Longevity of sport development programmes is dependent on highly reliable and respected local, contextual knowledge. Empower voices 'from the field' in the design and delivery of community programmes.

## 70   Ben Gould and Carlotta Giussani

- Use of pedagogies which reflect the needs of the context. In this example non-linear approaches provided an open and creative philosophy to coaching and coach education. Other projects may investigate alternative pedagogic approaches which dovetail to the needs of the specific context. Some of which are made explicit in other chapters of this book.

## Notes

1 A 'line' is a skate or BMX colloquialism for a chain of stunts, moves or tricks performed in sequence.
2 For a further breakdown of Bourdieu's forms of capital, see Skinner et al. (2008).

## References

Althusser, L. (1971). *Ideology and ideological state apparatus (notes towards an investigation). Lenin and philosophy and other essays, 127–186)*. New York: Monthly Review Press.

Atkinson, W. (2011). 'From sociological fictions to social fictions: Some Bourdieusian reflections on the concepts of "institutional habitus" and "family habitus".' *British Journal of Sociology of Education*, 32 (3), 331–347.

Berry, J., Abernethy, B., and Côté, J. (2008). 'The contribution of structured activity and deliberate play to the development of expert perceptual and decision-making skill.' *Journal of Sport and Exercise Psychology*, 30 (6), 685–708.

Bourdieu, P. (1978). 'Sport and social class.' *Information (International Social Science Council)*, 17 (6), 819–840.

Bourdieu, P. (1984). *Distinction: A social critique of taste*. Trans. Richard Nice. Cambridge, MA: Harvard University Press.

Bourdieu, P. (1988). 'Program for a sociology of sport.' *Sociology of Sport Journal*, 5 (2), 153–161.

Bourdieu, P., and Wacquant, L. (1992). *An introduction to reflexive sociology*. Chicago: University of Chicago.

Chow, J.Y., Davids, K., Button, C., Shuttleworth, R., Renshaw, I., and Araújo, D. (2007). 'The role of nonlinear pedagogy in physical education.' *Review of Educational Research*, 77 (3), 251–278.

Clark, B.R. (1972). 'The organizational saga in higher education.' *Administrative Science Quarterly*, 178–184.

Coalter, F. (2007a). 'Sports clubs, social capital and social regeneration: "Ill-defined interventions with hard to follow outcomes"?' *Sport in Society*, 10 (4), 537–559.

Coalter, F. (2007b). *A wider social role for sport: Who's keeping the score?*. Abingdon: Routledge.

Dolecki, R., and Ramsdell, L. (2018). *Catching up with Greg Illingworth*. https://digbmx.com/features/catching-up-with-greg-illingworth [Accessed 17 December 2018].

Fletcher, R. (2008). 'Living on the edge: The appeal of risk sports for the professional middle class.' *Sociology of Sport Journal*, 25 (3), 310–330.

Gibson, E.J., and Pick, A.D. (2000). *An ecological approach to perceptual learning and development*. Oxford: Oxford University Press.

Giulianotti, R. (2015). *Sport: A critical sociology*. Cambridge : John Wiley & Sons.

Green, M. (2009). 'Podium or participation? Analysing policy priorities under changing modes of sport governance in the United Kingdom.' *International Journal of Sport Policy and Politics*, 1 (2), 121–144.

Harris, K., and Adams, A. (2016). 'Power and discourse in the politics of evidence in sport for development.' *Sport Management Review*, 19 (2), 97–106.

Honea, J.C. (2013). 'Beyond the alternative vs. mainstream dichotomy: Olympic BMX and the future of action sports.' *The Journal of Popular Culture*, 46 (6), 1253–1275.

Irwin, S. (2009). 'Family contexts, norms and young people's orientations: Researching diversity.' *Journal of Youth Studies*, 12 (4), 337–354.

Mcdonough, P.M. (1997). *Choosing colleges: How social class and schools structure opportunity*. Albany : Suny Press.

Navarro, Z. (2006). 'In search of a cultural interpretation of power: The contribution of Pierre Bourdieu.' *IDS Bulletin*, 37 (6), 11–22.

Noble, G., and Watkins, M. (2003). 'So, how did Bourdieu learn to play tennis? Habitus, consciousness and habituation'. *Cultural Studies*, 17 (3–4), 520–539.

Putnam, R.D. (2001). *Bowling alone: The collapse and revival of American community*. New York : Simon and Schuster.

Renshaw, I., Chow, J.Y., Davids, K., and Hammond, J. (2010). 'A constraints-led perspective to understanding skill acquisition and game play: A basis for integration of motor learning theory and physical education praxis.' *Physical Education and Sport Pedagogy*, 15 (2), 117–137.

Rhinehart, R. (2000). 'Emerging arriving sport: Alternatives to formal sport.' In: Dunning, E., and Coakley, J., eds. *Handbook of sports studies*, 504-519 London: Sage Publications.

Rieke, M., Hammermeister, J., and Chase, M. (2008). 'Servant leadership in sport: A new paradigm for effective coach behavior.' *International Journal of Sports Science and Coaching*, 3 (2), 227–239.

Ritzer, G., and Stepnisky, J. (2017). *Contemporary sociological theory and its classical roots: The basics*. Thousand Oaks : Sage Publications.

Sandford, R.A., Duncombe, R., and Armour, K.M. (2008). 'The role of physical activity/ sport in tackling youth disaffection and anti-social behaviour.' *Educational Review*, 60 (4), 419–435.

Skinner, J., Zakus, D.H., and Cowell, J. (2008). 'Development through sport: Building social capital in disadvantaged communities.' *Sport Management Review*, 11 (3), 253–275.

Spaaij, R., and Jeanes, R. (2013). 'Education for social change? A Freirean critique of sport for development and peace.' *Physical Education and Sport Pedagogy*, 18 (4), 442–457.

Tomlinson, A. (2004). 'Pierre Bourdieu and the sociological study of sport: Habitus, capital and field.' In: Giulianotti, R., ed. *Sport and modern social theorists*. London: Palgrave Macmillan UK, 175–190.

# 6 A structural shift in voluntary work with refugees

## A case study of sports clubs in Germany

*Sebastian Braun, Katrin Albert,*
*Mareike Alscher and Stefan Hansen*

## Introduction

The number of people in Germany with a refugee background increased significantly in 2015 and 2016. In fact, Germany was the country with the most asylum seekers worldwide during both of these years (UNHCR, 2016, p. 39f.). It did not take long for these growing numbers to be associated with questions surrounding integration policy in Germany, with extremely controversial discussions still ongoing. It is interesting to note here that sports clubs are viewed as local organisations within civil society that hold plenty of potential as a way of helping people with a refugee background to integrate. In actual fact, data from the 2015/2016 sport trends report, which is based on the results of a survey conducted regularly amongst sports clubs in Germany, reveals that 'sports clubs in Germany have taken on an exceptionally active role in the refugee crisis' (Breuer, Feiler and Nowy, 2017, p. 47).

These findings demonstrate that sports clubs have responded swiftly to current challenges by taking relevant, practical measures in the field of sports-related work with refugees. Given that there are relatively few paid positions within sports clubs in Germany, it is safe to assume that the work involved is mainly performed on a voluntary basis by members who make up a key economic and cultural resource, as far as sports clubs are concerned. Although the empirical findings relating to volunteer work within sports clubs are far from consistent, the majority of relevant studies reveal that the number of people involved in sports clubs, and the number of people in long-term club positions, in particular, is in decline (cf. Braun, 2017a; Breuer, 2017; Simonson, Vogel and Tesch-Römer, 2017, for example).

On the basis of this background information, we decided to use this study[1] to explore the question of how sports clubs approach their work with refugees, which often extends beyond the actual purpose of a sports club, and which methods and 'strategies' sports clubs use to make the all-important time and knowledge of its members and presumably non-members available as required on a voluntary basis. In order to address these questions, we conducted an explorative qualitative study on a number of sports clubs based in Berlin.

## Sports clubs and volunteers in Germany

### Sports clubs under the umbrella of sports associations

There are around 91,000 local sports clubs in Germany, which are indirectly linked to the German Olympic Sports Confederation (DOSB) through regional sports associations. The German Olympic Sports Confederation (DOSB) is the umbrella organisation for sport and exercise within Germany. It was first formed in 2006 when the German Sports Federation (DSB, founded in 1950) and the National Olympic Committee (NOK, founded in 1949) merged. Since then, the DOSB has assumed the role of an umbrella body for some 100-member organisations, which include many sports associations that work with specific or multiple sports. All of these member organisations are independent in the work they do as well as in how they are organised and financed. They have the specific legal status of organisations registered in the register of organisations. Taking the DOSB's 2017 figures as a point of reference, with around 27.4 million memberships in sports clubs (cf. DOSB, 2018, p. 1), it is safe to say that there is no other major association-based organisation in Germany that can boast more links to people than the DOSB given its status as an umbrella organisation overseeing a complex structure of member organisations (cf. Braun, 2018).

As a general rule, sports clubs are members of regional sports confederations (through district, regional and town/city sports associations), which may, for instance, represent the overarching interests at the state level or educate coaches. Sports clubs are also members of national sports governing federations that represent the interests within the field of a specific sport. Every sport that is represented within the DOSB has such a national sports governing federation, which, depending on the state, is broken down into district, regional and town/city sports associations and is a direct member of the DOSB. In this way, all sports clubs in Germany are members of associations, through which they are linked to association-based sport (cf. Haring, 2010).

### Subsidiary state funding

Within this context, a complex nationwide system of state funding for sports has arisen in conjunction with the federal state structure and the different responsibilities and levels of independence assigned at the federal, state and local levels. State funding for sports follows the principle of subsidiarity – on the basis of the status of autonomy held by sports associations and clubs. This underlying situation has allowed the DOSB and its member organisations to receive state funding for a wide range of projects aimed at various target groups for decades now (cf. Braun, 2018).

This also applies to specific programmes and measures designed to benefit people with a refugee background, which have been implemented in sports clubs with the aid of subsidiary state funding since 2015 in particular. This may include

74   *Sebastian Braun et al.*

opening up existing activities to refugees and creating new activities aimed explicitly at refugees as well as even arranging non-sporting activities and services, such as language courses and assistance with dealings with the authorities. However, measures implemented at sports clubs using subsidiary state funding still have to be put into practice by people who (usually) give up their time and donate their knowledge without being paid, making them volunteer workers within clubs.

### Structural shift in voluntary work

Who are the people involved in sports clubs, and how are they recruited? We have long seen in theory and practice here that the structure of voluntary work in Germany is changing in a specific way. This theory of the 'structural shift in voluntary work' can be summarised in simplified terms as follows: Whilst it was traditionally the case that members would get involved with a specific club and remain loyal in the long term, we see more and more cases of voluntary work on a temporary or project-by-project basis. It has been customary for members to have a long history and social background within a club that would make them qualified to volunteer. However, there are more and more volunteers who want to get involved when they find themselves in a suitable situation in their lives (e.g. when their career or family life is particularly settled) or in response to a specific political issue (e.g. the environment or the integration of people with a refugee background). Traditionally, volunteering has been viewed as a selfless, altruistic sacrifice on the part of members, but now more and more people are viewing voluntary work as a form of self-fulfilment or self-discovery or at least linking it with specific interests (e.g. personal development) (cf. summary in Braun, 2017a).

On this basis, opportunities for working with refugees in the context of a club should come about in the form of structures allowing for volunteers to commit for a limited amount of time or on a project-by-project basis in a way that fits in with their life in terms of their own motivations and availability. Volunteering with a sports club has become an attractive prospect even for the groups of the population who have been under-represented thus far.

Taking this background information into account, the underlying theory at the heart of this article is that sports clubs have put a lot of effort into experimenting with creative ideas by trying out and implementing alternative, unconventional 'recruitment strategies' that are far removed from the routine methods of getting volunteers on board (long-term effects of socialising within a club, strong feelings of loyalty to a club and its members, and so on). According to the extended theory, these 'strategies,' which have usually come about on an ad-hoc basis, will often be linked to the 'structural shift in voluntary work' that has been put forward for some time now, leading to new ways of getting volunteers on board for work within clubs and gaining their loyalty – an outcome that was originally intended.

In order to take an empirical look at these assumptions, our focus within the text that follows is on four research questions: (1) How and with whose help did sports clubs arrange sports-related, and possibly also non-sports-related activities, for refugees during the 'refugee crisis' in Germany in 2015/2016? (2) To what extent do sports clubs change when they arrange activities for refugees? (3) What difficulties do sports clubs face when putting on activities for refugees? (4) How easy was it to recruit people who were not already members of a club to volunteer within the corresponding activity structures of sports clubs?

## Methodology

In order to gain answers to our research questions, we conducted two mutually complementary case studies in the form of interviews with clubs and volunteers in Berlin in 2016.

When interviewing clubs, we followed the expert interview as set out by Meuser and Nagel (2009) and spoke to seven office-holders from different sports clubs with lots of members that arranged special activities for refugees in 2015/2016 and received dedicated funding for this from the 'Sport for Refugees' programme run by the Berlin State Sports Association. These interviews were audio-recorded and transcribed in full, before being analysed in three stages: single-case analysis, case comparison and generalisations/typification (cf. Meuser and Nagel, 2009, p. 476ff.).

When it came to speaking to volunteers, we conducted biographical interviews (following Schütze, 1983; Fuchs-Heinritz, 2010, pp. 85–104) with five people (four women and one man between the ages of 20 and 35 with an academic background) who were new recruits for voluntary work with clubs during the 2015/2016 'refugee crisis.' In other words, they were not members nor otherwise involved with the club before volunteering to help with the sports activities for refugees in question. Once the interviews had been transcribed, the analysis involved content segmentation, biographical case reconstruction and topic-related case comparisons.

## Results

The results of the research project are organised by the research question and summarised in an extremely concise format in the text that follows.

### (1) Which groups of members volunteer for sports-related projects with refugees within sports clubs?

Activities and services for refugees at the sports clubs interviewed depend largely on members volunteering. All groups of people in sports clubs are involved in planning, coordinating and organising the activities.

- *Board members* and *coaches* put in the most work, and no other group dedicates as much time to proactively organising and putting on sports-related events.
- *Dedicated members of sports clubs* also help to plan, coordinate and organise activities put on by their club for the benefit of refugees – regardless of whether they hold a position outside of the board.

76   *Sebastian Braun et al.*

- Some *members who were previously 'just' active* were also recruited for voluntary work. This shows that projects aimed at refugees can help rally the existing workforce who can offer their services on a voluntary basis.
- *Full-time members of staff* (if applicable at the sports club in question) are also involved in putting on activities for refugees – either as part of their employment contract or on a voluntary basis on top of their usual duties.

On the whole, it is clear to see that sports-related projects aimed at refugees give dedicated members of clubs the opportunity to have positive social/emotional experiences within their clubs (e.g. experience of helping and showing solidarity, rewarding contact with people they didn't know before, the experience of refugees demonstrating feelings of joy, gratitude, excitement and enjoyment).

### (2) Do clubs change when they arrange sports-related activities for refugees?

Planning, organising and putting on sports-related activities for refugees brought about some changes within some of the clubs interviewed that were considered to be both opportunities and challenges.

*Members of clubs have the opportunity to learn too* if the uncommon experiences that come about as a result of sports-related projects involving refugees offer them the opportunity to develop on a personal level and experience something new. According to those who were interviewed, this is largely a question of cultural learning processes relating to unfamiliar life skills and worldly knowledge, different values, and specific experience gained when planning activities and dealing with organisational and structural aspects.

*The club evolves as a whole* if the positive social/emotional experiences that go hand-in-hand with successful projects create a motivational space for everyone involved. In some cases, this can breathe life back into a club that may have been stagnating a little (e.g. new activities, public attention and awareness, structural improvements).

*Sports-related activities for refugees bring about change in the range of activities offered by sports clubs.* Whether activities are introduced as the extension of existing activities or as something brand- new, the scope of the activities on offer undergoes a change. This can incur extra costs and bring about additional burdens, with the additional expense to be borne by the clubs themselves.

*The level of interaction at sports clubs changes* when refugees revitalise the dialogue within a club as well as between clubs and other organisations. Members of clubs can enter into discussions, giving them the opportunity to reflect on their own views and attitudes and inspiring them to come up with ideas for further new projects. The club as a whole comes into contact with other organisations in cases where networking is necessary or may be helpful. As a result, all processes of exchange within and between organisations are put into action and stepped up a gear.

*Changes can be seen amongst active members of a club* when their numbers increase. All of the clubs managed to attract refugees to take part in their activities. Some of the clubs have already taken refugees on board as members or are aiming to do so, and they have managed to recruit new volunteers and even new trainers. It can therefore be assumed that the numbers of members and volunteers have risen in many respects as a result of showing commitment to refugees in the sporting activities on offer. Equally, some clubs refer to potential conflict with their members in relation to the refugee situation on the whole or specifically the activities on offer. In some cases, people decided to end their membership and there was a certain level of discontent amongst members, which is assumed to be the result of limited management opportunities within clubs and possibilities for members to participate.

*Changes in responsibilities are reflected* in a shift and/or extension of the scope of work conducted by the board and by members/volunteers for the benefit of refugees. Tasks relating to refugees are taken on by different members of clubs and other tasks that do not have anything to do with refugees are postponed or continued alongside them.

### (3) What difficulties do sports clubs face in their work?

According to the people interviewed, sport clubs' commitment to refugees is linked inextricably to a situation filled with all kinds of uncertainty. There are three main points to look at in more detail here:

- The *lack of structure at the start* of the 2015/2016 refugee crisis meant that sports clubs had to react in the face of an overall lack of clarity surrounding the situation from the very start. Crucial legal issues had not been clarified (e.g. in relation to membership status, insurance cover and liability, residency status). Some clubs found themselves in difficult situations owing to flexibility not being exercised in allocating sports areas or areas being occupied by refugees. The situation was made even more complicated by the steadily increasing number of refugees and the lack of availability of points of contact for clubs at the time. At this stage, sports clubs tended to deal with things themselves and found their own ways of helping refugees through their own initiatives and financing in conjunction with volunteering and network-building.
- *Structural framework conditions* that offered sports clubs support in their activities for refugees going forward in particular then included funding for projects, information on refuge and asylum and voluntary work performed by board members, coaches, members and other people. The challenge now is stabilising what is on offer. There are, however, a number of factors that can make this particular challenge even more difficult to overcome, including insufficient funding, a lack of staff resources who can provide constant support to refugees, limitations to volunteer work and a reduced ability to plan ahead, and the role of refugee shelters that clubs are working with. The

78  *Sebastian Braun et al.*

success of a partnership with shelters depends on the points of contact available there and the supporting structures in place.

- The *uncertainty surrounding refugees' situations* makes for another challenge when arranging sports-related activities. Refugees' lives are not stable if their residency status has not been confirmed. Clubs often have to deal with irregular daily routines and the fact that refugees cannot be relied upon to show up on a regular basis. In extreme cases, sports clubs simply do not know who will end up turning up for an activity, how many participants there will be or for how long each person will be able to take part in an activity.

### (4) Is it possible to attract new members and volunteers by arranging sports-related projects aimed at refugees?

Our attempts to find people who got involved with the relevant sports clubs for the first time to work on sports-related projects for refugees proved to be fairly tough despite extensive research. On that basis, it would seem that the clubs relied on making use of the existing volunteering potential amongst their members when arranging sports-related projects for refugees rather that recruiting volunteers externally – despite a wave of people willing to offer their assistance in 2015 and 2016, as reported on heavily by politicians and the media.

Nevertheless, we did manage to conduct interviews with five people who were recruited by clubs as new volunteers specifically for sports-related projects for refugees in 2015/2016. The volunteers were between 20 and 35 years old. Three have been migrants (Brazil, France, the United States). All volunteers had a high school diploma, three were studying, two had completed their studies and worked employed or self-employed. Following our analysis of the interviews, it became clear that these new volunteers were people who had expressed an interest in volunteering for a specific cause (in this case to help refugees) who had an affinity for sports and were looking for a suitable, low- threshold opportunity to make a difference. Social connections and online announcements were used by sports club members to recruit these former non-members as volunteers for activities with refugees. The volunteers neither had to present a certain qualification as coach nor meet any safeguarding requirements (for example police clearance certificates). All that was need was a willingness to volunteer in sport-related projects for refugees.

The following are typical of this type of 'socially committed volunteer':

- *Voluntary work is seen as a moral duty.* In this specific case, those interviewed wanted to help refugees in their time of need.
- *Voluntary work is believed to give meaning to the individual's life.* This sees the people we interviewed link their voluntary commitment to their own instrumental individualistic interests, including involvement in a social situation of historical relevance, expectations of picking up knowledge and expanding their own range of experience, and hope of finding 'inner balance.'

- *Voluntary work with a sports club fits in with their life.* Everyone who we interviewed has experience in the worlds of volunteering and sport, making their work with a sports club something that is familiar to them in a more or less familiar field. This voluntary commitment fitted in with the living situation of the people we spoke to.

Sports-related activities for the benefit of refugees in sports clubs provided the perfect opportunity for these 'socially committed volunteers' to get involved because the activities already had a solid structure, the voluntary work could be flexible and there were chances for them to have their say and shape the work they did without them having to take on a lot of responsibility or feel too great a sense of duty. The sports clubs themselves were of very little relevance to the people we interviewed. For them, they were merely a platform that allowed them to fulfil their wish to get involved in voluntary work for a specific cause.

*It is difficult to find new volunteers who stay loyal to a club in the long term.* It should really be clubs that see themselves as 'social service providers' that can manage to offer new volunteers the type of platform they are looking for in the long term since they offer other services beyond activities for refugees, which new volunteers might see as making sense given their life and experience. However, changes in our lives are not linear or possible to predict. With that in mind, working with refugees and even voluntary work on the whole may seem ideal based on a person's past experience and current life status one minute and then turn out to be disruptive and obtrusive the next minute.

## Conclusion and recommendations

One of the focal points of the empirical research was the question of how sports-related activities, potentially alongside non-sports-related ones, were arranged in sports clubs that responded in a specific way for the benefit of refugees during the 'refugee crisis' of 2015/2016. We also looked into how people who were not already members of a sports club were recruited to volunteer within the corresponding activity structures of sports clubs. In the text that follows, some of the results from the club and volunteer interviews have been used to derive some recommendations.

### Points that relate to the clubs

Clubs have flexible basic structures that allow them to respond to external crisis situations in a relatively unbureaucratic way as voluntary organisations. However, the results from the interviews conducted with clubs do show that a lack of stability as far as structures are concerned can limit the sports activities put on for refugees. From this point of view, the following recommendations can be put forward:

- Clubs sometimes only had limited details on organisational and legal matters (including insurance) relating to 'refuge, refugees and asylum' made

80  *Sebastian Braun et al.*

available to them and the lack of information stopped them acting quickly in some cases. *It is therefore recommended that clubs are provided with points of contact in administration and associations who can work with them on the information they need, responding on a case-by-case basis and making the relevant information available as required. This should lead to dialogue between administration and key players in civil society being institutionalised.*

- Unstable structures come about when projects are taken on that require quick and on-going funding and when the available payments are only made following a huge delay and for a limited period of time, with the current demand not being sufficiently covered. *In order to ensure that clubs can respond to issues in society, including crisis situations in particular, it is recommended that suitable forms of funding are offered and deployed. This will involve identifying and establishing forms of funding that allow for money to be used quickly in line with the current demand. On this basis, it is advisable that the current form of project funding provided by state parties is developed further in terms of the content and in line with the current situation. Furthermore, ways of financing clubs' plans that rely on the parties involved in projects playing a greater role should be brought into play. Consequently, mechanisms that give key players in civil society the scope to get involved and have a say in the structure and allocation of funds could be looked into in greater depth in the future.* Some related ideas have already been tried out at the local level. For example, public funding for civic engagement has been made available in the form of funds and foundations. Local citizens and/or club representatives are involved in the allocation of these resources.
- A large number of clubs have worked with refugee aid organisations. Certain framework conditions must be put in place if these kinds of partnerships are to continue to be effective going forward. The most important factor in guaranteeing a successful partnership is on-going close coordination with sports clubs on the part of the staff working at shelters. The evidence we have suggests that these employees have two important roles to play. Firstly, they can make refugees aware of the activities on offer by providing them with detailed information. They can then keep reminding them or even take on admin tasks such as signing refugees in and out of their designated shelter. The points of contact for sports clubs at shelters can also help by informing other members of staff about the activities on offer. This may lead to employees at shelters offering their services as volunteers for sports-related projects. *It is therefore recommended that points of contact are established at shelters and familiarised with clubs and, most importantly, the activities they have on offer. This will involve making staff resources available, including people who can be made responsible for tasks relating to communications, organisational work and civic engagement.* It would seem as though another factor determining the success of a partnership between a club and a shelter is the shelter's supporting body. Collaborations seem to be most fruitful when shelters are supported by not-for-profit organisations as then there is usually access to extensive experience of volunteer work, which in turn ensures that there is a level of understanding as far as the voluntary project work being conducted by sports clubs is

concerned. *With this in mind, it seems logical to ensure that charitable shelters are supported with a view to boosting collaborative links between not-for-profit organisations and associated civic engagement.*

- At the sports clubs we looked at, activities and projects relating to refugees in 2015 and 2016 were generally organised very quickly with a lot of improvisation. *It is recommended that, following the dynamic set-up phase, appropriate quality standards are gradually refined for the activities on offer over time and implemented for (new) volunteers as a benchmark. A top-down approach must be avoided when introducing these standards. Instead, they should be developed together with volunteers at clubs on the basis of the experience of the volunteers themselves.*

### Points that relate to the volunteers

Considerations on recruiting volunteers for work with refugees within clubs may be linked to application-based concepts of 'volunteer management' (cf. Biedermann, 2012; Reifenhäuser, Hoffmann and Kegel, 2009, for example), 'voluntary post management' (cf. Stamer, 2014, for example) or 'engagement management' (cf. Braun, 2017b) as far as practical recommendations are concerned. These concepts refer to a systematical management tools for organisations regarding the work with volunteers. In on-going discussions on civic engagement, these form tools a working focus that is becoming more and more relevant with a view to linking engagement modernisation processes up with recruitment and loyalty strategies for voluntary work within local club structures. Considering the results of the interviews conducted with volunteers from this perspective, at least six recommendations can be put forward:

- According to the results of the club interviews, sports-related activities for refugees are mainly arranged by people who are already on board as active members of a club. On that basis, encouraging existing club members to get involved with specific activities aimed at refugees seems to be an effective way of getting volunteers on board. *It is therefore recommended that the specific tasks and the club's own expectations for these activity formats aimed at certain target groups are identified, revealed and communicated to members with as much reach as possible.*
- It is also possible to recruit volunteers who have not previously been members of a sports club. In this case, we are talking about people wishing to get involved as 'socially engaged volunteers' to help refugees specifically. The following recommendation applies at least to the group of volunteers that were interviewed in this context, that is young and middle-aged adults, socialised in the West, with an academic background, an interest in sport, and the characteristics typical of volunteers involved within the sporting sector: *Communications should focus on activities that are clearly related to the issue at hand and include a description of clearly defined tasks. Systematic, targeted face-to-face communications (e.g. by people in key positions) and other formats*

82    *Sebastian Braun et al.*

*such as digital media (e.g. volunteer portals and the sports club's website) should also be capitalised on.*

- The main draw for new volunteers is the opportunity to help young refugees. Sports clubs are used as a platform for this because their activities and low-threshold structures for opportunities make for an appealing field in which to work. The ease of access to clubs and their activities for refugees comes down to having solid structures already in place, placing low requirements on the amount of time and expertise volunteers have to commit to combined with the chance to flexibly increase this, offering volunteers the chance to have a say on what exactly the work they do covers, and, for example, not forcing people to feel too great a sense of duty. *With this in mind, it appears to be a good idea to maintain low-threshold structures for opportunities as a way of encouraging external parties to get involved with sports clubs in general and, most importantly, of recruiting volunteers for sports-related work with refugees.*

- 'Socially engaged volunteers' offer their services on a project-by-project basis without integrating fully into a club. This means that their involvement with a club has a time limit to start with. If, however, the new volunteers' underlying motivations line up with the focus and the structures for opportunities of a specific activity being offered by the club they will continue to volunteer and, what's more, they will be willing to take on more responsibility. *In this respect, it would appear to be worthwhile to appoint someone in the club who is responsible for new volunteers and can determine how compatible tasks and skills are. This might involve, for example, asking new volunteers about their requirements in relation to specific issues or motivation as well as the amount of time and the knowledge they have at their disposal. Adjustments can then be made to the activities and tasks assigned to them. They should also inform new volunteers about details relating to the club.*

- New volunteers give thought to the organisation and development of sports-related activities for refugees, but they will sometimes find themselves faced with challenges that they cannot overcome using what they know alone. They may be thankful for the opportunity to share ideas and experiences with like-minded people and they may also be interested in relevant training without having much knowledge about what is on offer. This kind of training may already be organised by sports associations. *It is therefore recommended that sports club board members or other responsible parties in the club inform new volunteers about (newly introduced) training sessions and seminars covering relevant topics.*

- As mentioned previously, new volunteers are willing to provide their services within a club for a limited amount of time to help out with a specific project relating to a selected issue. *It is therefore advisable that clubs systematically plan for these 'socially engaged volunteers' to leave them once the project has come to an end. In some cases, this planning may involve offering volunteers the opportunity to work on subsequent projects or ensuring that volunteers are given due credit for their service to the refugee community.*

## Note

1 The research project was conducted at the Humboldt University of Berlin within the framework of the 'Solidarity in Change?' research and intervention cluster run by the Berlin Institute for Integration and Migration Research (BIM) and funded by the German Federal Government's Commissioner for Migration, Refugees and Integration. The work on the project was completed by employees within the 'Integration, Sport and Football' department of the BIM and the Department of Sport Sociology within the Department of Sport Sciences at the Humboldt University of Berlin (cf. Braun, Albert, Alscher and Hansen, 2017).

## References

Biedermann, C. (2012). 'Die Zusammenarbeit mit Freiwilligen organisieren. Eine Handlungsanleitung (Guidelines for organising work with volunteers).' In: Rosenkranz, D., and Weber, A., eds. *Freiwilligenarbeit. Einführung in das Management von Ehrenamtlichen in der Sozialen Arbeit (Volunteer work. An introduction to the management of volunteers in social work)* (second edition). Weinheim: Juventa, 57–66.

Braun, S. (2017a). *Ehrenamtliches und freiwilliges Engagement im Sport im Spiegel der Freiwilligensurveys von 1999 bis 2009. Zusammenfassung der sportbezogenen Sonderauswertungen (Voluntary work in sport on the basis of volunteer surveys from 1999 to 2009. A summary of the sports- related special analyses)* (second edition) (accessible at http://my.page2flip.de/2895682/9813109/9815155/html5.html#/1).

Braun, S. (2017b). 'Engagement und Engagement-Management im Sportverein: von Problem- zu Potenzial-Diskursen (Engagement and engagement management in sports clubs: shifting discourses from problem to potential).' In: Thieme, L., ed. *Der Sportverein. Versuch einer Bilanz (Sports clubs – finding a balance)*. Schorndorf: Hofmann, 173–204.

Braun, S. (2018). 'Organisierter Sport in Bewegung. Neokorporatistische Strukturen, gesellschaftliche Funktionen und bürgerschaftliche Selbstorganisation in pluralisierten Sportlandschaften (Organised sport in motion. Neo-corporate structures, social functions and citizens' self-organisation in pluralised sporting landscapes).' *Forschungsjournal Soziale Bewegungen (Social Movements Research Journal)*, 1–2, 234–240.

Braun, S., Alscher, M., Albert, K., and Hansen, S. (2017). 'Strukturwandel des Ehrenamts in der Geflüchtetenarbeit von Sportvereinen (A structural shift in voluntary work with refugees within sports clubs).' In: Berlin Institute for Integration and Migration Research (BIM), ed. Research Report. *'Solidarity in Change?' research and intervention cluster*. Berlin: Berlin Institute for Integration and Migration Research (BIM) Humboldt University of Berlin, 144–164. https://www.bim.hu-berlin.de/media/Forsc hungsbericht_BIM_Fluchtcluster_23032017.pdf (accessed 24th March 2017).

Breuer, C., ed. (2017). *Sportentwicklungsbericht 2015/2016, Band I und II. Analyse zur Situation der Sportvereine in Deutschland (2015/2016 sport trends report, volume I and II. An analysis of the status of sports clubs in Germany)*. Cologne: Sportverlag Strauß.

Breuer, C., Feiler, S., and Nowy, T. (2017). 'Sportvereine, Sportbünde und Flüchtlinge. (Sports clubs, sports associations and refugees.).' In: Breuer, C., ed. *Sportentwicklungsbericht 2015/2016, Band I und II. Analyse zur Situation der Sportvereine in Deutschland (2015/2016 sport trends report, volume I and II. An analysis of the status of sports clubs in Germany)*. Cologne: Sportverlag Strauß, 47–100.

84 *Sebastian Braun et al.*

DOSB. (2018). Willkommen im Sport [Welcome to sports]. Retrieved from: https://in tegration.dosb.de/inhalte/projekte/wis-willkommen-im-sport-fuer-gefluechtete on (6th February 2020)

Fuchs-Heinritz, W. (2010). 'Biographieforschung. (Biography research.).' In: Kneer, G., and Schroer, M., eds. *Handbuch Spezielle Soziologien (Handbook of special sociologies).* Wiesbaden: VS Verlag für Sozialwissenschaften, 85–104.

Haring, M (2010). *Sportförderung in Deutschland: eine vergleichende Analyse der Bundesländer (Sport promotion in Germany: A comparing analysis of the federal states),* Wiesbaden: VS Verlag für Sozialwissenschaften.

Meuser, M., and Nagel, U. (2009). 'Das Experteninterview – konzeptionelle Grundlagen und methodische Anlage (The expert interview – conceptual basics and methodological approach).' In: Pickel, S., Pickel, G., Lauth, H.-J., and Jahn, D., eds. *Methoden der vergleichenden Politik- und Sozialwissenschaft: Neue Entwicklungen und Anwendungen (Methods of comparative political and social sciences: New developments and applications).* Wiesbaden: VS Verlag für Sozialwissenschaften, 465–479.

Reifenhäuser, C., Hoffmann, S.G., and Kegel, T. (2009). *Freiwilligen-Management (Volunteer management).* Augsburg: ZIEL.

Schütze, F. (1983). 'Biographieforschung und narratives Interview (Biography research and narrative interview)'. *Neue Praxis (New Practices),* 13 (3), 283–293.

Simonson, J., Vogel, C., and Tesch-Römer, C., eds. (2017). *Freiwilliges Engagement in Deutschland (Voluntary work in Germany).* Wiesbaden: Springer VS.

Stamer, K. (2014). *Ehrenamt-management. Impulse und praktische Hilfestellungen zur Förderung des Ehrenamts in Sportvereinen (Voluntary post management. Insights and practical guidelines for supporting voluntary work in sports clubs).* Göttingen: Cuvillier Verlag.

UNHCR (2016). 'Global trends. forced displacement in 2016.' http://www.unhcr. org/5943e8a34.pdf (accessed on 8 May 2018).

# 7 The importance of sport in engaging refugees

'It's only a game?'

*Mark Doidge*

'Who is better? Messi or Ronaldo?', the Afghan teenager said in perfect English. I had just brewed him and his friend a cup of tea on the gas camp stove. His friend poured an inordinate amount of sugar into the steaming liquid as the football conversation started. We sat around the plastic camping table inside the wooden medical clinic. Outside was 'The Jungle' refugee camp on the outskirts of an industrial zone in the Northern French port of Calais. The contrast between the brutal conditions outside of the clinic contrasted with the relative serenity inside the four wooden walls. Likewise, the mundanity of the conversation contrasted sharply with the lives and journeys of the two teenagers sipping tea in front of me. Anywhere in the world, at any moment, there are thousands of people having similar conversations about the relative merits of star players. In recent years, that debate has been around two of the modern stars, Lionel Messi and Cristiano Ronaldo. As the tea cooled, the conversation shifted from the skills and attitude of star players to the previous night's game. *El Clásico* had been played the evening before between Spain's top two clubs, Barcelona and Real Madrid; coincidently, the two teams that Messi and Ronaldo played for. In an abnormal situation, here was a moment of relative normality.

This chapter makes no magical claims on the 'power' of football or sport more generally. It demonstrates some examples of how sport can provide a safe, mundane space in which to engage refugees and asylum-seekers and the principles that are presented will also facilitate more inclusive environments for *all* participants. Overall, the coach has an important social role to play. They can play an active role in creating an inclusive environment, fostering positive social interaction and allowing participants to enjoy themselves. From this starting point we can begin to build strong foundations of trust and relationships, which can then help develop other forms of engagement. Too often, as will be briefly discussed later, grand myths are propagated about the power of sport. Sport is not, and never will be, the panacea that solves the social integration, education and medical needs of migrants, refugees and asylum-seekers (or other minority groups). We should not forget that for some people, talking about or playing football is an end in itself. However, it can provide a valuable social space where relationships can be forged and developed.

86   *Mark Doidge*

I write this chapter as an academic-activist, not as a practitioner (Doidge, 2018). There are many volunteers and coaches who have more experience and practical ideas borne from their involvement in delivering activities on the ground. I am a sociologist who has had some practical experience in 'The Jungle,' rather than coming from a coaching, NGO or social work background. The basis of this chapter comes from my involvement as a volunteer in 'The Jungle,' as well as research associated with various sport and education projects, including the University of Brighton's Football 4 Peace (F4P)[1] programme and a Sport England funded refugee integration project with Brighton Table Tennis Club (see Doidge and Sandri, 2018). Whilst these show that sport can have a beneficial influence on breaking down cultural barriers in divided societies, the sporting context has to be carefully managed with clear communication and training to coaches, off-pitch team-building exercises and carefully managed competition which emphasises team work, cross-cultural understanding, gender-equality and individual empowerment. Consequently, this is more of a call to critically consider the role sport can play in supporting refugees and asylum-seekers, as well as outlining some ideas on how to engage refugees with sport. Primarily, the voices of refugees should be central so they have a say in what activities work for them. At the same time, this should be done in collaboration with a wide range of support organisations. Sport is merely one minor solution within a much wider holistic approach. This chapter, therefore, is not putting sport into a wider context, nor is it proposing coaching exercises. These can be found elsewhere. In arguing for the consideration of the role of sport for refugees, this chapter will briefly outline the relatively recent role that sport has taken in community projects. It will then outline some of the opportunities and issues affecting the use of sport, before presenting the three main arguments: (1) that coaches should play an active role in developing inclusive environments; (2) these environments should be 'trauma-informed'; and (3) that positive social interaction should be encouraged for community benefits.

## The growth of sport in community development

There is a long history of football being used to help integrate young refugees in the United Kingdom. Eighty years ago, young male refugees from the Basque Region were given exile during the Spanish Civil War and some of these players went on to become the first Spanish professional footballers in England (Westland, 2012). Across Europe, there are numerous examples of groups and organisations that are using sport to help refugees and communities to connect (SPIN, 2012). In Britain, many of these have been founded by groups of individuals, often fans, who identified the importance of football in engaging refugees and host communities. Elsewhere in Europe, clubs have taken the initiative, such as Athens-based Olympiacos who have supported the establishment of Hope FC and likewise in Babelsberg, Potsdam where Welcome United has been created. In other countries, organisations have taken a lead, such as the Italian Sport for All organisation, UISP, helping with the refugee team Liberi Nantes in Rome. Projects have also been set up by sports clubs that specialise in sports activities other than football. Brighton Table Tennis Club has created a welcoming, inclusive atmosphere and actively engaged with many different communities, including refugees and asylum-seekers. Elsewhere, the Refugee Cricket project in London has given Afghan boys a safe social space in their strange new environment.

These initiatives build on a recent tradition of using sport for community development. Variously called, 'Sport for Development' (SFD; S4D); 'Sport for Development and Peace' (SDP), 'Sport in Development' (SiD), or 'Sport and Development' (Schulenkorf and Adair, 2014; Hayhurst et al., 2016), this growing sector deploys sport, play and physical activity as interventionist, socio-cultural tools to promote social development and peaceful relations across the world. The majority of the S4D programmes use sport in a recreational and non-competitive manner. Coalter (2010) highlights how some programmes focus primarily on sport ('sport plus'), whilst others add sport to programmes that address specific social or developmental aims ('plus sport'). Both are based on the belief in sport as something inherently good and valuable to individuals and the whole society. We have to be careful of inscribing sport with the functionalist myth that it will solve all social problems (Coalter, 2007). Ultimately, sport is 'value neutral' (Sugden, 2010), it holds no power in or of itself. It merely provides a space where social aims can be addressed.

The field of Sport for Development is broadly divided between projects organised in communities in the global north and those in the global south. The majority of academic analyses of sport for development are on projects predominantly undertaken in Africa, Asia or Latin America. Usually NGOs and volunteers from the global north run these projects (Gliulianotti and Armstrong, 2014; Darnell and Hayhurst, 2014). This results in a range of specific power relations, underpinned by colonial legacies and specifically impacting ethnic, racial and gendered understandings of the self. It is important to acknowledge these power relations when working with refugees. Whatever the location of the interaction, sport is inscribed with certain cultural understandings of who should or should not play. Gender, in particular, can be a major obstacle when implementing sport programmes (Chawansky, 2011; Hayhurst, 2014). Often there are significant cultural barriers to sport participation for girls and women. Programmes have to be carefully designed to ensure that these obstacles can be overcome. This is not to say that it is easier for boys. For a start, not all boys like sport. Additionally, sport can act as a liminal space where certain behaviours are tolerated or exposed. As will be discussed later, this can be an excellent way of revealing and/or managing trauma in young boys. But it can also create problematic situations, like anger or physical intimidation, that need to be carefully managed. Designing a programme with trauma and social interaction placed centrally can help sport be used as a powerful tool to support refugees and asylum-seekers.

There is a relatively small range of literature on sport for development projects for refugees ( Olliff, 2008; Nathan et al., 2010, 2013; Spaaij, 2012, 2015; Werge-Olsen and Vik, 2012; Ha and Lyras, 2013; Stone, 2013; Doidge, 2018; Doidge and Sandri, 2018; McGee and Pelham, 2018). Despite this, sport programmes

88   *Mark Doidge*

have been demonstrated to provide a range of positive benefits that include mental, emotional, social and physical wellbeing, opportunities for cultural and social integration, opportunities for pro-social interactions and friendships, access to wider social networks for support and access to employment, and increased self-esteem and feelings of empowerment.

Here we return to a key argument that permeates the chapter: sport does not have causal powers. Sport is a process of participation and practice that can promote certain positive experiences when combined with other support (Coalter, 2007). Sport programmes for refugees therefore need to be carefully planned, in line with socio-political circumstances and needs and experiences of their targeted group. Sport in itself is not a sufficient tool for refugee settlement and it can only provide benefits for refugees in the context of addressing other barriers for refugees' full participation and inclusion in the host society, including but not limited to: education and employment opportunities, language training, offering affordable housing and health services, supporting refugee families, and making sure the police and justice systems are fair and responsive Olliff, 2008). Sport can play an important role in supporting refugees. The following sections outline some ideas of how sport can help, primarily focussing on three areas: the role of the coach; trauma-sensitivity; and social interaction. By keeping these three aspects central, practitioners can provide a supportive environment for refugees and asylum-seekers as well as building the foundations for other development work, as long as this is carefully managed.

### Active coaching

Successful Sport for Development projects rely on the hard work and dedication of the coaches and volunteers who run them. Invariably community-orientated individuals run them, which means there is a focus on social skills as well as sporting skills. Sport offers a rare social space where there are individuals specifically tasked with intervening over people's behaviour and actions (Doidge and Sandri, 2018). This isn't just about setting up coaching sessions that are inclusive, but actively creating an environment where participants are welcomed on their own terms, treated with respect and made to feel comfortable. Some specific practical examples will be laid out in the following two sections on taking a trauma-informed approach and facilitating social interaction. Moreover, 'sensitivity to the emotional experiences of others permits people to actively develop a sense of collective identity and social solidarity in ways that can positively impact upon social and psychological wellbeing' (Potrac et al., 2017: 136). Working with the individual emotional needs of participants can have a beneficial outcome for the individual, team, and club. This can be as simple as just letting someone play, rather than forcing them to socialise, or making them feel welcome by greeting them in their native language.

It should be recognised that undertaking this more nuanced and emotionally engaged role takes emotional resources. Recent scholarship, including this volume, has challenged the notion that coaching is merely about technical

*Importance of sport in engaging refugees* 89

rationality (Jones, Armour and Potrac, 2004; Potrac and Marshall, 2011; Nelson et al., 2013; Wallis and Lambert, 2016). Coaching and volunteering in sport projects requires 'emotional labour' (Nelson et al., 2013; Lee et al., 2015; Hayton, 2017; Potrac et al., 2017). This is especially true when working with groups that may have experienced trauma, like refugees (Doidge and Sandri, 2019). Emotional labour is the emotion work employees do to manage their own emotions for their job (Hochschild, 1983). The emotion work is done in response to a perceived disconnect between how an individual feels and how they think they should feel. Coaching requires intense social interaction with participants. The social relationships are infused with power as the coach has to assert themselves, build trust and respect, and even coerce players to act in certain ways (Nelson et al., 2013). This can lead to an intense learning curve, particularly for young coaches (Hayton, 2017). Coaching courses invariably focus on the physical and technical skills rather than the emotional and social skills (Doidge and Sandri, 2018). Being submerged in a sports development project with participants that the coaches may perceive as difficult often requires a lot of emotional labour and reflection (Hayton, 2017).

Coaches are not simply service sector employees who have to perform a specific role for their customers; they are more intimately engaged with their participants. Coaches are specifically tasked with altering individuals' behaviour and skills (Lee et al., 2015). Coaches do this in connection with a host of others, including carers and parents, opposing teams, fans, referees, and youth workers (Lee et al., 2015). All of these interactions have an impact on the emotional resilience of coaches. If players are experiencing difficulties due to issues away from the sport, then coaches need to perform extensive emotional labour. Although coaches are in a unique and trusted position, they do not have to perform the role of social worker, counsellor or carer. Where possible, coaches should try linking to specialists who are used to working with the target group, like refugees. By linking with social workers and specialist grassroots organisation, coaches can signpost any particular issues to the specialists, as well as gaining much needed emotional support. For example, in Brighton, there are a range of grassroots and municipal organisations that can support refugees. These include council social workers, caseworkers at charities like Pathways to Independence, Voices in Exile or Brighton Migrant Solidarity, or other grassroots groups, like Migrant English Project or Global Social Club to provide language or social activities.

## The trauma-informed approach

Refugee children are particularly susceptible to trauma. Many have endured difficult experiences at home, and this has led them to undertake arduous journeys (UNICEF, 2017). As they cross countries and continents they may have witnessed and experienced events that will undoubtedly leave their marks, both physically and mentally. Being sensitive to this trauma is a fundamental role of volunteers, youth workers and coaches working with refugees.

90   *Mark Doidge*

This chapter does not argue that sport can help heal trauma. There are many complex reasons for trauma, especially for refugees. Sport can become part of the healing process and clinical referrals are absolutely still required. Sport can help bring symptoms of trauma to the surface. The playful aspect of sport creates a different space in which social interaction occurs. As a result, coaches and volunteers should look out for certain signs and refer when required. Those volunteers and coaches should not take that responsibility, unless suitably qualified. Symptoms of trauma can appear through the physical interactive aspects of sport. The combination of physical and verbal engagement in sport provides many potential flashpoints. Physical aggression, quickly escalating arguments and violence, or an inability to adhere to the rules when things go against the player can all be signs of emotional dys-regulation. This can also surface through a social and emotional distance where the individual struggles to make friends or pro-social relationships with coaches or teammates. Attachment avoidance issues are also indicative of trauma related concerns. Yet these can be supported through sport.

Following trauma-sensitive design principles will help provide a solid foundation for your activities. The guidelines outlined in *Playing to Heal: Designing a Trauma-Sensitive Sport Program* (Bergholz, 2013) provide an excellent tripartite framework that addresses design, approach and support. It is imperative to have robust support for the programme. To reiterate that sport is just one part of a holistic approach, having a strong referral system can help recruit participants, but also allow those running sessions to refer to the necessary social and medical services as required. The success of any programme is only as good as the support given to those running it and their emotional wellbeing is paramount. And this support should also extend to caregivers who should be involved in the programme if possible.

Within the curriculum, there should be three guiding principles; play; skills, and strengths. Sport can enable a young person to develop skills and strengths that can build their self-esteem (Northcote and Casimiro, 2009; Bergholz, 2013; Bergholz et al., 2016; Doidge and Sandri, 2018a). Stone (2013, p. 77) argues, 'Self worth comes from mastery within the context of the match.' Trauma often leads to feelings of guilt and shame, so positive encouragement of strengths can assist the healing process. Skills-based sessions can also help develop those competences and provide positive teachable moments. Fundamentally, the sessions should include play-based activities. The philosopher Huizinga (1949) suggested that humans were fundamentally playful animals. Sport for refugees should be a playful space, particularly at the start. Developing a range of activities that maintain the playful and fun aspect of sport helps cultivate meaningful social interactions through the sport programme (Football 4 Peace International, n.d.a; n.d.b). There may be some athletes who wish to push themselves and referrals to more 'professional' teams may be required, but for many participants, just taking part is all that is required.

Designing and creating a supportive environment is fundamental when supporting refugees through sport. Providing normalcy and structure is a key part of helping to overcome trauma. Refugees and asylum-seekers are often in vastly different spaces to where they feel comfortable. They can be in refugee camps, which are beset with their own oppressive feelings and issues. If they are lucky enough to have reached a final destination, they may be placed in a new community, often one that doesn't want them, and in accommodation that is unsuitable. In many European countries, asylum-seekers are not permitted to work. When removed from the usual rhythms of daily life, programmes that provide structure help to create some semblance of normality. Mundane conversations about football, like the one at the start of this chapter, go a little way to building some familiarity and ordinariness in the lives of those whose lives are anything but ordinary.

Creating a safe neutral space is paramount in supporting young refugees (Spaaij and Schulenkorf, 2014). The sports field is a liminal space. If one were to rugby tackle someone on the street there would be serious repercussions, but on the rugby field it is positively encouraged. Even within a refugee camp, the sports field can become a temporary safe space, even if it is not physically demarcated. Ideally, there would be separate spaces for the young people to reinforce the difference, but failing that, it is important to ensure that the sports field is used only by the young people and is not a free-for-all for others. This helps establish a set of rules, and also reiterates the focus on the young people. Once again, this requires the active engagement and awareness of the coach. They need to establish the rules, enforce them as well as policing the boundary of that safe space and challenge anyone that infringes the rules. This safe space does not mean that difficult conversations cannot take place, but that there are agreed rules for tackling issues.

Creating a safe space is important for two main reasons. The first is that young people affected by trauma do not feel safe. Their primary points of safety – home, family, etc. – are no longer there. Without these physical points of anchorage, the young people can feel hypersensitive to perceived threats. The emotional space of sport could heighten this sensitivity, so creating a safe space helps mitigate some of these issues. Second, the safe space creates a zone that is different from other parts of their daily lives. Within this zone, it can encourage the interactions where fun, discipline and teamwork can be promoted. When refugees and asylum-seekers move to new places, language and culture can be unfamiliar, so promoting friendly and supportive interaction in a safe space can help promote a sense of normality. Over time, these safe spaces can provide anchorage as the young people settle into a routine. Youth centres, sports clubs, and even football stadia, can provide a physical space that imbues feelings of belonging and safety (Stone, 2013).

The combination of a physical safe space and fun environment helps create a cathartic space where participants can 'switch off' from their daily tribulations. There is a 'mindfulness' in participating in sport that allows for the individual to focus on the immediate, embodied experience, rather than dwell on emotional or mental anxieties. 'In lives that are unfamiliar in so many other ways,' as Stone (2013, p. 15) states, 'this unthinking understanding of what is taking place during a match relieves the constant pressures of managing daily life. The emotions and experiences are carried through the week to provide positive means of reflection

92 *Mark Doidge*

and anticipation.' When combined with the link between physical health and mental wellbeing, the combination of physical activity and cathartic games can be a useful way of combatting stress.

Communication is vital for the creation of the safe space. On the one hand, clear communication provides the rules and framework of engagement that structures the safe space. Volunteers and coaches need to have clear and unambiguous rules of behaviour that help to give clear guidance to participants (Football 4 Peace International, n.d.b). This ensures that the space is safe for all players, coaches and volunteers. Clear communication can also draw on the various teachable moments that sport can provide. When there are issues and challenges, these incidents can be highlighted and reflected upon. In a similar fashion, positive behaviour can be encouraged which help build self-esteem and self-confidence. At all times, the coach or youth worker should provide space for reflection. Asking questions, giving time to reflect and offering feedback is a continuous process that maintains dialogue. Language can be a major obstacle for communication with refugees (Olliff, 2008; Spaaij, 2012, Werge-Olsen and Vik, 2012; Ha and Lyras, 2013), so simple language and hand gestures are very important. Positive encouragement and time for reflection combined with observation and anticipation can help the coach support participants.

## Positive social interaction

Sport is one space where social connections can be fostered (Coalter, 2007, 2013, 2014; Nathan et al., 2010; Sugden, 2006, 2010, 2014; Giulianotti, 2011; Stone, 2013). This is where coaches have a unique role; they can help foster social interaction between players by facilitating dialogue through their sessions. Social wellbeing is important for everyone, not just those suffering from trauma. Engaging in a shared activity can help form pro-social relationships and overcome some of the impact of trauma. The shared space can also highlight the symptoms of trauma as individuals may struggle to make social connections. In this case, empathy and support is required to build those relationships and potentially refer individuals for clinical supervision. Initially, new members gravitate towards similar ethnic, religious, or linguistic groups. Monoethnic teams can help refugees find acceptance and familiarity among other refugees or immigrants who share their culture and language (Spaaij, 2015). In the short term, this can help new members feel a sense of belonging and comfort in the group, but over the long term, these intra-ethnic groupings need to be carefully managed. For example, Khan (2013) observed that clan/tribal divisions in the Afghan refugee diaspora in Brighton impeded their ability to form a broader Afghan community organisation through which they could organise sport programmes for migrants, refugees and asylum-seekers. Additionally, ethnic or linguistic divisions can exacerbate intolerance or racism, reiterating the argument that sport does not solve problems.

This is where sport can provide the space to overcome these divisions, when carefully managed. Sport programmes should work to overcome these differences through team-building exercises and games prior to matches taking place.

Brighton Table Tennis Club work hard to break down these divisions between different communities be they refugees, older people, less physically able or others (Doidge and Sandri, 2018). They create spaces where different people will play against each other, or if they see two friends playing together all session, the coaches actively intervene to mix the pairings. Analysis of the Football United programme in New South Wales, Australia found that boys taking part showed significantly more positive levels of other-group orientation, more pro-social behaviour and less problems with their peers than the comparison group (Nathan et al., 2010, 2013). F4P (Football 4 Peace International, n.d.b) has developed an 'Off-pitch Manual' to provide ideas for games and activities to help overcome social divisions of religion, class, gender, ethnicity and sexuality. These can include a variety of ice-breakers to learn each other's names, trust-building games like blindfolding partners and leading them, to activities such as treasure hunts. Placing young people in situations where they have to work together, solve problems, and develop practical knowledge can also help promote mutual understanding, respect and trust. These values can then be transferred onto the sports field and referred back to during teachable moments. Ultimately, it is hoped that these values are then taken into wider society (Sugden, 2010).

These activities are not restricted to intra-refugee programmes but can be undertaken with the various groups that make up host communities (Doidge and Sandri, 2018). Care must be taken that there is not an assumption of assimilation as this can entrench feelings of inadequacy or difference and potentially trigger trauma. As well as being fun, these games and activities should also highlight the importance of a diverse range of opinions and insights and encourage co-operation. Even the use of the term 'integration' is contested as it is often seen as a one-way process, rather than a two-way dialogue where refugees become part of the social, political, cultural and economic fabric of the society ( Ha and Lyras, 2013; Spaaij, 2015). This requires efforts from both the refugees and the host society and ensures 'the ability to participate fully in economic, social, cultural and political activities while maintaining one's cultural identity' (Spaaij, 2012, p. 1519). Programmes therefore need to ensure mingling of participants from different ethnic groups, their teamwork and orientation towards common goals (Nathan et al., 2010).

With sustained interaction, friendships can develop over time. Schulenkorf (2010), through his research on ethnically divided communities in Sri Lanka, indicated that carefully monitored sports events can establish friendships and inclusive social identities by creating moments of togetherness for members of disparate ethnic groups. As Stone (2013: 77) highlights:

> Friendships develop over time and football provides the motivation for people to meet regularly. Whether training, playing, going to matches or watching on television, there is a timetable that for many refugees and asylum-seekers may be absent in the rest of their lives. The development of friendships, or friendly relationships with interconnecting networks of acquaintances, is part of the communality attached to belonging.

94   *Mark Doidge*

Sport programmes provide structure in an otherwise unstructured life. As asylum-seekers are not permitted to work and are restricted on what voluntary activity they can undertake, sport provides an opportunity to meet on a regular basis. For this reason, sport programmes should be scheduled and predictable (Bergholz et al., 2016). For many, this can be the highlight of their week and provides some much needed relief throughout the Kafa-esque asylum process (Stone, 2013).

Sport programmes need to be long-term. Although resources are often in short supply, the success of sport is that it provides regular, sustained interaction between participants. This is also important for the healing process from trauma. This is a long process and long-term engagement helps provide the stability and support that sufferers require in order to anchor themselves in their new community. Similarly, time is also required to build trusting relationships and friendships. One-off tournaments can be very useful in providing a shared focal point for participants and to raise awareness of specific issues. But only sustained programmes can develop the social, physical and emotional benefits that sport can provide. Additionally, long-term projects can be linked to other projects, such as language courses, which also require regular sustained engagement.

Furthermore, routine helps to entrench sport as a mundane activity. As the opening paragraph to this chapter demonstrated, football is a commonplace and ordinary activity that is shared by millions around the world. Healing from trauma can be facilitated by 'The re-establishment of daily patterns of living that supply structure and support such as participation in work, school and community activities' (Lawrence et al., 2010). Sport provides this structured environment and can help children overcome trauma (Henley, 2005). Emphasising the routine can help bring normality back to participants. As Stone (2013, p. 77) states:

> The routines and discipline attached to football help with the management of life from one day to the next. Football represents something like 'normality' amongst the unfamiliarity and inactivity that dominates life for new arrivals. Simple things like the exchange of 'banter' amongst teammates has the effect of just feeling like 'one of the guys.' Being mocked for missing a shot has nothing to do with the systemic oppression felt by many asylum-seekers. It is both meaningful and meaningless within the mundanity of day to day life providing it remains within acceptable boundaries.

Just being a fan or player can help lessen the stigma of being an asylum-seeker and reiterate the normality of daily life. This can help overcome some of the social and emotional dislocation experienced by refugees and asylum-seekers.

Sport can therefore become a powerful site for those seeking trusting relationships. Facilitating attachment is an important factor in providing a trauma-sensitive programme (Bergholz, 2013). Caring adult relationships within the programme can help create a healing environment. This also allows for the development of trusting relationships, particularly when arriving in new communities (Olliff, 2008; Werge-Olsen and Vik, 2012, Spaaij, 2015). As Whitley and Gould (2011) highlight, this is of particular relevance for refugee children,

*Importance of sport in engaging refugees* 95

since by participating in sport they get a chance to build a trusting relationship with adult figures in their new country, which is important for their further socio-psychological development. Coaches and volunteers should get to know participants, learning their names. Ice-breakers and trust-building games can help build the links between participants and coaches, as well as creating a fun environment (Football 4 Peace International, n.d.b).

Awareness of cultural practices helps maintain the supportive structure of the programme. Being respectful of the cultural background of participants is important for two reasons (Bergholz, 2013; Bergholz et al., 2016). First, different cultures have different ways of dealing with grief and trauma. This can help the produce a supportive environment rather than imposing specific methods on the individuals that might lead to emotional disengagement. Secondly, rooting activities in the cultural games and activities of the participants can reproduce feelings of normalcy and continuity with the past. For example, cricket is popular in Afghanistan, whereas baseball is more popular in Venezuela. It is for this reason that football has become the most common activity of sport for development programmes as it is the world's most popular sport. But programmes should also be aware that football also comes with a lot of cultural baggage. It can be seen as heavily gendered, and also comes with pre-existing identities attached, such as racism or violence. But as the opening of this chapter attests, it also provides a *linga franca* that enables people to speak across cultures.

Other sports can be used as long as they provide all the other ingredients of a safe and supportive environment, long-term engagement and engaged coaches. An excellent example of this is Brighton Table Tennis Club who has used table tennis as a way of engaging young refugees, as well as linking the sport to language and maths lessons.[2] Many of the boys at the club had never played table tennis before, but the supportive environment ensured that they had good retention, and the fun atmosphere, and relatively quick skills mastery meant that self-confidence quickly grew. A clear and supportive structure within the club meant that players could undertake coaching qualifications that not only developed their self-esteem, but also provided sustainability. Table tennis is an excellent sport as it is a relative leveller. Skills can be quickly acquired, and games are not restricted to the same demographic. Games can take place between people of different genders, ethnicities, dis/abilities and ages. Consequently, a range of different sports can be used to engage refugees and asylum-seekers. Ultimately, involving them and placing their needs central can help determine which approach to take.

## Conclusion: The importance of sport

As the opening paragraph to this chapter attests, football is a universal language that is popular across a wide range of social, political and geographical contexts. It is something many (particularly young male) refugees have done as a way of occupying and socialising themselves in their home countries, and this experience and activity can be extended to their new communities. It is for this reason that sport does not have to be about elite performance. Coaching for social and personal development helps build on the collaborative and cordial aspects of sport. Football enjoys the status of being the most popular and most widely played sport in the world. This is due to its accessibility. It is relatively inexpensive, its rules are fairly simple, and it can be played almost anywhere (grass, streets, sand etc.). It is played by all genders and can be designed as non-violent sport. In doing so it promotes teamwork and can be used to educate on values (Nathan et al., 2010; Sugden, 2006, 2010). As with other sports, football allows for participants to be seen as fans or footballers first, and refugees second. This plays an important role in developing self-esteem within their new communities.

Sport can be used as a hook for a variety of people who see it as a fun, engaging and relaxing activity (Sherry et al., 2015). Whilst physical activity may be a low priority for refugees who have endured long physically and mentally demanding journeys, as Murray (2014) points out, many refugees have expressed a desire for sport and physical activity, especially when settling down in a new society with an aim to stay. Ultimately, their voices should be paramount. Sport projects should not be forced on participants, but if they express a desire for sport and physical activity, then there are numerous benefits. Some will want to push themselves and want to have elite coaching accordingly; others will just want to have fun with their friends. This hook also allows sport to be used a metaphor to explain cultural practices, or even their asylum process. Drawing on game situations, or the broader context of the game, can help paint a picture that allows asylum-seekers to locate themselves. Referring to the asylum process as a league campaign, or cup run, can help the young person to understand where they are.

It is important to reiterate that sport does not provide a complete solution; it can create divisions around gender, ethnicity, sexuality, dis/ability and faith. That said, if carefully managed, it can provide a space where these differences can be addressed and overcome. As Sugden (2010, p. 258) states, 'sport is intrinsically value neutral and under carefully managed circumstances it can make a positive if modest contribution to peace building.' Whilst acknowledging this, sport does offer considerable advantages for supporting refugees:

In brief, sport for development programmes can promote safe environments for refugees and asylum-seekers. Focussing on social and individual development, rather than sport performance, coaches can take an active role in facilitating social interaction and promoting fun and inclusive spaces. In this way sport becomes a positive location for *all* participants and helps build strong foundations for trusting relationships, which can then help develop other forms of engagement. Framing all this within a trauma-sensitive programme can help the healing process. This can require a certain degree of emotional labour as coaches and volunteers may not be expert in potential trauma and mental health issues associated with those seeking asylum, particularly children. Linking into wider support networks of social workers and specialist grassroots organisations will take some of this pressure off sport projects. Ultimately, the mundanity of sport is important when supporting refugees. Simple conversations, such as arguing about whether Ronaldo or Messi is better, helps to create sense of normality that can be incredibly supportive.

## Notes

1 Further information about the research and approach can be found via www.football-4peace.eu.
2 For more information, see https://blogs.brighton.ac.uk/alumni/2016/07/26/batty-about-inclusivity/.

## References

Bergholz, L. (2013). *Playing to heal: Designing a trauma-sensitive sport program*. Boston, MA: Edgework Consulting.

Bergholz, L., Stafford, L., and D'Andrea, W. (2016). 'Creating trauma-informed sports programming for traumatized youth: Core principles for an adjunctive therapeutic approach.' *Journal of Infant, Child, and Adolescent Psychotherapy*, 15 (3), 244–253.

Chawansky, M. (2011). 'New social movements, old gender games?: Locating girls in the sport for development and peace movement.' *Research in Social Movements, Conflicts and Change*, 32, 121–134.

Coalter, F. (2007). *Sport a wider social role: Who's keeping the score?* London: Routledge.

Coalter, F. (2010). 'The politics of sport for development: Limited focus programmes and broad gauge problems?' *International Review for the Sociology of Sport*, 45 (3), 295–314.

Coalter, F. (2013). *Sport for development: What game are we playing?* London: Routledge.

Coalter, F. (2014). 'Sport-for-development: Pessimism of the intellect, optimism of the will.' In: N. Schulenkorf and D. Adair, eds. *Global sport-for-development: Critical perspectives*. Basingstoke: Palgrave Macmillan, 62–78.

Darnell, S., and Hayhurst, L. (2014). 'De-colonising the politics and practice of sport-for-development: Critical insights from post-colonial feminist theory and methods.' In: N. Schulenkorf, and D. Adair, eds. *Global sport-for-development: Critical perspectives*. Basingstoke: Palgrave Macmillan, 33–61.

Doidge, M. (2018). 'Refugees United: The role of activism and football in supporting refugees.' In: T. Carter, D. Burdsey, and M. Doidge, eds. *Transforming sport: Knowledge, structures, practice*. London: Routledge, 79–93.

Doidge, M., and Sandri, E. (2018). *Active integration: Brighton Table Tennis Club, Refugee Integration Project*. Brighton: University of Brighton.

Doidge, M., and Sandri, E. (2019). '"Friends that last a lifetime": The importance of emotions amongst volunteers working with refugees in Calais.' *British Journal of Sociology*, 70 (2), 463–480.

Football 4 Peace International (n.d.a). *Teaching values through sport: A manual for community football*. Eastbourne: Football 4 Peace.

Football 4 Peace International (n.d.b). *Teaching values through sport: A handbook for off pitch activities*. Eastbourne: Football 4 Peace.

Giulianotti, R. (2011). 'Sport, peacemaking and conflict resolution: A contextual analysis and modeling of the sport, development and peace sector.' *Ethnic and Racial Studies*, 34 (2), 207–228.

Giulianotti, R., and Armstrong, G. (2014). 'The sport for development and peace sector: A critical sociological analysis.' In: N. Schulenkorf and D. Adair, eds. *Global sport-for-development: critical perspectives*. Basingstoke: Palgrave Macmillan, 15–32.

Ha, J.-P.., and Lyras, A. (2013). 'Sport for refugee youth in a new society: The role of acculturation in sport for developing and peace programming.' *South African Journal for Research in Sport, Physical Education and Recreation*, 35 (2), 121–140.

## 98 Mark Doidge

Hayhurst, L. (2014). 'The "girl effect" and martial arts: Social entrepreneurship and sport, gender and development in Uganda.' *Gender, Place and Culture*, 21 (3), 297–315.

Hayhurst, L., Kay, T., and Chawansky, M. (2016). *Beyond sport for development and peace: Transnational perspectives on theory, policy and practice*. London/New York: Routledge.

Hayton, J. (2017). '"They need to learn to take it on the chin": Exploring the emotional labour of student volunteers in a sports-outreach project in the North East of England.' *Sociology of Sport Journal*, 34 (2), 136–147.

Henley, R. (2005). 'Helping children overcome disaster trauma through post-emergency psychosocial sports programs.' *Working Paper*. Biel/Bienne: Swiss Academy for Development.

Hochschild, A.R. (1983). *The managed heart: commercialization of the human feeling*. Berkeley: University of California Press.

Huizinga, J. (1949). *Homo ludens: A study of the play element in culture*. London: Routledge and Keegan Paul.

Jones, R., Armour, K., and Potrac, P. (2004). *Sports coaching cultures: From practice to theory*. London: Routledge.

Khan, N. (2013). 'From refugees to the world stage: Sport, civilisation and modernity in out of the Ashes and a UK Afghan diaspora.' *South Asian Popular Culture*, 11 (3), 271–285.

Lawrence, S., De Silva, M., and Henley, R. (2010). *Sports and games for post-traumatic stress disorder (PTSD)*. London: The Cochrane Collaboration.

Lee, Y.H., Chelladurai, P., and Kim, Y. (2015). 'Emotional labour in sports coaching: Development of a model.' *International Journal of Sports Science and Coaching*, 10 (2–3), 561–575.

McGee, D. and Pelham, J. (2018). 'Politics at play: Locating human rights, refugees and grassroots humanitarianism in the Calais Jungle, *Leisure Studies* 37 (1), 22–35.

Murray, D. (2014). The challenge of home for sexual orientation and gendered identity refugees in Toronto, *Journal of Canadian Studies*, 48 (1), 132–152.

Nathan, S., Bunde-Birouste, A., Evers, C., Kemp, L., Mackenzie, J., and Henley, R. (2010). 'Social cohesion through football: A quasi-experimental mixed methods design to evaluate a complex health promotion program.' *BMC Public Health*, 10, 587–599.

Nathan, S., Kemp, L., Bunde-Birouste, A., MacKenzie, J., Evers, C., and Shwe, T.A. (2013). '"We wouldn't of made friends if we didn't come to Football United": The impacts of a football program on young people's peer, prosocial, and cross-cultural relationships.' *BMC Public Health*, 13, 399–415.

Nelson, L., Potrac, P., Gilbourne, D., Allanson, A., Gale, L., and Marshall, P. (2013). 'Thinking, feeling, acting: The case of a semi-professional soccer coach.' *Sociology of Sport Journal*, 30 (4), 467–486.

Northcote, J., and Casimiro, S. (2009). 'A critical approach to evidence-based resettlement policy: Lessons learned from an Australian Muslim refugee sports program.' *Tamara Journal of Critical Organisation Inquiry*, 8 (1/2), 173.

Olliff, N. (2008). 'Playing for the future: The role of sport and recreation in supporting refugee young people to "settle well" in Australia.' *Youth Studies Australia*, 27 (1), 52–60.

Potrac, P., and Marshall, P. (2011). 'Arlie Russell Hochschild: The managed heart, feeling rules and emotional labour: coaching as an emotional endeavour.' In: R. Jones, Potrac, P., Cushion, C., and Ronglan, L.T., eds. *The sociology of sports coaching*. London: Routledge, 55-66.

Potrac, P., Smith, A., and Nelson, L. (2017). 'Emotions in sport coaching: An introductory essay.' *Sport Coaching Review*, 6 (2), 129–141.

Schulenkorf, N. (2010). 'Sport events and ethnic reconciliation: Attempting to create social change between Sinhalese, Tamil and Muslim sportspeople in war-torn Sri Lanka.' *International Review for the Sociology of Sport*, 45 (3), 273–294.

Schulenkorf, N., and Adair, D. (2014). *Global sport-for-development: Critical perspectives.* Basingstoke: Palgrave Macmillan.

Sherry, E., Schulenkorpf, N., and Chalip, L. (2015). 'Managing sport for social change: The state of play.' *Sport Management Review*, 18 (1), 1–5.

Spaaij, R. (2012). 'Beyond the playing field: Experiences of sport, social capital, and integration among Somalis in Australia.' *Ethnic and Racial Studies*, 35 (9), 1519–1538.

Spaaij, R., and Schulenkorf, N. (2014). 'Cultivating safe space: Lessons for sport-for-development projects and events.' *Journal of Sport Management*, 28 (6), 633–645.

Spaaij, R. (2015). 'Refugee youth, belonging and community sport.' *Leisure Studies*, 34 (3), 303–318.

SPIN. (2012). 'Inclusion of migrants in and through sports: A good practice guide.' Accessed online at: www.dge.mec.pt/sites/default/files/Projetos/Agenda_Europeia_Migracoes/Documentos/inclusion_in_spor t_guidelines.pdf.

Stone, C. (2013). 'Football – a shared sense of belonging.' Accessed online at: www.furd.org/resources/Final%20Research%20Report-%20low%20res.pdf.

Sugden, J. (2006). 'Teaching and playing sport for conflict resolution and co-existence in Israel'. *International Review for the Sociology of Sport*, 41 (2), 221–240.

Sugden, J. (2010). 'Critical left realisms and sport interventions in divided societies.' *International Review for the Sociology of Sport*, 45 (3), 258–272.

Sugden, J. (2014). 'The ripple effect: Critical pragmatism, conflict resolution and peace building through sport in deeply divided societies.' In: N. Schulenkorf and D. Adair, eds. *Global sport-for-development: Critical perspectives.* Basingstoke: Palgrave Macmillan, 79–96.

UNICEF. (2017). *Harrowing journeys: Children and youth on the move across the Mediterranean Sea, at risk of trafficking and exploitation.* New York: UNICEF.

Wallis, J., and Lambert, J. (2016). *Becoming a sports coach.* London: Routledge.

Werge-Olsen, I., and Vik, J. (2012). 'Activity as a tool in language training for immigrants and refugees.' *Scandinavian Journal of Occupational Therapy*, 19 (6), 530–541.

Westland, N. (2012). 'How Gernika's bombs spawned the first Spanish footballers to play in England.' Accessed online at: http://elpais.com/elpais/2012/05/22/inenglish/1337 695459_091784.html.

Whitley, M., and Gould, D. (2011). 'Psychosocial development in refugee children and youth through the personal–social responsibility model.' *Journal of Sport Psychology in Action*, 1 (3), 118–138.

# 8 Addressing the under-representation of BAME coaches

## An examination of the EFL mandatory code of coach recruitment in professional football club youth academies

*Steven Bradbury and Dominic Conricode*

### Introduction

Over the past 50 years, the higher echelons of men's professional sport has become characterised by the increasing racial, ethnic and cultural diversity of its playing workforce. As a result, in some sports in the United States and in Western Europe (including the United Kingdom) the incidence of elite level (mainly black) racial minority sports performers has become comparable to or exceeded national racial population demographics (Bradbury et al., 2011, Lapchick 2016). However, during this period there has also been a limited throughput and consequent under-representation of coaches from racial minority backgrounds across a range of sporting and national contexts (Bradbury et al., 2011, 2014, 2018, Branham 2008, Cunningham 2010, Norman et al., 2014, Rankin Wright et al., 2016, 2017, Sagas and Cunningham 2005, Singer et al., 2010). Where there has been a steady incremental growth in the numbers of racial minority coaches in some (mainly US-based) sports, these statistical gains seem largely restricted to peripheral support coach positions with lower levels of formal authority or decision making powers and where opportunities for upward career mobility remain limited (Braddock et al., 2012, Cunningham et al., 2010, Day and Mcdonald, 2010, Day and Mcdonald, 2015, Lapchick 2016). These more general patterns of under-representation and occupational segregation seem especially evident in professional football in England where there has historically been a minimal throughput of racial minority (hereafter referred to as BAME) players into senior coaching positions at the elite club level. For example, since 1992 just 29 BAME coaches have held 'head coach' positions at all 92 professional clubs and just seven have held positions of this kind at 20 clubs competing annually in the English Premier League (LMA 2017). Furthermore, between 2014 and 2017 the levels of BAME representation in senior coaching positions at professional clubs have remained stagnant at around 4% at first team level and around 5% at youth academy level (SPTT 2014, 2015, 2016, 2017). More promisingly, recent research has indicated that around 17% of the overall professional club youth academy coaching workforce is drawn from BAME backgrounds. However, just 27% of this cohort are employed on a full-time basis and 73% are in lower status part-time or sessional coaching positions with limited occupational permanence or clearly structured opportunities for career advancement (Conricode and Bradbury, forthcoming 2020). Taken together, the levels of representation of BAME coaches in first team and youth academy settings in professional football compares unfavourably with that of BAME youth academy players (around 40%), BAME professional players (around 30%), and the BAME population of England more broadly (around 15%).

Recent research has drawn on the informed experiential testimonies of elite level BAME coaches and other key stakeholders to examine the reasons for the under-representation of BAME coaches in professional football in England (Bradbury 2018, Bradbury et al., 2014, 2018, Cleland et al., 2011, Kilvington 2020, forthcoming). The work of Bradbury has been particularly instructive in making visible some of the historically embedded and relatively unshifting practices of racially inflected institutional closure which have impacted negatively in constraining the extent and scope of BAME progression across the 'transition pipeline' from playing to coach education to coach employment at first team and youth academy level in the professional game. In doing so, it has identified three inter-related barriers. First, limited opportunities for identification, selection, mentoring and financial support to access high-level coach education courses and negative experiences of intentional and unintentional racism at courses of this kind. This is argued to have limited the potential of BAME coaches to achieve high-level coaching qualifications deemed requisite for employment at professional clubs and to have positioned them at a competitive disadvantage in the professional football coaching marketplace. Second, the continued over-reliance on networks (rather than qualifications) based methods of coach recruitment at professional clubs premised on personal recommendation, patronage, and sponsored mobility. This is argued to have favoured the recruitment of white coaches from within dominant social and cultural insider networks and to be evidenced in the frequency in which, often less qualified or experienced, white coaches access paid coaching positions at professional clubs. Third, the continued existence of conscious and unconscious racial bias and stereotyping in the coaching workplace and the incidence of misplaced cultural perceptions regarding the attitudes, behaviours, intellect and suitability of BAME coaches. This is argued to have led some key decision makers at professional clubs to falsely conceptualise BAME coaches in terms of misperceived ethnic and cultural traits rather than engaging in a reflexive and considered analysis of their coaching qualifications, experiences and abilities as coaches. Taken together, these processes and practices of racialised exclusion are considered to constitute a form of institutional discrimination which has thus far limited the potential for and realisation of equality of opportunities and outcomes for BAME coaches in professional football. As a result, it is argued that any measures designed to address these racialised imbalances should seek to challenge, disrupt and dismantle the normative institutional arrangements and everyday practices of hegemonic whiteness embedded within the senior organisational tiers of football which underpin this inequitable state of affairs (Bradbury et al., 2018).

Promisingly, in recent years, a number of key stakeholders in professional football in England have developed a series of new programmes and initiatives designed to increase the numbers of BAME coaches in the professional game. These targeted interventions have emerged in part as a result of growing external pressures from high profile equality campaign groups including Kick It Out, the Sports People's Think Tank and the Football Against Racism in Europe Network and national media sources and differ markedly in their resource, scope, focus and intended outputs. Some programmes such as the FA BAME COACH Bursary programme (2012–2015) and the more expansive FA Coach Inclusion and Diversity programme (2016–2021) have focused on providing financial and practical resource support to enable and empower BAME coaches to achieve high-level coach education qualifications and to enhance their employability in the coaching marketplace. Evaluation of these programmes has indicated some partial success on this score and also in engendering a series of wider developmental benefits for participants, inclusive of increased confidence, communication, organisation and leadership skills, and an increased knowledge and understanding of the professional football coaching and coach education landscape (Bradbury 2016, 2017). Other programmes have focused on dismantling some of the aforementioned institutional barriers to coach recruitment and have sought to adapt in principle (rather than adopt in full) bespoke versions of the much vaunted 'Rooney Rule' which was first implemented in the NFL in 2002 and which has been hailed as a key mechanism through which the numbers of racial minority head coaches have increased significantly over time (Collins 2007, Duru 2011). Arguably, the most notable efforts on this score have been undertaken by the English Football League (EFL) which in June 2016 launched the 'voluntary' and 'mandatory' codes of coach recruitment following an extensive period of consultation with key football stakeholder bodies and equality campaign groups. The voluntary code of coach recruitment is targeted specifically at first team operations and was first implemented at ten pilot clubs during the 2016–2017 season. It has been argued that despite its laudable aims, the voluntary code features a series of embedded caveats in its wording which position it as a 'discretionary' rather than 'must do' consideration forcing mechanism and that its implementation at club level thus far has been limited and problematic (SPTT 2017). In contrast, the mandatory code of coach recruitment is targeted specifically at professional club youth academies and was first implemented during the 2016–2017 season at all 72 EFL member clubs. The mandatory code stipulates that all EFL club youth academies must run a full recruitment process for any position that requires an individual to hold an FA UEFA B or FA UEFA A licence, and that such positions should be advertised publicly on the EFL and club website for a minimum of seven days. Furthermore, clubs must include at least one suitably qualified BAME candidate on the interview shortlist for that position where an application has been received but will be permitted to opt out of this full recruitment process when promoting a suitably qualified internal candidate regardless of ethnicity. To this end, the mandatory code can be understood as a distinctly positive action (rather than positive discrimination) measure as outlined in sections 158 and 159 of the 2010 UK Equality Act, which allows for employers to implement targeted practices of promoting and interviewing for vacancies in order to redress historical disadvantages and experiences of under-representation on the basis of ethnicity and other 'protected characteristics' (Government Equalities Office, 2010).

The findings presented in this chapter are drawn from an extensive and in-depth evaluation of the first year of the implementation of the EFL mandatory code of coach recruitment at professional football club youth academies. They are drawn from a quantitative online survey of academy managers at EFL club academies (n = 23) and qualitative semi-structured interviews with academy managers, organisational stakeholders and BAME coaches (n = 40). More specifically, the findings presented in this chapter seek to identify and examine the extent of procedural adherence to and effectiveness of the implementation of the mandatory code at club academies and to measure the impact the code has had on increasing the levels of representation of BAME coaches in academy settings. In doing so, the findings presented in this chapter will focus on the following four inter-related elements of the code: *advertising, applications, interviews,* and *appointments.*

## The findings

### Advertisements

Overall, survey and interview findings indicated that during the 2016–2017 season the mandatory code of coach recruitment had engendered a broadly positive impact in increasing the incidence and scope of publicly advertising coaching positions at professional club youth academies. For example, the overwhelming majority of club academies reported publicly advertising coaching positions on 'every occasion' (86%) and a smaller number on 'some occasions' (14%) during this period. Whilst almost all club academies publicly advertised these positions on their own club website (91%), around three-fifths of clubs also utilised other online mediums such as the EFL website (64%) and FA Licensed Coaches Club website (59%). Whilst these formalised approaches to advertising were often enacted alongside – rather than instead of – informal 'word of mouth' methods of vacancy promotion, they were nonetheless felt by interviewees to have become a much more permanent and standardised feature of the coach recruitment process at club academies during the period under review. One academy manager at a category two status club academy reflects on these changing practices below:

> *Actually, because of that [mandatory code] intervention, the jobs now go on the EFL website, which I'd say is a massive step forward in the fact that probably around 18 months ago, before this came in, that never happened.* (Interviewee, Academy Manager)

For some interviewees, this more open and transparent approach to advertising coaching positions was felt to have increased the potential of club academies to attract and recruit a more ethnically diverse cohort of candidates than had been the case in the past. One highly qualified BAME coach with extensive experience of working in club academy settings comments on this potential below:

> One of the things now is that jobs are advertised. You know, at academies, for all sorts of positions. And that's a major difference. That just wasn't the case in the past and so that has to be a good thing. Because getting into academies was a real problem for BAME coaches for a long time. You had to be 'in the know.' (Interviewee, BAME Coach)

The overwhelming majority of club academies also reported they had gone beyond the stipulated seven-day period for publicly advertising coaching positions and had extended the 'reasonable time frame' for advertising to between 8 and 14 days (62%), 15 and 21 days (24%) or 22 and 28 days (14%). This was felt by a number of interviewees to have increased the potential for all aspiring coaches to become aware of vacancies at club academies and to provide an extended period in which to prepare and submit high quality applications for positions of this kind. This was felt by some interviewees to have a particular resonance for BAME coaches whose marginality to dominant social and cultural insider football coaching networks meant that they were more likely than their *social capital heavy* and *better connected* white counterparts to rely solely on these formalised processes of submission. One BAME coach presently working at a category one status club academy reflects on the importance of the temporal relationship between advertising and applications below:

> Sometimes you see a job and you want to go away and think about how you're going to apply for that particular job and how you're going to edit your CV and your covering letter. And that might take some [BAME] individuals a little longer. So I think it's definitely fair and important to have that time period. (Interviewee, BAME coach)

### Applications

Despite the increased incidence and scope of advertising referred to above, survey and interview findings indicated that during the 2016–2017 season this had not yet translated to engendering a markedly greater number of applications for coaching positions at club academies from BAME coaches. For example, club academies reported that during this period just 9% of all applications for coaching positions were from suitably qualified BAME coaches: inclusive of applications for full-time (6%) positions and part-time (21%). For some interviewees, these figures were deemed to be reflective of the relatively low numbers of BAME coaches perceived to have FA UEFA B or high-level youth coaching qualifications considered as requisite for employment at club academies. Such assertions

Addressing under-representation of BAME coaches    105

are borne out to some partial extent by prior research in this area, at least in relation to some specific (mainly South Asian) BAME groups and in less ethnically diverse locales nationally where many lower division EFL clubs are based (Bradbury 2018). One academy manager at a category three status club academy illustrates these points further:

> At any one time, I might have a number of positions available in the academy, but it's tough now. You need to have your UEFA B [coaching qualification] at the very least and probably more. And how many ethnic minority coaches have that. Especially Asian coaches. Probably very few. And so we just don't get applications from those groups. (Interviewee, Academy Manager)

In other cases, a number of interviewees felt that beyond the senior organisational tiers of the EFL and professional club youth academy hierarchies there was little wider knowledge or awareness of the recent implementation or procedural content of the mandatory code of coach recruitment. This was felt to be the case amongst BAME coaches within and outside of the professional game and for whom potential opportunities embodied in the code to ensure an interview to a suitably qualified BAME coach remained 'hidden' and 'unknown.' These perceptions are summarised below by one BAME coach with extensive experience of working for and with national football stakeholder bodies and club youth academies in varying capacities over time:

> I don't think many ethnic minority coaches know about the mandatory code. I mean, there has been some talk in the media about the 'Rooney Rule' but I think the assumption is that it's about managers, you know, at first team level. But at academies? Who knows about it? How is it publicised? (Interviewee, BAME coach)

As a result, there was a general consensus amongst interviewees that the limited promotion of the code beyond the 'inner circle' of football industry professionals had thus far limited its potential to 'reach out' to or increase the numbers of applications from BAME coaches in the short term. Or, at least, up until such a time as the code might become more widely publicised by the EFL and its member club youth academies. One academy manager at a category three status club academy comments further in this respect:

> 'I think it will [increase applications] but I don't think you will see that until the next two or three years. And the only reason I say that is again because it goes back to the whole, have they got the word out, do black and ethnic minority coaches know about this rule?' (Interviewee, Academy Manager)

### Interviews

Despite the relatively low levels of applications for BAME candidates referred to above, survey and interview findings indicated that during the 2016–2017 season there was a more positive correlation between the number of applications made by – and interviews awarded to – suitably qualified BAME coaches. For example, club academies reported that during this period a total of 27% of all coaches interviewed for coaching positions were from BAME backgrounds: inclusive of interviews for full-time (19%) and part-time (35%) positions. Findings here indicate a strong procedural adherence to the mandatory code amongst club academies and a resultant identifiable sea-change in the levels of BAME coaches progressing through the previously blocked applications 'entry passage' pipeline to the interview selection stage of the recruitment process. This was felt by some interviewees to have helped neutralise some of the unconscious racial bias and related preference for homologous reproduction inherent within the interview selection criteria at club academies and which was reported to have impacted negatively in limiting opportunities for some (especially South Asian and Arab) BAME coaches to access interviews in the past. One BAME coach presently working at a category two status club academy articulates these themes further:

> I think something as little as a name that's foreign can be pushed aside. Whereas I think if they are progressing to an interview and you're giving that individual an opportunity to sit down and get to know the coach, and see them coach and see how good they are, you know, trying to overcome the obstacle of the name barrier, I think it's a good thing. (Interviewee, BAME coach)

A number of interviewees also felt this more strongly regulated process of being selected for (and then attending) interviews had enabled BAME coaches the 'interactional space' in which to showcase their qualifications portfolio and experiential achievements directly to key decision makers at club academies. These face to face opportunities to 'make the case' as to their vocational suitability for coaching positions was considered to be an essential factor in increasing the likelihood of securing employment at club academies thereafter. One BAME coach presently working at a category two status club academy comments further on this score:

> If the clubs are following the BAME guidelines then there is at least a chance there is an opportunity for one person as minimum to get in front of people and sell their strengths. (Interviewee, BAME coach)

Furthermore, opportunities to undertake interviews were felt by some interviewees to offer valuable learning experiences for BAME coaches in enabling the development of improved presentational skills over time. This was felt to be especially important for BAME coaches with little or no prior experience of being in interview situations in club academy settings. In this respect, the regulatory opportunities for interview embodied within the mandatory code were felt to have a potentially positive medium to longer term impact in providing interactional experiences through which BAME coaches can better develop the relevant 'interview nous' to secure coach employment over time. One highly qualified BAME coach recently appointed as a full-time coach at category one status club academy offers some personal reflections on this process below:

> I've had a couple of interviews now, and it's been a real learning experience. Invaluable really. Each academy wants something different, what they're looking for, their philosophy, and so on. But you learn from it and you get better at it. I mean, I wouldn't be at the academy where I'm at now, if I hadn't gone through those interviews. Because by the time I did that interview, all the creases were ironed out. I knew what they wanted. I knew how to sell myself. I was ready. (Interviewee, BAME coach)

### Appointments

Overall, survey and interview findings indicated that during the 2016–2017 season the mandatory code of coach recruitment had also engendered a strongly positive impact in enabling increased numbers of BAME coaches to become successfully appointed to coaching positions at professional club youth academies. For example, club academies reported that during this period BAME coaches accounted for around one-half (49%) of all new coaching appointments: inclusive of appointments for full-time (37%) and part-time (57%) coaching positions. These annual snap-shot figures compare favourably with and show a marked upturn when set against figures drawn from the same survey which indicated that BAME coaches accounted for 16.7% of the overall club academy coaching workforce: inclusive of full-time (11%) and part-time (21%) coaching positions. For a number of interviewees, this 'season-specific' upsurge in the numbers of BAME coaching appointments was felt to be underscored by the procedural adherence to and effectiveness of the mandatory code in ensuring interviews for suitably qualified BAME candidates, then enabling them with opportunities to promote their skill-sets and abilities to key decision makers at club academies. One BAME coach appointed as a phase lead coach at a category three status club academy during this period offers some personal reflections on this score:

> You could argue due to this rule at [club academy], I had the opportunity to sit down in front of the powers that be and from there I was able to make my case to say, 'this is why you need to hire me.' So you could argue that if the rule wasn't there and they didn't have to interview some-one from a BAME background, would I be the new foundation phase lead at the [club academy]. Probably not.' (Interviewee, BAME coach)

Furthermore, there was a general sense amongst interviewees that numerical success on this score was likely to have continued longevity if such findings were more widely publicised to aspiring coaches from BAME backgrounds. In particular, in acting as a potential catalyst for increasing the number of applications for coaching positions from BAME coaches, which, as alluded to earlier in this chapter, in the first year of the implementation of the code have remained relatively

108 *Steven Bradbury and Dominic Conricode*

low. One BAME former coach and organisational stakeholder comments below on the prospective potential of the code to increase the levels of representation of BAME coaches at club academies over time:

> *I think it will increase appointments by virtue of the numbers, because more BAME people will go for these roles. And the more people see there is a chance, the better it will be.* (Interviewee, BAME organisational stakeholder)

However, in contrast to these more positive assertions, a number of interviewees questioned the extent to which the mandatory code was being enacted in a meaningful and transparent – rather than rhetorical and tokenistic – way at all club academies. These more critical accounts were posited by BAME coaches who felt that despite being selected for and performing well in interview situations, they had still not been appointed to coaching positions at club academies. In some cases, interviewees reported that the coaching positions for which they had applied had been awarded instead to previously 'known' and 'preferred' white candidates drawn from within dominant localised insider networks and with strong social and cultural connections to senior staff at club academies. As a result, the interview processes in which they had been involved were considered to have been a 'façade' and a 'sham' and to have been undertaken by club academies to performatively satisfy the regulatory requirements of the mandatory code whilst simultaneously ignoring the central principles of inclusivity to which it aspires. One highly qualified and experienced BAME coach below reflects on some deeply negative personal experiences on this score:

> *I was invited for an interview as an academy manager at [the club]. I was pretty confident going into it because I had all the qualifications and lots of experience and I was working at a higher status academy at the time. The evening beforehand, a good friend of mine called me to tell me he'd just been offered the academy managers job at [same club]. A job I was supposed to be having an interview for the following day. It wasn't his fault. He didn't know. Now, he isn't as qualified as me. Nowhere near. But he knows the people there. So he got the job. I went to the interview anyway the following day and I just knew by the way it was conducted. I sat there thinking 'this is a farce, this job has already gone, I'm just here to fill a quota.'* (Interviewee, BAME Coach)

## Conclusions

This chapter has sought to identify and evaluate the procedural adherence to and effectiveness of the first year of the implementation of the EFL mandatory code of coach recruitment at professional football club youth academies, and to evaluate its initial impact in increasing the levels of representation of BAME coaches in club academy settings. In doing so, the findings presented in this chapter have focused on four inter-related elements of the code: advertising, applications, interviews, and appointments. Taken together, the findings have indicated that in the early stages of its implementation there has been a generally strong procedural adherence to the central regulatory principles embodied in the code at club academies. This is most notably the case in terms of the work of most club academies to formalise and broaden their advertising procedures and ensure that at least one suitably qualified BAME candidate is awarded an interview. Whilst these more equitable and inclusive processes of coach recruitment have not yet engendered a significant increase in applications for coaching positions amongst BAME coaches more broadly, there is strong statistical evidence to suggest they have had a positive correlative impact in enabling increased opportunities for BAME coaches to progress through the previously blocked applications to appointments pipeline at club academies. For example, during the period under review almost all (98%) BAME applicants were awarded an interview and three-fifths (58%) were appointed to coaching positions. These findings suggest that the implementation of and adherence to the mandatory code on the part of the majority of club academies has provided a policy-based platform on which to successfully begin the process of dismantling some of the key institutional barriers which have previously constrained the career progression of BAME coaches. Not least of all, in engendering a notable processual shift from networks to qualifications-based methods of coach recruitment and in enabling opportunities for BAME coaches to showcase their technical and experiential abilities and to consequently challenge unconscious racial bias and stereotyping.

On this latter score, it is important to note that survey and interview data indicated a stronger procedural adherence to and effectiveness of the implementation of the mandatory code at club academies where senior decision making staff exhibited a greater level of 'problem awareness' of – and more 'progressive' attitude towards addressing – the under-representation of BAME coaches in the academy game. This was especially at club academies situated in ethnically diverse locales and where senior academy staff had prior professional experience of working in other vocational settings such as education and sports development. At these club academies, senior staff were much more likely to recognise the importance and value of cultural diversity in the coaching workplace and to view BAME coaches as a potentially positive resource through which to attract and develop talented young players from a range of BAME and white backgrounds and for whom experiences of 'everyday multiculturalism' are the norm. It is argued here that it is at these 'more enlightened' club academies where the central principles embodied in the mandatory code are likely to become a normative – rather than exceptional – feature of the coach recruitment landscape and where the initial statistical advances in BAME representation are likely to have greater longevity over time. In contrast, survey and interview data also indicated some ideological and procedural resistance to the redistributive principles embodied in the mandatory code amongst senior staff at other club academies, reflective of a general view that positive action measures of this kind represented a form of 'racial favouritism' or 'reverse racism.' Such perspectives were informed by a set of uncritical ideas and beliefs that the pre-existing coach recruitment process was inherently 'meritocratic' and 'fair' and that issues of BAME coach under-representation had resulted from wider societal exclusions and/or the negatively conceptualised properties of BAME coaches, rather than as being shaped and maintained by the processes and practices of dominant individuals and organisations within professional football. It is argued here that it is at these 'less enlightened' club academies where the principles of equality and inclusivity embodied in the mandatory code remain deprioritised and where institutional forms of racial exclusion are likely to be effortlessly reproduced and the predominantly white landscape of the club academy coaching environment perpetuated over time.

In conclusion, it is argued here that any meaningful efforts to increase the racial diversity of the coaching workforce in professional football club youth academies need to remain cognisant of the symbiotic relationship between under-representation of BAME coaches, processes and practices of institutional racism, and the underlying and unremarked normative power of whiteness embedded within the senior organisational tiers of professional football (and in other sports). In this respect, the principles of the mandatory code of coach recruitment (and its policy informant the 'Rooney Rule') square firmly with the claims of Critical Race Theory that liberalism alone is not enough to address institutional forms of racism and that 'colour-blind' ideologies and the application of 'neutral-criteria' approaches to all forms of recruitment tend to sustain rather than redress patterns and experiences of racial disadvantage. From this perspective, the mandatory code can be understood as a distinctly interventionist and politically progressive positive action measure which actively seeks to ensure that a full consideration of equality of opportunities *and* outcomes become a central and prioritised feature of recruitment practices at club academies. However, it is argued here that for the initial procedural adherence to and effectiveness of the mandatory code to be maintained and expanded over time, greater efforts are needed on the part of the EFL to encourage a stronger and more consistent level of attitudinal and organisational 'buy-in' at club academies to the central principles of equality and inclusivity on which the code is premised. Such efforts should include the delivery of relevant cultural awareness training for senior staff at club academies with a focus on engendering an increased understanding of the social and economic value and beneficial impacts of cultural diversity in the coaching workplace. This pedagogical work should also be supported by the production of a standardised guidance document and checklist of good practice in relation to each of the inter-related stages of the procedural process of coach recruitment, with particular respect to advertising, applications, interviews, and appointments. Relatedly, much more should be done to ensure that the demographic make-up of selection and interview panels at club academies are more reflective of the ethnic and cultural diversity of the playing workforce of first team and academy football and of society more broadly. Taken together, it is argued here that these procedurally adaptive and culturally reflexive measures will help to ensure that issues of racial equality and diversity sit at the heart of – rather than as being peripheral to – the decision making process and will better inform the work of club academies to adopt a more inclusive operational approach to coach recruitment. This chapter simply concludes that the adoption of a more holistically considered and complementary procedural and attitudinal approach is likely to engender more meaningful and sustainable social change for the benefit of BAME coaches and club academies over time and to have significant transferability as a model of equitable recruitment practice across other football, sporting and societal contexts in the United Kingdom and beyond.

## References

Bradbury, S., Amara, M., Garcia, B., and Bairner, A. (2011). *Representation and structural discrimination in football in Europe: The case of minorities and women*. Loughborough: Loughborough University and the FARE Network.

Bradbury, S., Van Sterkenburg, J., and Mignon, P. (2014). *Cracking the glass ceiling? Levels of representation of 'visible' minorities and women in leadership and coaching in football in Europe and the experiences of elite level 'visible' minority coaches*. Loughborough University and the FARE Network.

Bradbury, S. (2016). 'The progression of Black and Minority Ethnic footballers into coaching in professional football: A case study analysis of the COACH bursary programme'. In: Allison, W., Abraham, A., and Cale, A., eds. *Advances in coach education and development: from research to practice*. London/New York: Routledge, 137–148.

Bradbury, S. (2017). *Evaluation of the FA coach inclusion and diversity programme: First annual review*. Loughborough: Loughborough University.

Bradbury, S. (2018). 'The under-representation and racialised experiences of minority coaches in high level coach education in professional football in England.' In: Hassan, D., and Action, C., eds. *Sport and contested identities*. London: Routledge, 11–29.

Bradbury, S., Van Sterkenburg, J., and Mignon, P. (2018). 'The under-representation and experiences of elite level minority coaches in professional football in England, France and the Netherlands.' *International Review of the Sociology of Sport*, 53 (3), 313–334.

Braddock, J., Smith, E., and Dawkins, M. (2012). 'Race and pathways to power in the National Football League.' *American Behavioural Scientist*, 56 (5), 711–727.

Branham, D. (2008). 'Taking advantage of an untapped pool: Assessing the success of African American head coaches in the National Football League.' *The Review of Black Political Economy*, 35 (4), 129–146.

Cashmore, E., and Clelland, J. (2011). 'Why aren't there more black managers.' *Ethnic and Racial Studies*, 34 (9), 1594–1607.

Collins, B.W. (2007). 'Tackling unconscious bias in hiring practices: The plight of the Rooney rule.' *New York University Law Review*, 82, 870–911.

Conricode, D., and Bradbury, S. (forthcoming 2020). 'Game changer or empty promise: An examination of the EFL mandatory code of coach recruitment.' In: Bradbury, S., Lusted, J., and Van Sterkenburg, J., eds. *Race, ethnicity and racisms in sports coaching*. London: Routledge.

Cunningham, G.B. (2010). 'Understanding the under-representation of African American coaches: A multilevel perspective.' *Sport Management Review*, 13 (4), 395–406.

Day, J.C. (2015). 'Transitions to the top: Race, segregation, and promotions to executive positions in the college football coaching profession.' *Work and Occupations*, 42 (4), 408–446.

Day, J.C., and McDonald, S. (2010). 'Not so fast, my friend: Social capital and the race disparity in promotions among college football coaches.' *Sociological Spectrum*, 30 (2), 138–158.

Duru, J.N. (2011). *Advancing the ball: Race, reformation and the quest for equal coaching opportunities in the NFL.* Oxford: Oxford University Press.

Government Equalities Office. (2010). *Equality act 2010.* London: Government Equalities Office.

Kilvington, D. (forthcoming 2020). 'British Asian football coaches: Exploring the barriers and advocating action.' In: Bradbury, S., Lusted, J., and Van Sterkenburg, J., eds. *Race, ethnicity and racisms in sports coaching.* London: Routledge.

Lapchick, R. (2016). *The 2016 racial and gender report card.* Institute of Diversity and Ethics. Orlando: University of Central Florida.

League Managers Association. (2017). *Black, Asian and Minority Ethnic (BAME) football Managers.* Burton upon TrentLeague Managers Association.

Norman, L., North, J., Hylton, K., Flintoff, A., and Rankin, A.J. (2014). *Sporting experiences and coaching aspirations among Black and Minority Ethnic (BME) groups.* Leeds: Sports Coach UK and Leeds Metropolitan University.

Rankin-Wright, A.J., Hylton, K., and Norman, L. (2016). 'Off-colour landscape: Framing race equality in sport coaching.' *Sociology of Sport Journal,* 33 (4), 357–368.

Rankin-Wright, A.J., Hylton, K., and Norman, L. (2017). 'The policy and provision landscape for racial and gender equality in sport coaching.' In: Long, J., Fletcher, T., and Watson, B., eds. *Sport, leisure and social justice.* London: Routledge, 194–208.

Sagas, M., and Cunningham, G.B. (2005). 'Racial differences in the career success of assistant football coaches: The role of discrimination, human capital, and social capital.' *Journal of Applied Social Psychology,* 35 (4), 773–797.

Singer, J., Harrison, K., and Buksten, S. (2010). 'A critical race analysis of the hiring process for head coaches in NCAA college football.' *Journal of Intercollegiate Sport,* 3 (2), 270–296.

Sports People's Think Tank. (2014). *Ethnic minorities and coaching in elite level football in England: A call to action.* Loughborough: Sports People's Think Tank, FARE Network and Loughborough University.

Sports People's Think Tank. (2015). *Levels of BAME coaches in professional football in England: 1st annual follow report.* Loughborough: Sports People's Think Tank, FARE Network and Loughborough University.

Sports People's Think Tank. (2016). *Levels of BAME coaches in professional football in England: 2nd annual follow report.* Loughborough: Sports People's Think Tank, FARE Network and Loughborough University.

Sports People's Think Tank. (2017). *Levels of BAME coaches in professional football in England: 3rd annual follow report.* Loughborough: Sports People's Think Tank, FARE Network and Loughborough University.

# 9 Coaching and teaching LGBT youth

*Gillian Teideman and Graham Spacey*

## Introduction

Current UK legislation and government policy foregrounds the need for equity and social justice in education yet applying these guidelines in practice is not without its challenges. Many young people from the lesbian, gay, bisexual, and transgender (LGBT) community experience ongoing verbal, emotional and physical bullying resulting in mental health problems such as anxiety, depression and self-harm, and damaging educational outcomes connected to disciplinary problems and truancy (McCabe and Rubinson, 2008; Dyson et al., 2003). Set within learning contexts that endorse cultural and institutional heteronormativity, transforming practice to support inclusivity, fostering a sense of belonging and protecting against harassment is vital. This chapter focuses its discussion on issues affecting LGBT youth and how educators can establish safe, supportive environments by addressing attitudes and perceptions in preparation for working with these students. The chapter provides contextual background that illustrates how LGBT people experience discrimination before drawing on a case study from the 'Football4Peace v Homophobia campaign' (F4PvH), that provides evidence-based guidance for practitioners on good practice in developing and implementing coaching and teaching strategies that utilise diversity as a pedagogic resource and promote LGBT advocacy.

LGBT is used as an umbrella term for people who self-identify as lesbian, gay, bisexual, transgender or as having any other minority sexual orientation or gender identity. Furthermore, the differences between cisgender and trans (individuals who self-identify as a man/woman but were assigned the opposite gender at birth) is an important distinction to be aware of, and in sport coaching or teaching invites certain questions about equality of access in an environment where a person's physical appearance does not necessarily represent their personal identity, as illustrated in the following quote:

> My experience of PE in school was fairly positive, I wasn't out as trans and was considered good at most sports. My PE teacher was brilliant and always offered me plenty of opportunities within sport and with gaining experience teaching PE. However, when I came out as trans at 17 these opportunities stopped. She stopped

114 *Gillian Teideman and Graham Spacey*

*interacting with me around the school and gave the opportunities to other class members. This was my first negative experience of being trans in PE, I put it down to her not understanding or educating herself on what it means to be transgender. Another negative experience I had in sport was in Taekwondo. In my first competition at 17 I had to compete as a girl, against girls which was uncomfortable for me. I won the competition and wanted to compete again but as a boy. Unfortunately, I was told that I couldn't because I had not started to medically transition and because I was now 18, I would be competing against grown men which they would not allow. I did ask if, because of my light weight, I could compete with the under 18 boys but that was also not allowed. I have not competed since. In my taekwondo classes I have been accepted for who I am and feel very comfortable when training, there is also another trans guy at my club which makes pairing up and sparring much easier.*

(BA (Hons) Physical Education Student,
University of Brighton)

As depicted in the quote above, despite significant advances in tackling issues of equity and inclusion in sport coaching and teaching environments, action that specifically addresses the needs and experiences of lesbian, gay, bisexual and transgender (LGBT) youth continues to lag behind. Discrimination against LGBT people has been common for decades and it has multiple impacts (Dragowski, McCabe and Rubinson, 2016). LGBT bullying remains a problem in schools and sports settings; accompanied by widespread assumptions that all students are heterosexual, and cisgender (personal sense of identity and gender corresponds to sex at birth) means the precise support required by LGBT students is often poorly understood and left unaddressed.

Gordon, Reid and Petocz (2010) suggest that educators occupy a philosophical space based on their 'conceptions of student diversity in the context of teaching and learning' (p. 956). These two dimensions are related and multi-dimensional; they characterise what student diversity *means* to an educator and how this influences their pedagogic choices. In its most limited form, students are viewed as homogenous and teaching is characterised by a 'one size fits all' approach. At the most aspirational level, both group and individual diversity is appreciated and utilised as a pedagogic resource.

Reflecting upon how diversity is conceptualised matters because it influences pedagogic decision-making. Teaching and learning occur within a context that has already been culturally defined. We make sense of the world through our engagement with it, and through our interactions find meaning and become meaningful (Heidegger, 2010). Past experiences determine the frames of reference used to regulate actions and behaviour in the present, our perception and expectations of others and how we approach the future. As practitioners working with LGBT students, teachers and coaches need to be aware that how they behave and make decisions determines a performer's experience of the world, and therefore how they make sense of who they are. Awareness of how 'my' being directly impacts upon 'their' being is fundamental to responding to the issues encountered by the LGBT community and in advocating for inclusivity from a position of knowledge and understanding.

This chapter considers how the culture of sporting environments situated in the broader context regarding equity and inclusion in adolescent educational settings can undermine the safety and development of LGBT participants. It begins by contextualising how LGBT people experience discrimination before exploring the behaviour of those inhabiting such environments. The chapter raises issues that can be addressed through appropriate LGBT advocacy, specifically the effect of language and the value of safe spaces. With reference to the F4PvH initiative embedded throughout the chapter, it demonstrates how teachers and coaches can utilise diversity as an essential pedagogical resource.

## Contextualising LGBT discrimination

The following section gives background to LGBT discrimination by drawing on evidence from surveys to illustrate the disconnection between what is expected by law and the prejudice encountered by many LGBT people. Bullying and the impact of discrimination on educational outcomes and mental health are highlighted as key issues associated with LGBT participation in sport. The evidence presented is then contextualised by considering heteronormative culture and role of the people that inhabit the sports coaching and teaching environment.

### Evidence of discrimination from LGBT Surveys

In July 2018 the UK government published findings from the National LGBT Survey (Government Equalities Office (GEO), 2018a), a large scale project aimed at identifying the contemporary challenges encountered by LGBT people in the United Kingdom and to gather evidence about their experiences following previous legislation designed to protect their rights. Despite legislation aimed at targeting discrimination in the United Kingdom including the Equality Act (2010), evidence presented in the survey suggests there is a disconnection between what is expected by law and the prejudice many LGBT people continue to experience on a daily basis. Policy documentation intended to recognise and remove barriers encountered by LGBT people in all aspects of life (DfE, 2017; GEO, 2011a; DCSF, 2009) and efforts to raise the profile of LGBT athletes through the Sports Charter (GEO, 2011b) seemed also to have had limited impact.

While it is fundamentally important that LGBT rights are legally protected, findings from the survey (GEO, 2018a) demonstrate that homophobia and transphobia remain an omnipresent cultural phenomenon. Respondents in the survey cited reticence at being open about their sexual orientation or gender expression, particularly with teaching staff, and were fearful of the unsanctioned disclosure of their LGBT identity. Statistics show that verbal and physical harassment including assault frequently occurred:

83% of the most serious incidents experienced by respondents in educational institutions had not been reported, primarily because respondents had considered them too minor, not serious enough or to 'happen all the time,' or because they had felt that nothing would happen or change as a result. (GEO, 2018a, p. 100)

The survey confirms the findings of Stonewall's[1] 'Schools Report' (2014) and 'Universities Report' (2018). These found that 45% of pupils (rising to 64% of trans pupils) in school are bullied specifically for being LGBT, whilst at university 36% of trans students and 7% of LGB students reported that they 'faced negative comments or conduct from university staff' (Stonewall, 2018, p. 3). A further 7% of trans students at universities reported that they were the victim of physical attacks by a fellow student or a member of staff. These are worrying statistics considering staff are the very people who are in place to protect them and confirms that discrimination is a problem that permeates all stages of education.

Securing inclusivity must involve consideration of how policy is enacted. Transforming the way LGBT youth experience sport begins by recognising practice that excludes; it demands a critique of personal bias and a willingness to question the social processes that underpin and define the ethos of an institution (DePalma and Jennett, 2010; Gordon et al., 2010; McCabe and Rubinson, 2008). Respondents in the National LGBT Survey (GEO, 2018a) reported feeling unsafe in a school setting and being unprepared for life beyond school age as an LGBT person, while in this case it referred to formal education, a coaching environment is likely to foster similar emotions. Education plays a vital role in promoting equality, both in terms of utilising effective pedagogy to support the learning of others, but also in developing professional practice which begins by understanding how actions at a micro and macro level are either complicit in sustaining or serve to challenge discrimination.

### Bullying and the LGBT community

In 2014, Stonewall reported that 86% of secondary school and 45% of primary school pupils had experienced some form of homophobic, biphobic or transphobic bullying regardless of sexual orientation and gender identity (Stonewall, 2014). Progress has been made but there remains consensus that LGBT bullying persists and more can be done to tackle continued lack of understanding and acceptance (GEO, 2018a). Conducted by an individual or group against others, a person becomes a victim of bullying when they are exposed to repeated verbal (e.g. name-calling, threats, taunting, malicious teasing), psychological (e.g. spreading rumours, engaging in social exclusion, extortion, intimidation) or physical aggression (e.g. hitting, kicking, spitting, pushing, taking personal belongings) (O'Higgins-Norman, Goldrick and Harrison, 2009; Nansel et al., 2001). Yet bullying is not a straightforward dichotomous relationship between victim and perpetrator; it permeates deep into the socio-cultural environment and concerns many players. The Gender Identity and Research Society (GIRES) (2008) suggest the targets of bullying are diverse. Victims may be:

- LGBT children and adolescents
- children of LGBT people
- LGBT teachers, coaches and other members of staff
- LGBT community members

The list extends to those who are perceived as being LGBT because their appearance or behaviour sits outside of the heteronormative binary that defines the environment (DePalma and Jennett, 2010). Perpetrators of bullying include those who directly intend to cause harm, threaten or humiliate others. It may include the principle ringleader and agitators or those who can be held indirectly complicit, from the authority figure to the bystander who through ignorance or fear fails to act. All who witness bullying are affected by it, which explains why the response to bullying is of crucial importance.

### Educational outcomes and mental health

There is compelling evidence that connects homophobic, biphobic and transphobic bullying with long-term social, emotional and psychological damage (Stonewall Education Equality Index, 2016; Office for National Statistics, 2017). Schools provide the context where LGBT youth report experiencing persistent, targeted abuse that frequently goes unnoticed or is met with an ambivalent response from staff and school leaders (GEO, 2018a; DePalma and Jennett, 2010). Nervousness around peers and feeling unsafe may initiate self-isolating behaviour; issues with punctuality degenerates to truancy and possible school 'drop-out' which severely damages educational outcomes and prospects post formal education (Aragon et al., 2014).

The impact on well-being can be severe resulting in escalating mental health issues. Over the past decade the proportion of children and young people suffering with mental health problems has increased. The Nuffield Trust (2018) found 1 in 20 young people in England report having a mental health condition, and the Youngminds charity (2019) has declared a 'crisis' where three children in every classroom have a diagnosable mental health disorder. Evidence suggests that LGBT youth are more likely to experience problems such as loss of confidence, loss of self-esteem, anxiety, depression and suicidal thoughts than non-LGBT peers (Mental Health Foundation, 2016). Without appropriate support, coping mechanisms such as self-harm, alcohol and substance misuse exacerbate the problems encountered. In 2017 Childline provided over 13,700 counselling sessions about anxiety and 22,400 related to suicidal thoughts, an increase of 17% and 15%, respectively, on the previous year (NSPCC, 2017). The authors do not deny that heterosexual youth encounter similar issues and the Childline statistics are not exclusively LGBT, but the risks are intensified through the additional stressors associated with acknowledging their sexual orientation, fractured

118    *Gillian Teideman and Graham Spacey*

identity development and fear of perceived or genuine rejection (O'Higgins-Norman et al., 2009; Athanases and Comar, 2008; McCabe and Rubinson, 2008).

There is expanding research that connects physical activity and sports participation with improved mental health and well-being (Biddle, 2016; Clow and Edmunds, 2014). A range of psychological benefits has been reported including enhanced mood, improved self-esteem and a decline in depression. Although further research is required, a recent study by Dore et al. (2018) indicates that the social context of team sports and group physical activity holds greater benefit to improved mental health outcomes than individual physical activity. It would seem appropriate that increasing opportunities for social sports participation would promote interaction and counter the isolation felt by many LGBT youth; indeed, such interventions may be considered a moral responsibility but would only be desirable if the socio-cultural and environmental conditions support an inclusive ethos. The F4PvH case study examples used in this chapter illustrate how such an environment can be facilitated.

### Heteronormative culture

When considering how gender and sexuality are viewed in society, it is predominantly from a perspective that promotes heterosexuality as the governing orientation. Heteronormativity is the belief that people occupy a gender binary (male / female, boys / girls) and the assumption that the world [we] inhabit should be grounded in, and reproduce this model (Price and Taylor, 2015). Heteronormative narratives shape how young people experience childhood and adolescence; 'traditional' conceptions of masculinity (bravery, coolness, sportiness, machismo) and femininity (physically attractive and ornamented, sexualised but controlled) are often openly encouraged (Athanases and Comar, 2008; Martino and Pallotta-Chiarolli, 2005) and also subliminally permeate everyday lives through language, images and symbols.

As teachers and coaches, it is important to question and challenge heteronormative practice. Heterosexuality is not called into dispute; rather the ideas that privilege conformity and, by implication, position LGBT people as different and 'outside' of the orthodox community. Ordinarily people are assumed to be heterosexual unless they declare otherwise; which in itself is a heteronormative presupposition where people on the 'inside' know others will make correct inferences about their lifestyle. LGBT people are faced with the decision whether to let people know about their identity, sexual orientation and relationships. The anxiety associated with 'coming out' at worst elicits fears associated with becoming a victim of homophobia, biphobia or transphobia, and even well-meaning individuals can cause discomfort. It is not uncommon for LGBT people to become the subject of gossip, speculation and unsolicited interest, fielding questions such as 'what made you gay,' or 'are you a boy or a girl?.'

Finding a sense of belonging when being treated differently and regarded as strange, even abnormal, is challenging. Belonging acknowledges individuals' subjective feelings of acceptance and inclusion by others within a social environment

Coaching and teaching LGBT youth 119

(Kahu, 2014; Thomas, 2012). Drawing on Lave and Wenger's (1991) theory of 'Situated Learning,' it is possible to view learning as a socially mediated process that takes place within a framework of participation. Sense is made through interaction and learning in a sporting context and is fundamentally anchored in a social world. Relationships between people, events and the environment serve to influence how the participants feel about their 'self' and therefore engage with opportunities.

Self can be understood as the associated affective beliefs held by an individual that come into view by means of experience, and through which people make meaning of [their] world. If the organisational structures in schools and sporting environments support heterosexuality LGBT people are implicitly labelled as deviant. Young people will process experiences in the context of the essence of 'who they are' (Baxter Magolda, 2003) so by default become equally aware of 'who they are not.' Yet self does not exist in isolation; self comes into being through a world of relationships, and as a point of reference, is partly defined by context and through comparison to others (Baumeister, 2011; Heidegger, 2010). DePalma and Jennett (2010, p. 16) argue that 'gender and sexuality are purposefully enacted rather than passively experienced.' From this perspective as adolescents grapple with figuring out who they are, they may find it easier to comply with heteronormative assumptions thereby reinforcing inequalities and legitimising discrimination, rather than risk alienation by not fitting in. For young LGBT people this can result in fractured identities and poor health outcomes. Therefore, the pursuit of inclusive practice needs to challenge heteronormativity at source by publicly and proactively supporting those who are not heterosexual or gender conforming. Achieving this requires willingness to understand and act upon key issues experienced by LGBT people.

### The role of teachers, coaches and peers

Occupying the role of teacher or coach brings professional responsibilities associated with protecting and safeguarding the welfare of all young and vulnerable people. It demands accountability for the quality of provision; this necessitates reflection on not simply *what* students learn but *how* they learn and are taught. Being a role model may prove challenging when encountering situations that fall outside of personal frames of reference, or in some instances conflict with personal belief systems, but lack of understanding is not an excuse for discrimination. It is perhaps unsurprising that peers have been cited as being responsible for carrying out 88% of bullying incidents, but the National LGBT Survey (GEO, 2018a) also reports 9% of perpetrators being teachers or non-teaching staff. LGBT students describe being excluded from activities and events, involuntary outing, and experiencing shaming, physical harassment and even violence from staff. Racism and sexism would be openly challenged so why not homophobia, biphobia and transphobia?

Reluctance to engage in meaningful discourse seems to be a fundamental barrier to resolving issues encountered, yet inaction remains due to the fears associated with the consequences of initiating dialogue. From a student perspective, under half of respondents in the National LGBT Survey (GEO, 2018a) felt able to be open with staff, with 68% citing a lack of understanding of the issues faced. If seeking help is met with ignorance or alienation, remaining in invisible silence is perhaps a more appealing option. Reasons given by staff in defence of their hesitancy in addressing LGBT equality centre around lack of knowledge, training and resources, yet a quick search of the internet reveals numerous training programmes for professionals delivered by reputable providers (www.theproudtrust.org; www.stonewall.org.uk). The problem seems to rest with deeper concerns, most notably fear of repercussions from being associated with LGBT advocacy, regardless of the member of staff's own sexual orientation or gender identity (Athanases and Comar, 2008). LGBT staff often retain concerns that prevent role-modelling; fears about job security, respect and safety driven by personal experiences of homophobia, biphobia and transphobia that impede confidence in disclosing their own sexual identity and the ability to provide support and advocate for LGBT youth (McCabe and Rubinson, 2008; Sykes, 2004; Butler et al., 2003). The 75-point LGBT Action Plan (GEO, 2018b), which is part of the National LGBT Survey (GEO, 2018a), commits the UK government to addressing these barriers but progress will only be made if all stakeholders are willing to challenge discrimination and take corrective action.

Paradoxically, although peers are the main perpetrators of discrimination, they can also perform an important role in acting as allies for young LGBT people (Poteat, 2015). More research is needed to understand the personal dispositions and social conditions that prompt heterosexual peers to behave in an LGBT affirmative manner, but adolescence represents a critical point where individuals display willingness to vocalise and demonstrate support and it would seem prudent to actively nurture the proclivity of youth to act as allies. Acceptance (and tolerance) for young LGBT people will only be achieved if their existence is normalised. Simply speaking about LGBT people and the issues they encounter in terms of 'hypothetical' reasoning camouflages and marginalises the realities of a very real sector of society. A cultural shift is required to ensure LGBT pupils are able to access the full range of educational opportunities and experience learning from an equitable and inclusive position. Becoming an advocate for LGBT inclusivity requires the development of learning situations that foreground the intersection of pedagogy with interpersonal relationships (Gordon et al., 2010). The F4PvH project described in the following section provides an example of a constructed learning situation through which strategies for LGBT advocacy can be applied.

## LGBT advocacy

The following section considers key aspects of practice that should be addressed when targeting homophobic, biphobic and transphobic behaviour. Background to the purpose and development of the F4PvH project highlights action undertaken at the University of Brighton[2] (UoB) in its training of PE teachers and

Coaching and teaching LGBT youth   121

coaches which constitutes a case study of work that has been used to raise awareness of LGBT issues within sport and learning environments. Embedded in both the F4P methodology and UoB practices are examples of performative pedagogy that can make sporting and learning environments more hospitable and inclusive places for all participants, not solely LGBT people. The practices adopted can be clustered around two key elements of advocacy; the creation of *safe spaces* and adoption of more inclusive *language*, both of which are at the heart of the Football 4 Peace International's F4PvH campaign.

### Football 4 Peace International and F4P v Homophobia

The F4PvH programme by Football 4 Peace International (F4P) has its roots in the Justin Campaign, the forerunner of the Football v Homophobia project now led by Pride Sports (www.pridesports.org.uk). F4P is a multi-dimensional research, education and community engagement platform that employs sport and physical activity to deliver values-based training and coaching interventions for those living in areas with 'high levels of cross-community conflict and various forms of political disorder and social disintegration' (www.footbal4peace.eu). The work started in divided communities in Israel and has since been adopted in various other locations across the world. It has also been adapted for the training of Physical Education teachers and sport coaches at the University of Brighton enabling the use of the F4P values-based methodology within their teaching and coaching in schools and clubs across the country. The following quote illustrates how one student participant in the programme translates the global objectives of F4P for use in an applied local setting. The language demonstrates an appreciation of the importance of inclusion and awareness of diversity that informs pedagogic decision-making:

> *The values that we have in Football 4 Peace are not just used in places in conflict like Israel, they are designed to be used by coaches in other situations ... we can use values to teach understanding. Like in a school situation – we can use the [F4P] values to teach understanding and getting everyone involved ... equity and inclusion is really the main one for the campaign. It doesn't matter if you are gay, straight, or anything else – we can bring people together using the values and football as a universal method to understand that people have the right to play together and respect each other and take responsibility for each other.*
>
> (BA (Hons) Physical Education with Qualified
> Teacher Status student, University of Brighton)

F4P v Homophobia began in 2012 when two UoB staff set about exploring how the F4P values and methodology could be used in relation to social justice issues, specifically LGBT representation in sport (Caudwell and Spacey, 2018). The National Union of Students, along with the University of East London had recently published research entitled 'Out in Sport' (2012) which highlighted the issues encountered by LGBT students in relation to their experiences within sport at university. The report found that discriminatory language (often referred to as banter) within university sports teams created a participatory barrier to those not openly 'out.' Findings showed that 20.5% felt 'worried it [being LGBT] might result in verbal or physical abuse,' whilst 12.9% were 'concerned they might be ostracised within the team, not get picked or ejected' (NUS, 2012, p. 18).

When asked 'why don't you currently participate in university sport?' the top two responses had nothing to with sexuality or gender focusing instead on a lack of interest and time constraints. The next two responses, however, were more revealing as the answers implied heteronormativity. Respondents found 'the culture around the sport alienating or unwelcoming' (2012, p. 20) and cited past, negative experiences at school as a reason for choosing to not participate. Despite these concerns 58.2% of LGBT students said they did not feel that coming out was relevant and that the vast majority of those that had come out were having positive experiences.

The report clearly highlighted a need to act upon the views held by a significant proportion of the respondents. Change was required to alleviate fears preventing LGBT participation in sport signalling a need for advocacy, role models, the creation of safe spaces and the eradication of negative language within sport settings.

With connections to the Justin Campaign, Caudwell and Spacey (2018) used the F4P project festival as a template for F4PvH festivals which have been held regularly at the University of Brighton, Bournemouth University and in various adapted versions at sixth form colleges in the south east of England. F4PvH is centred on festivals of football where mixed teams come together to play against other mixed teams, and 'Fair Play' points are accumulated in order to become champions. Alongside the festivals are public lectures, symposiums and art installations, sometimes linked to a wider event such as LGBT History Month, where the festival becomes one of a series of events. The transcending aim of the festival is to create a safe space and to advocate for positive and non-discriminatory language with a determination for these to become the norm within university sport and beyond.

## Safe spaces

*Safe space* cannot be defined in terms of geographical or a physical location, instead it refers to a psychological concept where learning is both situated and relational (Heidegger, 2010; Wenger, 1998). Individuals are indelibly located within the world which they inhabit; they are part of their own reality therefore efforts to promote LGBT inclusivity must foster a climate where participants experience individual affirmation free from heteronormative behaviours that can dominate sporting environments. Additionally, *space* is an expression of proximity where what matters most is brought close to an individual, whilst matters of least concern appear more distant (Heidegger, 2010; Moran, 2000). The safe space metaphor 'does not offer a concrete educational method, but rather a way of thinking about education' (Spaaij and Schulenkorf, 2014, p. 634). As the teacher or coach, it is imperative that our own proximal concerns do not obscure the needs of others and that opportunities for positive and appropriate experiential learning occurs.

Spaaij and Schulenkorf (2014) separate the notion of *safe space* into interconnected physical, affective and socio-cultural dimensions, useful when considering how to develop inclusive practice and strategies that advocate for LGBT. The physical dimension refers to the environment and resources; for example, access to appropriate changing facilities and clearly defined rules for participation. The University of Brighton have fostered toilets 'for everyone' across all its campuses to make ensure that all genders feel comfortable in any facility. Posters and presentations increase the visibility of LGBT athletes and issues and are often used to construct a welcoming environment giving an impression of inclusivity. F4PvH takes over sporting spaces during the build up to the festival and symposium, with posters and LGBT inspired art installations that disturb the status quo (Caudwell and Spacey, 2018). Music inspired by gay anthems and culture is played during the festival and the football pitch is decorated in rainbow flags and pink balls, and black and pink bibs baring Justin Fashanu's face are used. Teams wear fancy dress to create a 'carnival' atmosphere akin to Pride.

These adaptions to the environment can quickly become meaningless if the prevailing culture within the walls that display these images ignores or fails to respond to discrimination. It is important, therefore, to design curricula and select pedagogic methods that remove barriers to participation, for example, structuring group activities to purposefully counter the heteronormative gender bias found in traditional sports. Learning modules for those on sport and physical education courses at the University of Brighton have always incorporated issues surrounding gender and sexuality. Starting in 2019, the annual F4P v Homophobia Festival has been aligned to a module focusing on sport and activism, social justice, development and peace where students have been tasked to plan, prepare and deliver the festival to their peers. A similar approach can be adopted when planning curriculum in different sports teaching and coaching contexts.

The affective dimension of safe space refers to the emotional and psychological atmosphere. Participants need to feel able to engage with the activity, and it is important to nurture interest, curiosity and a willingness to take risks without fear of ridicule (Subramanian, 2010). Opportunities to meet proximal goals aligned to the shared aims of the group help with the development of self-efficacy (Bandura, 1995). Self-efficacy refers to an individual's confidence in their capacity to meet performance objectives, essentially adopting a 'can do' attitude when facing a challenge. Here, inclusive pedagogy demands personalisation and differentiation whereas use of any exclusionary methods, specifically those defined by gender, automatically alienates and reinforces heteronormativity. F4P utilises the affective domain through the application of its values ethos. Trust, Respect, Responsibility, Equity and Inclusion are the focus of the F4P 'fair play values' and are highlighted to participants and spectators during the F4P v Homophobia Festival. Positive associated behaviours are aligned to each value which gives rise to an expectation of how to act and interact. The values-based methodology has been adopted by some staff that work at the University of Brighton as content within modules associated with social justice, coaching pedagogy and teacher training and it influences the way they approach their own content delivery. For example, when engaging in games that teach values, like ice-breaker 'trust games,' the lecturer is sensitive to teachable moments, at key points pausing the activity to reflect upon and discuss associated issues of co-operation and communication among the participants.

Within the festival teams are made up of 'mixed squads' of up to eight playing five- or six-a-side. This encourages substitutions and allows more people to participate (inclusion), the squad can define the term 'mixed' without the need to justify the make-up of their team (equity). Individuals who register on the day are placed into a team who often have a spare fancy dress outfit for them. The games are self-refereed with teams providing, and justifying, a fair play score to their opponents based upon the values and their associated behaviours (both negative and positive) manifested in the game.

Relationships of trust are essential in fostering the affective dimension, as when all students trust their teachers / coaches, they are more likely to report any negative incidents and therefore break the spiral of damaging behaviour. The University of Brighton staff have the option to wear rainbow lanyards and / or pin buttons that state their nouns (e.g. him, hers, theirs) as a signal to others that they are open, allied and approachable with regards to LGBT issues. University staff play in teams and are joined by members of the public including individuals from the LGBT community and at times community representatives from the Police, Fire and Ambulance services. Students then get to mix with a wide variety of people playing in the tournament. Often, these invited individuals share their knowledge and experiences with students prior to the event in a symposium or public lecture allowing a safe space for students to interact with a variety of individuals and create positive sporting role models.

The adoption of the F4P values-based methodology is also closely linked to the socio-cultural meaning of safe space which refers to individuals finding a sense of belonging regardless of any perceived roles or hierarchy within the participating community. Often practitioners refer to 'a level playing field' as a metaphor where participants are not advantaged by inequities in prior experience or skill. This can also be applied to how we think about identity and work towards establishing mutual respect and appreciation of diversity. Pedagogy that promotes co-operation, and teamwork through problem-solving and shared goals contributes to a sense of collaboration and collegiality, where all members of the community hold value. Manipulating the learning experience to provide entry points [teachable moments] stimulates opportunities for discussion where differences and misunderstandings can be explored. For example, the process of forming equitable teams may initially be undirected allowing players to align themselves with others based on friendship groups or who [they believe] will be most effective in scoring more goals. As children are introduced to a variety of conditioned small-sided games the players are given the opportunity to review team selection based on fair play and the core F4P values. Bias and prejudice are

Coaching and teaching LGBT youth    125

brought into the open and through creative dialogue the prevailing culture can be challenged [and changed]. The players begin to develop an appreciation of one's own individuality and the value of others in a context of social diversity. It is the task of the practitioner to role model and manage these difficult conversations, rather than avoid them.

During the festival, students are encouraged by other students to make statements on camera about LGBT issues within sport. They are encouraged to have their photographs taken alongside LGBT signs, symbols and guest speakers and post and comment on social media. By spreading the message wider and to their peers not in attendance, students are being taught about peaceful activism and how their voice can make a difference.

These statements also allow students to ask questions, to form an opinion, to voice their opinions, and to challenge the opinions of others in a safe and constructive manner. Acknowledging the diverse experiences of individuals helps to create open and fair dialogue. It is reasonable to have disagreements if these are utilised for examining alternative perspectives. For example, tensions may arise where individuals hold strong opposing views for religious or cultural reasons. Students need to view each other as partners, not competitors in the learning experience. In the pursuit of advocacy, balancing inclusion with the potential exclusion of a different sub-group is challenging and demands awareness on behalf of the practitioner. Effectively, the panacea can become the poison if actions intended to address LGBT discrimination inadvertently cause harm to others. The following section addresses the complexity of language and helps to illustrate the importance of planning that demonstrates care and sensitivity for all.

## Language

Language is widely accepted as a significant influence on the social-cultural dimension of creating a safe space. It is also still regarded as a potential barrier to LGBT inclusion within sport. Research suggests that name-calling and the use of hostile remarks and homophobic slurs remains prevalent in educational settings (Athanases and Comar, 2008; GEO, 2018a). Understanding the reasons why such language is used is the foundation upon which interventions that confront deleterious speech can be built.

Words are purposefully selected and used intentionally and they are the medium through which education and sporting cultures either protect or undermine the safety and development of LGBT students. Through language youth mimic societal discourses. Words preserve group membership by marking others as undesirable, serve to establish control, furnish a sense of superiority, regulate behaviour and can be used to protect heterosexual identity (Martino & Pallotta-Chiarolli, 2005; Pascoe 2005; Franklin, 2000).

McCormack (2012, p. 109) stated that 'understanding of the issue is all too frequently based on a simplistic conceptualisation of language that is (or is not) homophobic' and argued that this can lead to an over exaggeration of the prevalence of homophobic language. In his research McCormack (2012, pp. 115–117) found that seemingly homophobic taunts were a form of social bonding between English secondary school aged boys and often used within friendship groups in a welcoming manner regardless of sexuality, and was used to bond the students together lessening any negative meaning associated the words used. Likewise, Anderson's study of homophobic language in sport settings (2011) showed that openly gay athletes found no negative social effect of banter and gay slurs, they were not indicative of homophobia and held very different meanings. In this context, not being on the receiving end of banter is perceived as exclusionary, harmful and serves to highlight the complexity of discrimination.

Unlike other forms of discriminatory abuse, language is often dismissed as 'banter' or the result of joking relationships where the notion of intent is far more complex than homophobic language. This often results in it deemed too insignificant for an objection to be raised. For example, the term 'gay' is frequently used to signify incompetence or another negative characteristic; an unwarranted association that can be psychologically damaging and if left unchecked legitimises and obscures the underlying derision held within such insults. Whilst McCormack argues that teenage boys have changed the meaning of the word 'gay' within their friendship circles, including those with 'out' individuals, evidence from surveys (GEO, 2018a, Stonewall, 2017) show that this type of language creates a perception that the sporting arena is homophobic and unwelcoming. It is important to acknowledge that the intention of words can vary and can be used to provoke as well as to joke. This nuance is what educators have to navigate whilst also teaching their subjects the power of language. When words are challenged, often it is the speaker who is held accountable, but it is equally important to question the origin of language; to not simply address the issue as an isolated event but to critically reflect on how the impact of language augments cultural inequities.

Athanases and Comar (2008) identify a continuum illustrating the range of meaning associated with the way LGBT slurs are used by young people (Figure 9.1) but this can also be applied to perceptions held by an adult population.

'Innocuous banter' represents a single performance where discriminatory language is dismissed as a 'joke' or trivial habit. For example, it can be argued that the phrase 'that's so gay' has become meaningless through routine use, often without any intentional link to LGBT. Where homophobic name-calling is perceived as a 'slur against LGBTs present,' language becomes performative in its nature, tied to larger socio-cultural discourses that perpetuate heteronormative behaviour (Athanases and Comar, 2008; Rasmussen and Harwood, 2003). For example, 'that's so gay' is intentionally used to hurt and discriminate.

*Figure 9.1* Students' perceptions of homophobic name-calling among peers, adapted from Athanases and Comar (2008, p. 20).

The movement from performance to performativity (when language has an effect on social action and leads to change) may be subtle in nature and demonstrates the significance of linguistic advocacy. Helping young people understand the meaning and power behind words can be achieved through 'teachable moments,' providing opportunity for discussion and reflection that foreground language and avoids judging the person. The power of performative cultural reproduction perhaps explains why people join in or ignore offensive language, but to do so is indefensible. Teachers and coaches are role models with a responsibility to foster a safer environment for LGBT students. Prohibiting homophobic, biphobic and transphobic speech seems appropriate, but censure is problematic without encouraging debate where young people can understand the harmful impact of language. Engineering discussions where students can learn about performativity may seem daunting, and for practitioners who feel nervous about initiating such dialogue, embedding LGBT issues within a wider exploration of social justice can provide a framework for the development of critical thinking, reflection, and collaborative skills that foster understanding of discrimination at micro and macro levels. However, successful conversations only happen in an environment where participant voices, ideas, and opinions are valued and respected by all present.

## Conclusion

Throughout this chapter, F4PvH has been drawn upon as a case study to illustrate approaches that can be used to tackle discrimination and promote LGBT advocacy. The significance of *safe space* is undeniable in fostering a sense of belonging and the strategies employed for cultivating the physical, affective and socio-cultural dimensions of safe space can be adapted and applied in locally specific sport teaching and coaching settings. Encouraging interaction with others is fundamental in developing a shared understanding of the issues encountered by the LGBT community and *language* is a critical factor in transforming social relationships. The authors recognise that different contexts hold specific challenges and change requires insight and careful planning. Change may not be instant and addressing the issues raised in this chapter may prove both a contentious and satisfying endeavour for the practitioner, but ultimately it will be worthwhile if the outcome leads to inclusive and equitable sports opportunities for all.

## Notes

1 Stonewall (officially Stonewall Equality Limited) is a LGBT rights charity in the United Kingdom who work to empower individuals, transform institutions and communities, and to change/protect laws to create inclusive and accepting cultures.
2 The School of Sport and Service Management at the University of Brighton houses the BA in Physical Education with Qualified Teacher Status, Undergraduate Physical Education and Sports Coaching degrees, PGCE Physical Education and PGCE Dance initial teacher education (ITE) courses.

## References

Anderson, E. (2011). 'Updating the outcome: Gay athletes, straight teams, and coming out in the educationally based sports teams.' *Gender and Society*, 25 (2), 250–268.

Aragon, S.R., Poteat, P.V., Espelage, D.L., and Koenig, B.W. (2014). 'The influence of peer victimization on educational outcomes for LGBTQ and non-LGBTQ high school students.' *Journal of LGBT Youth*, 11 (1), 1–19.

Athanases, S.Z., and Comar, T.A. (2008). 'The performance of homophobia in early adolescents' everyday speech.' *Journal of LGBT Youth*, 5 (2), 9–32.

Bandura, A. (1995) *Self-efficacy in changing societies*. Cambridge: Cambridge University Press.

Baumeister, R.F. (2011). 'Self and identity: A brief overview of what they are, what they do, and how they work.' *Annals of the New York Academy of Sciences*, Issue, *Perspectives on the Self*, 3, 48–55.

Baxter Magolda, M.B. (2003). 'Identity and learning: Student affairs' role in transforming higher education.' *Journal of College Student Development*, 44 (1), 231–247.

Biddle, S. (2016). 'Physical activity and mental health: Evidence is growing.' *World Psychiatry*, 15 (2), 176–177.

Butler, A.H., Alpaslan, A.H., Strumpher, J., and Astbury, G. (2003). 'Gay and lesbian youth experiences of homophobia in South African secondary education.' *Journal of Gay and Lesbian Issues in Education*, 1 (2), 3–28.

Caudwell, J., and Spacey, G. (2018). 'Football 4 peace versus (v) homophobia: A critical exploration of the links between theory, practice and intervention'. In: Pringle, R., Larsson, H., and Gerdin, G., eds. *Critical research in sport, health and physical education: How to make a difference*. 106-121 Abingdon: Routledge.

Clow, A., and Edmunds, S. (2014). *Physical activity and mental health*. Champaign, IL: Human Kinetics.

DePalma, R., and Jennett, M. (2010). 'Homophobia, transphobia and culture: Deconstructing heteronormativity in English primary schools.' *Intercultural Education*, 21 (1), 15–26.

Department for Children, Schools and Families. (2009). 'Guidance for schools on preventing and responding to sexist, sexual and transphobic bullying.' Available at: http://publications.dcsf.gov.uk [accessed 29 October 2018].

Department for Education. (2017). *Preventing and tackling bullying: Advice for headteachers, staff and governing bodies*. London: DfE, Gov.UK.

Doré, I., O'Loughlin, J.L., Schnitzer, M.E., Datta, G.D., and Fournier, L. (2018). 'The longitudinal association between the context of physical activity and mental health in early adulthood.' *Mental Health and Physical Activity*, 14, 121–130.

Dragowski, E., McCabe, P., and Rubinson, F. (2016). 'Educators' reports on incidence of harassment and advocacy toward LGBTQ students.' *Psychology in the Schools*, 53 (2), 127–142.

Dyson, S., Mitchell, A., Smith, A., Dowsett, G., Pitts, M., and Hillier, L. (2003). 'Don't ask, don't tell. Hidden in the crowd: The need for documenting links between sexuality and suicidal behaviours among young people.' *Monograph Series*, Number 45. London: Mental Health Foundation.

Equality Act 2010. Available at: http://www.legislation.gov.uk [accessed 29 October 2018].

Franklin, K. (2000). 'Antigay behaviours by young adults: Prevalence, patterns and motivators in a noncriminal population.' *Journal of Interpersonal Violence*, 15 (4), 339–362.

Gender Identity and Research Education Society. (2008). 'Transphobic bullying: Could you deal with it in your school?' Available at: www.gires.org.uk/assets/Schools/TransphobicBullying.pdf [accessed 29 October 2018].

Gordon, S., Reid, A., and Petocz, P. (2010). 'Educators' conceptions of student diversity in their classes.' *Studies in Higher Education*, 35 (8), 961–974.

Government Equalities Office. (2011a). *Working for lesbian, gay, bisexual and transgender equality: Moving forward*. Available at: www.gov.uk/government/publications [accessed 29 October 2018].

Government Equalities Office. (2011b). *Tackling homophobia and transphobia in sport: The charter for action*. Available at: www.gov.uk/government/publications [accessed 29 October 2018].

Government Equalities Office. (2018a). *National LGBT Survey*: Research Report, Available at: www.gov.uk/government/consultations/national-lgbt-survey [accessed 29 October 2018].

Government Equalities Office. (2018b). *LGBT action plan: Improving the lives of lesbian, gay, bisexual and transgender people*. Available at: www.gov.uk/government/publications [accessed 29 October 2018].

Heidegger, M. (2010). *Being and time* (translated by Stambaugh, J.). Albany: State University of New York Press. (originally 1927 and published 1953 by Max Niemeyer Verlag).

Kahu, E. (2014). 'Increasing the emotional engagement of first year mature-aged distance students: Interest and belonging.' *The International Journal of the First Year in Higher Education*, 5 (2), 45–55. Available: 10.5204/intjfyhe.v5i2.231 [accessed 29 October 2018].

Lave, J., and Wenger, E. (1991). *Situated learning: Legitimate peripheral participation*. New York: Cambridge University Press.

Martino, W., and Pallotta-Chiarolli, M. (2005). *Being normal is the only way to be: Adolescent perspectives on gender and school*. Sydney: University of New South Wales Press.

McCabe, P.C., and Rubinson, F. (2008). 'Committing to social justice: The behavioural intention of school psychology and education trainees to advocate for lesbian, gay, bisexual, and transgendered youth.' *School Psychology Review*, 37 (4), 469–486.

McCormack, M. (2012). *The declining significance of homophobia: How teenage boys are redefining masculinity and heterosexuality*. New York: Oxford University Press.

Mental Health Foundation. (2016). *Fundamental facts about mental health 2016*. London: Mental Health Foundation.

Moran, D. (2000). *Introduction to phenomenology*. London: Routledge.

Nansel, T., Overpeck, M., Pilla, R., Ruan, W., Simons-Morton, B., and Scheidt, P. (2001). 'Bullying behaviours among US youth: Prevalence and association with psychosocial adjustment.' *Journal of the American Medical Association*, 285 (16), 2094–2100.

National Union of Students (NUS). (2012). *Out in sport: LGBT student's experiences of sport*. London: University of East London.

NSPCC. (2017). *Childline annual review 2016/17: Not alone anymore: What children and young people are talking to Childline about, London: England*. NSPCC Knowledge and Information Services.

Nuffieldtrust. (2018). 'Striking increase in mental health conditions in children and young people.' Available at: www.nuffieldtrust.org.uk/news-item/striking-increase-in-mental-health-conditions-in-children-and-young-people [accessed 25 April 2019].

O'Higgins-Norman, J., Goldrick, M., and Harrison, K. (2009). 'Pedagogy for diversity: Mediating between tradition and equality in schools.' *International Journal of Children's Spirituality*, 14 (4), 323–337.

Office for National Statistics. (2017). *Personal well-being and sexual identity in the UCK 2013–2015*. London: Gov.UK.

Pascoe, C.J. (2005). 'Dude, you're a fag.' *Adolescent Masculinity and the Fag Discourse, Sexualities*, 8 (3), 329–346.

Poteat, P.V. (2015). 'Individual psychological factors and complex interpersonal conditions that predict LGBT-affirming behaviour.' *Journal of Youth and Adolescence*, 44 (8), 1494–1507.

Price, L. and Taylor, J. (2015) 'Heteronormativity in the Lives of Lesbian, Gay, Bisexual, and Queer Young People', *Journal of Homosexuality*, 3, 98–109.

Rasmussen, M.L., and Harwood, V. (2003). 'Performativity, youth and injurious speech.' *Teaching Education*, 14 (1), 25–36.

Spaaij, R., and Schulenkorf, N. (2014). 'Cultivating safe space: Lessons for sport-for-development projects and events.' *Journal of Sport Management*, 28 (6), 633–645.

Stonewall. (2014). *The teachers report 2014: Homophobic bullying in Britain's schools*. London: Stonewall.

Stonewall. (2017). *An introduction to supporting LGBT young people: A guide for schools*. London: Stonewall.

Stonewall. (2018). *LGBT in Britain – university report*. London: Stonewall.

Stonewall Education Equality Index. (2016). *Celebrating difference and preventing and tackling homophobic, biphobic and transphobic bullying in Britain's schools*. London: Stonewall.

Subramaniam, P.R. (2010). 'Unlocking the power of situational interest in physical education.' *Journal of Physical Education, Recreation and Dance*, 81 (7), 38–49. Available at: 10.1080/07303084.2010.10598507 [accessed 29 October 2018].

Sykes, H. (2004). 'Pedagogies of censorship, injury, and masochism: Teacher responses to homophobic speech in physical education.' *Journal of Curriculum Studies*, 36 (1), 75–99.

The Proud Trust. (2019). *Training and education*. Available at: www.theproudtrust.org/training-and-education/ [accessed 25 April 2019].

Thomas, L. (2012). *Building student engagement and belonging in higher education at a time of change: Final report from What works? Student retention and success programme*. London: Higher Education Funding Council for England.

Wenger, E. (1998). *Communities of practice: Learning, meaning, and identity*. Cambridge: Cambridge University Press.

Youngminds. (2019). *Wise up to wellbeing in schools*. Available at: https://youngminds.org.uk/get-involved/campaign-with-us/wise-up/ [accessed 25 April 2019].

# 10 Disability sport coaching

'You just coach the athlete not the disability'

*Chris Cushion, Tabo Huntley and Robert Townsend*

## Introduction

The importance of understanding the intersection of sport, impairment and disability is considerable. Disability and parasport play an important role in disrupting and challenging cultural beliefs and discourses about disability and disabled people (Howe and Silva, 2016). Indeed, disability and parasport provide a unique platform for the visibility and representation of disability and disabled people, providing a context in which cultural understandings of 'disability' can be challenged and reshaped (DePauw, 1997). Disability and parasport is often assumed a 'non-disabling' site or associated with disability 'empowerment' and identity work, that is, resisting and reconstructing negative disability-specific associations (Ashton-Schaeffer, Gibson and Autry, 2001; Howe and Silva, 2016). As such, the disability and parasport field is replete with the encouragement and development of 'athlete-first' or 'athlete-centred' discourses (Townsend, Huntley, Cushion and Fitzgerald, 2018). However, few critically interrogate these notions, and as a concept 'athlete-centred' has become 'taken-for-granted,' is presented uncritically and enthusiastically accepted as a 'good' for disability and parasport. A key tenet of an 'athlete-centred' approach is it purports to be 'power-free' or attempts to democratise power (Foucault, 1975). This means that disability and parasport is seen as a neutral, benign space where participation is a desirable activity to develop 'better' people who are 'empowered' or made 'autonomous' (Townsend et al., 2018; Cushion and Jones, 2014).

As a crucial part of disability and parasport, disability sport coaching was identified as a priority for research over 30 years ago (DePauw, 1986; DePauw and Gavron, 1991), and an emerging literature has begun discovering something of the complexity of coaching in disability sport (e.g. Tawse, Sabiston, Bloom and Reid, 2012; McMaster, Culver and Werthner, 2012; Taylor, Werthner, Culver and Callary, 2015). However, most of the established work in disability coaching tends to distance itself from discussions about impairment (e.g. Cregan, Bloom and Reid 2007; Tawse et al., 2012; McMaster et al., 2012) implicitly forcing disability into the background. Only recently has work looking at coaching in disability sport engaged with models of disability (e.g. Wareham, Burkett, Innes and Lovell, 2017; Townsend, Smith and Cushion, 2015). Hence, the

## 132   *Cushion, Huntley and Townsend*

interrelationships between disabled people and broader social relations and practices are so far largely unexplored in sporting contexts.

Interrogating disability sport through a critical lens is an important step as coaching is a de-limited field of practice that is 'imbued with dominant values and common beliefs that appear natural and are therefore taken-for-granted' (Cushion and Jones, 2014, p. 276). Coaching is a practice where situated discourses of disability, disabled athletes, and the knowledge-practices of coaches are enacted (Townsend, et al., 2018). Because many coaches have limited or no training in coaching disabled athletes (Townsend et al., 2017), they instead rely largely on experience and informal learning (McMaster et al., 2012) and therefore lack opportunities to make social and cultural sense of disability (cf. Casper and Talley, 2005). Understanding the ways that coaches think about, respond to, and integrate impairment into their coaching practice provides an important contribution to broader debates about impairment and bodies in the disability sport context (cf. Hughes and Paterson, 1997). Coaches draw on discourses that circulate in the wider culture to construct identities, interventions and practice for disabled athletes. As a result, sport and sport coaching provide a lens through which to analyse the social relations that 'construct, produce, institutionalise, enact and perform disability' (Smith and Perrier, 2014, p. 12). Taking 'disability' as both socially constructed, culturally fashioned, and lived (Smith and Perrier, 2014; Thomas, 1999), suggests that different cultural fields produce distinctive contextual understandings of disability. Sport as a distinctive cultural field creates some disruptive potential generated from the visibility of disabled people[1] (DePauw, 1997; Ashton-Schaeffer et al., 2001). However, there remains a tension between cultural perceptions of disability framed in medical model discourses (cf. DePauw, 1997, Silva and Howe, 2012; Howe and Silva, 2016) and sport, of which coaching is central and a defining practice (Townsend et al., 2018; DePauw, 1997; Silva and Howe, 2012). Therefore, if sport and coaching are to function as a platform for empowerment (Purdue and Howe, 2012a), it is crucial to examine how the social practices of coaching are 'generated and sustained within social systems and cultural formations' (Thomas, 1999, p. 44) such as disability sport. The purpose of this chapter therefore is to contribute to discourses on the social construction of disability in sport and through coaching. In particular extending debate on 'empowerment' in sport and highlighting the, sometimes unintended, consequences of well-intended actions. In other words, the chapter focuses on deconstructing taken-for-granted conditions that disabled people face, exacerbated in social formations where power relations mediate who has voice, autonomy and identity, and who does not.

## 'Coach the athlete not the disability'

In the disability sport context, coaches both produce and are the products of certain discourses about disability that have a direct impact on the coaching and training practices adopted. For instance, while disabled people are usually understood symbolically, only insofar as they 'deviate from a prescribed set of norms'

(Edwards and Imrie, 2003, p. 244) and disability sport itself is structured according to categorical approaches to disability (DePauw, 1997), within disability sport there is a tension between disabled identities and identities that have more symbolic value, such as 'Paralympian' or 'elite athlete' (Townsend, et al., 2018). To look past an athlete's impairment is commonly assumed to be an empowering position that transforms disabled athletes' identities from being 'disability-based to sport-based' (Le Clair, 2011, p. 1113). A more critical look at such rhetoric, however, reveals a nuanced position in which disability is understood in relation to able-bodied norms within the social structure of sport. Coaching, therefore, is a 'product of cultural rules about what bodies should be or do' (Garland-Thomson, 1997, p. 6) where coaches are afforded the power to impose the 'legitimate definition of a particular class of body' (Bourdieu, 1991, p. 362). The implications for claims of 'empowerment' are important because for disabled athletes, social structure and power are determining of their identity but not individual autonomy. Hence, by adhering to discourses such as 'coach the athlete, not the disability,' the range of agentic choices and strategies available for athletes to shape their experiences are limited. In other words, disabled athletes are required to adhere to particular definitions of self which may be oppressive rather than 'empowering' but are labelled as the latter.

The notion of empowerment is complex and contested within disability sport (e.g. Howe and Silva, 2016; Purdue and Howe, 2012b), mainly because there is no consensus as to a universal definition. However, a common feature evident within disability sport research is the notion of 'gaining' or 'having' power. Here, following Purdue and Howe's (2012) example, empowerment is defined as a 'multi-level construct that involves people assuming control and mastery over their lives in the context of their social and political environment' (Wallerstein, 1992, p. 198). In light of this definition an immediate issue arises with the facile nature of 'coaching the athlete not the disability,' when it contributes nothing of substance to the idea of 'control and mastery' over a person's life. Indeed, within the para coaching literature, there is an assumption that having a disability limits sporting potential (e.g. Tawse et al., 2012).

Consequently, to impose an identity on a disabled person as 'athlete' whilst seemingly progressive (e.g. Cregan et al., 2007; McMaster et al., 2012) and offering escape from the trappings of the disabled body in fact constructs a boundary of acceptance within the sporting context. For example, in Powis's (2018) study of disabled cricketers, players found that 'incorporating their disability into an athletic identity' removed the 'stigma' of being visually impaired and made it more 'palatable' (p. 12). However, a consequence of this was to be accepted as an 'athlete' meant disability was pushed to the background or denied. Similarly, Townsend et al. (2018) found that coaching in both Paralympic and disability sport constructed a logic of practice that acted as the 'principal locus' (Bourdieu, 1990, p. 89) for the production of generative schemes, hierarchies and classifying systems about disability. This included the production and maintenance of 'able-bodied high-performance values' that had important implications for the social construction of disability. 'Coaching the athlete not the disability' became

## 134  Cushion, Huntley and Townsend

a process of misrecognition that assimilated disability into more valued performance discourses assuming this to be 'empowerment.' This had a dual function. On one hand, coaches were encouraged to look beyond the 'disability' in order to challenge and develop the players. On the other hand, there were tensions whereby the distance between disability and sport was maximised. These conditions meant that the language of coaching framed in terms of 'empowerment' was, in fact, a method where coaches had the 'power to impose the legitimate mode of thought' (Bourdieu, 1977, p. 170) about coaching disabled athletes. For the athletes, the power to challenge these coaching discourses was not located in individual autonomy but constrained within stratified social configurations that had all the appearances of being a liberating structure that was actually oppressive. In this sense, under certain conditions 'coach the athlete not the disability as empowerment' is largely taken-for granted and is fundamentally linked to issues of power, ideology and domination.

This perspective has, in some respects, some familiarly with the application of the social model of disability, where 'empowerment' reflects access to a normative view of the social world – in this case sport – and in doing so disability arguably disappears. Hence several researchers promote the view of the '(in)visibility of disability' (DePauw and Gavron, 1991; Cregan et al., 2007; McMaster et al., 2012) to the extent that disabled athletes can be viewed as the same as their nondisabled counterparts. However, as the research described suggests, such an approach uncritically applied can have unintended consequence where able-bodied sporting and performance norms are projected onto disabled athletes without question. Therefore, empowerment in this case may mean leaving the 'disabled body' but does not provide individuals with control and mastery of their lives.

Importantly, once an athlete identity has been placed on the disabled participant, as Townsend et al. (2018) have shown, coaches act as gatekeepers, with the power to impose the values and expectations associated with the sport on their athletes. These expectations often centre on the need for professional approaches and elite lifestyles (e.g. Cregan et al., 2007; Powis, 2018; Tawse et al., 2012). For example, the coaches in the Tawse et al. (2012) study highlighted the need to foster an 'elite mindset' that reflected the increased professionalism of the sport. However, in this study of coaches of spinal cord injured players, the reality of the impaired body was integral to the coaching process. So, whilst a performance identity was the focus, coaches had to consider the disruptive nature of acquiring a SCI which required players regain confidence to undertake new and also return to previous exploits. The outworking of this meant players were encouraged to become independent or learn how to manage their new 'body's.' Consequently, the disabled body was not invisible but real and for players with newly acquired injuries, engaging with veterans in the sport offered opportunity to learn some mastery of their physical life. However, positioning impairment in this way aligns with medical model views of disability, where the focus is on overcoming the 'problem' of a changing dysfunctional body. The medical model has historically been dominant in understanding disability and positioning research (Smith and Perrier, 2014). The central focus of the medical model frames impairment as the *cause* of disability (Swain, French and Cameron, 2003) and therefore the only limiting factor in coaching. From a medical model perspective, the disabled athlete is an object to be 'educated ... observed, tested, measured, treated, psychologised ... materialised through a multitude of disciplinary practices and institutional discourses' (Goodley, 2011, p. 114). Medical model discourses in sport promote a dominant consciousness where all problems are instrumental or technical problems to be solved and that coaching is fundamentally about improving sporting performance against the limitations athletes with a disability have. These practices are often so accepted that they influence, to greater or lesser extent, coaching frameworks that coaches draw upon and as such complicate further notions of 'empowerment.'

A clear limitation of the research presented so far, is the exclusion of athletes' voices and the limited theoretical lens applied to understanding the complexity of empowerment. Townsend et al., (2018) revealed the powerful socialising effects of coaching on athletes in the disability sport context. As already discussed, coaches' notions of empowerment were based on performance ideals associated with rejection of disability and the foregrounding of ability. Subsequently, coaches reported giving ownership of the coaching process to their athletes. In this case, athletes had assimilated the coaches' message of rejecting their disabled identities in favour of a sporting identity 'an Olympian,' 'a pro'.' This meant that the discourse of empowerment centred on a 'disability-ability' continuum (Howe and Silva, 2016), where the level of athlete ability, and striving for a particular athlete identity overshadowed the need to associate or disassociate with disability. As such, coaches continually challenged their players to overcome their limitations literally pushing athletes to 'blood, sweat and tears' (Townsend et al., 2018), thus misrecognising notions of empowerment for coach defined ideals. Similarly, reflecting on the elite sport environment of visually impaired cricket players Powis (2018) concluded 'a number of participants did feel empowered by elite visually impaired cricket; yet their empowerment was at the expense of other less-able players' (p. 15). In these examples, coaching was paradoxically acting as a form of control over athletes. Thus, empowerment in some cases could be considered an illusion that masks the very nature of the workings of power.

Research within disability sport has allowed the notion of empowerment to be deconstructed which has implication for its derivatives such as 'athlete-centred' or 'holistic-coaching.' In this respect, whilst the disability sport field may be understood as a site of resistance, whereby disabled athletes can be 'empowered,' it may be further conceptualised as a site of domination whereby coaches and coaching position disability in opposition to certain sporting ideals around 'performance.' As Townsend et al. (2018) argue, these understandings are often accepted and unquestioned within the structural conditions, constituting a taken-for granted view of coaching that 'flows from practical sense' (Bourdieu, 1990, p. 68). This section has shown that notions of 'coaching the athlete not the disability' framed as 'empowerment' cannot be separated from, and must be considered in relation to, 'power' and how this is expressed and experienced within different contexts and by different relationships.

## 136  Cushion, Huntley and Townsend

### How coaches can foreground disability and issues of power – the social relational model

It has been suggested that sport provides a context that can challenge and influence the social and cultural perceptions of disability and disabled people (Howe and Silva, 2016). Indeed, disability sport provides a platform for the visibility of disability in ways that understandings of 'disability' can be challenged and reshaped (DePauw, 1997). This is because situating disability in disability sport produces a unique tension between disability identity and athletic ideals (Townsend et al., 2018). The disabled body is 'a bearer of symbolic value' (Shilling, 2004, p. 111), which has important considerations for coaches who act as powerful figures in enabling disabled people to access sport and provide inclusive opportunities for developing independence, respect and agency as athletes. In this sense, coaches act as central figures in constructing, producing, institutionalising and enacting ideas and beliefs about disability and disabled people (Smith and Perrier, 2014; Townsend et al., 2018).

While this chapter has highlighted the potentially subversive effects of 'athlete-first' ideals in terms of promoting ableism and 'normative' ideals about coaching (cf. Townsend et al., 2018) it is worth considering how coaches can act as advocates for disabled people, recognising the social barriers that are imposed *on top of* the very real and direct effects that impairment can have on disabled peoples' lives (Oliver, 1992; Thomas, 1999). Indeed, introducing the concept of disability, framed by models of disability, helps to shed light on issues of access, equity, inclusion while recognising that impairment can and does play a role in athletic performance. For instance, the social relational model (Thomas, 1999) is a key reflective tool for coaches to assimilate into their practice as it focuses attention on structural barriers that inhibit coaching practice. This model focuses on the various social mechanisms by which people with impairments can be disabled within sporting contexts. The focus of the social relational model therefore is on the social construction of disability in different contexts and its use helps to analyse the production of knowledge about disability where social relations comprise the 'sedimented past and projected future of a stream of interaction' (Crossley 2011, p. 35).

Using a social relational model in coaching is useful as it highlights the unique construction of knowledge between coaches, athletes and the contexts in which they are situated. The model enables researchers to analyse the understandings of disability at individual, social and cultural levels (Martin, 2013) of coaching and coach education. Recognition and acceptance of the effects of impairment, as described in the social relational model, is an important factor for coaches to consider. Impairment can and does limit engagement in sport. Indeed, the psycho-emotional factors associated with disability such as low self-esteem, low motivation and low self-efficacy can be understood as a product of what Fitzgerald (2005) termed the paradigm of normativity within sport, where disabled people are defined insofar as they deviate from ableist 'norms' of sporting ability. However, impairment effects can only be 'disabling' in social formations which do

Disability sport coaching 137

not account for them – by recognising the disablism embedded in such normative expectations, an affirmative environment can be created whereby athletes are celebrated for their ability to show progression and development. Furthermore, by attempting to shape a coaching environment that has high-levels of contact with the players and their support systems (e.g. families), create coaching sessions designed to facilitate player learning, independence and autonomy (Fitzgerald, 2005), and provide opportunities for feedback, the effects of impairment are considered, but are not the central focus of coaching. Using a social relational model can give greater appreciation, recognition and power to the athletes in the construction of their sporting experiences (Richard, Joncheray and Dugas, 2015).

Thinking about coaching in light of the social relational model can include, for instance, highlighting the disabling nature of access to facilities, lack of visible disability sport opportunities as well as a lack of or difficulty implementing inclusive policies in mainstream sports. Furthermore, Thomas (1999) highlights the impact of relational barriers on constructing disability. In coaching these might include disabling stereotypes, lack of coaching knowledge about routine adaptations to practice, and behaviours that inhibit full inclusion of disabled people (exclusive and disabling language, communication difficulties, attitudes towards inclusion). Finally, coaching within the social relational model emphasises a dialogue with athletes, parents, support workers and coaching and support staff to understand their individual needs and build individualised support systems. Such an approach promotes full participation and autonomy while avoiding criticisms about prescriptions *for* coaching based on generalised assumptions about impairment. With the potential of these examples, implementing models of disability into coach education and coaching practice might be considered an important first step in establishing genuine 'athlete-centred' coaching (Townsend and Cushion, 2018). Another important step in this process is the development of coach education and development.

## Coach education, issues and ways ahead

As Townsend and Cushion (2018) argue, whilst coach education is a crucial feature of coach development, coaches are generally not trained in the specific circumstances of many disability contexts (Bush and Silk 2012, Tawse et al., 2012). More often than not, disability coach education provision tends to occupy a separate and distinct 'space' from 'mainstream' coach education (Bush and Silk 2012) reflecting the 'highly fragmented' nature of disability sport (Thomas and Guett 2014, p. 390). This means that the on-going professionalisation of the disability coaching pathway is inhibited as coaches face a lack of structured, disability-specific coach education opportunities (McMaster et al., 2012, Taylor et al., 2015). Therefore, coaching knowledge and practices are often derived from informal and non-formal sources and coaches are left to self-medicate by taking knowledge generated outside of disability contexts and grounding their understanding in material and experiential conditions in disability sport. Furthermore, research investigating disability coach education has shown how the process of coach development in disability sport often focuses overly on impairment, to such an extent that coach education positions athletes as 'problems' for coaches and coaching to overcome. Such a perspective is reinforced when coach education reduces disability to 'adaptations' or 'modifications' designed to increase coaches' 'confidence' to work with disabled people (Townsend et al., 2017), thus perpetuating exclusion in coaching despite inclusive lexicon.

In disability sport, the training of coaches is considered one of the most pressing matters in sustaining and improving the quality of sports provision for disabled people (Townsend et al., 2017). The success of disability sport in realising wider social inclusion objectives is predicated on a high-quality, inclusive and appropriately trained coaches providing quality opportunities for disabled people. Currently, disability-specific coach education opportunities play only a minor role in coach development in disability sport meaning that coaches are often 'dropped in at the deep end' of disability sport (Townsend et al., 2017) and have to negotiate a learning process characterised by 'trial and error,' through a largely self-referential practice of reflection (Taylor et al., 2015).

There is a critical need then to understand and outline some ways forward for disability coach education. As discussed, the current system in which coaches are 'educated' about disability is largely 'compartmentalised,' meaning that disability coach education is often separate from mainstream coach education pathways (Townsend et al., 2017). This structural situation results in a proliferation of courses and workshops focusing on inclusion, adaptations to coaching practice and impairment-specific workshops that are delivered as reactions to the lack of disability content in formal coach education (cf. DePauw and Goc Karp, 1994). These 'additive,' passive learning episodes focus on exposure to disability content, and have been criticised for perpetuating generalised stereotypes about impairment and providing an illusion of 'best practice' for coaches (Townsend et al., 2017). Such approaches are characterised by separatist thinking and practices reflective of the medical model of disability. Such an educational system necessarily isolates components of a complex coaching process and collapses the distinction between disability and impairment. The result, understandably, is that many coaches highlight a 'fear of the unknown' in working with disabled athletes, thus limiting the opportunities for participation in competitive sporting structures and impacting on coaches' ability to provide the conditions for full inclusion.

In considering participation in sport and physical activity as a human right (Townsend et al., 2017), coach education directly contributes to a form of disablism. Conversely, educating coaches about the political, social and cultural conditions that impact on disabled peoples' lives enables coaches to better consider sport as a vehicle for challenging the conditions of disablism and an ableist culture (Haslett and Smith, 2019). However, as Townsend et al. (2017, p. 359) argue, 'as long as coach education positions disabled people as 'different' to the degree that separate structures are required to educate coaches, inclusive sports coaching remains elusive' (Townsend et al., 2017, p. 359).

In addressing this, first and foremost, the dominance of disability discourses in producing and sustaining many conceptions of coaching requires exposure,

Disability sport coaching 139

challenge and reflection as they can often become embedded in coaching consciousness. At a practical level, the lack of disability-specific coach education and development is an area for both concern and possibility, and further developments are required to bring the process of socialisation into coaching under critical control (Eraut, 1994). Furthermore, while it has been suggested that sport provides a context that can challenge and influence the social understanding of disability (DePauw, 1986), as this chapter has illustrated coaching rhetoric is often structured by binary understandings or tensions between 'coaching the athlete' and 'coaching the disability.' As such, coach education needs to display a better understanding of the production of disability in different coaching environments, to build working principles that coaches can utilise in practice. Connecting theory to practice (i.e. understanding models of disability) is invaluable in developing a much-needed transformative agenda in disability sport coaching.

The following reflective points provided by Townsend and Cushion (2018) suggest some guidance for coaches wishing to engage in disability sport, though as with all coaching approaches, should not be read as a prescriptive 'how to' guide, but are mediated by the sporting context, level of performance and individual coaches and athletes:

- Work *with* athletes, not *on* them.
- Recognise and accept impairment and adapt practice accordingly.
- Create coaching sessions that challenge and support in equal measure.
- Draw on multiple, integrated sources of knowledge to understand the athletes.
- Continually reflect on your beliefs and assumptions about coaching disabled athletes.

## Note

1 The use of the term 'disabled people' reflects our position that disability is a product of social relationships (cf. Thomas, 1999, 2004). This social relational perspective focuses on the various social mechanisms by which people with impairments face disablism within social and cultural contexts.

## References

Ashton-Schaeffer, C., Gibson, H.J., Autry, C.E., and Hanson, C.S. (2001). 'Meaning of sport to adults with physical disabilities: A disability sport camp experience.' *Sociology of Sport Journal*, 18 (1), 95–114.

Bourdieu, P. (1977). *Outline of a theory of practice*. Cambridge: Cambridge University Press.

Bourdieu, P. (1990). *The logic of practice*. Cambridge: Polity Press.

Bourdieu, P. (1991). 'Sport and social class.' In: C. Mukerji and M. Schudson, eds. *Rethinking popular culture: contemporary perspectives in cultural studies*. Oxford: University of California Press, 357–373.

Bush, A.J., and Silk, M.L. (2012). 'Politics, power and the podium: Coaching for paralympic performance.' *Reflective Practice: International and Multidisciplinary Perspectives*, 13 (3), 471–482.

Casper, M.J., and Talley, H.L. (2005). 'Preface: Special issue: Ethnography and disability studies.' *Journal of Contemporary Ethnography*, 34 (2), 115–120.

Cregan, K., Bloom, G.A., and Reid, G. (2007). 'Career evolution and knowledge of elite coaches of swimmers with a physical disability.' *Research Quarterly for Exercise and Sport*, 78 (4), 339–350.

Crossley, N. (2011). *Towards relational sociology*. London: Routledge.

Cushion, C.J., and Jones, R.L. (2014). 'A Bourdieusian analysis of cultural reproduction: Socialisation and the "hidden curriculum" in professional football.' *Sport, Education and Society*, 19 (3), 276–298.

DePauw, K.P. (1986). 'Toward progressive inclusion and acceptance: Implications for physical education'. *Adapted Physical Activity Quarterly*, 3 (1), 1–6.

DePauw, K.P., and Gavron, S.J. (1991). 'Coaches of athletes with disabilities.' *The Physical Educator*, 48, 33–40.

DePauw, K.P., and Goc Karp, G. (1994). 'Integrating knowledge of disability throughout the physical education curriculum: An infusion approach.' *Adapted Physical Activity Quarterly*, 11 (1), 3–13.

DePauw, K.P. (1997). 'The (in)visibility of disability: Cultural contexts and sporting bodies.' *Quest*, 49 (4), 416–430.

Edwards, C., and Imrie, R. (2003). 'Disability and bodies as bearers of value.' *Sociology*, 37 (2), 239–256.

Eraut, M. (1994). *Developing professional knowledge and competence*. London: Falmer Press.

Fitzgerald, H. (2005). '"Still feeling like a spare piece of luggage?": Embodied experiences of (dis)ability in physical education and sport'. *Physical Education and Sport Pedagogy*, 10 (1), 41–59.

Foucault, M. (1975). 'Interview on the prison: The book and its method.' In: J. Faubion, ed. *Michel Foucault: power: essential works of Foucault 1954–1984*, volume 3, 134–156. London: Penguin Books.

Garland-Thomson, R. (1997). *Extraordinary bodies: Figuring physical disability in American culture and literature*. New York: Columbia University Press.

Goodley, D. (2011). *Disability studies: An interdisciplinary introduction*. London: Sage.

Haslett, D., and Smith, B. (2019). 'Disability sports and social activism.' In: M. Berghs, T. Chataika, Y. Ellahib, and A.K. Dube, eds. *Routledge Handbook of disability activism*. 98–113 .London: Routledge.

Howe, P.D., and Silva, C.F. (2016). 'The fiddle of using the Paralympic Games as a vehicle for expanding [dis]ability sport participation.' *Sport in Society*, 21 (1), 125–136.

Hughes, B., and Paterson, K. (1997). 'The social model of disability and the disappearing body: Towards a sociology of impairment.' *Disability and Society*, 12 (3), 325–340.

Le Clair, J.M. (2011). 'Transformed identity: From disabled person to global Paralympian.' *Sport in Society*, 14 (9), 1116–1130.

Martin, J.J. (2013). 'Benefits and barriers to physical activity for individuals with disabilities: A social-relational model of disability perspective.' *Disability and Rehabilitation, Early Online*, 5, 1–8.

McMaster, S., Culver, D., and Werthner, P. (2012). 'Coaches of athletes with a physical disability: A look at their learning experiences.' *Qualitative Research in Sport, Exercise and Health*, 4 (2), 226–243.

Oliver, M. (1992). 'Changing the social relations of research production?' *Disability, Handicap and Society*, 7 (2), 101–104.

Powis, B. (2018). 'Transformation, advocacy and voice in disability sport research.' In: T.F. Carter, D. Burdsey, and M. Doidge, eds. *Transforming sport: knowledges, practices, structures*. London: Routledge, 248–259.

Purdue, D.E.J., and Howe, P.D. (2012a). 'Empower, inspire, achieve: (Dis)empowerment and the Paralympic Games.' *Disability and Society*, 27 (7), 903–916.

Purdue, D.E.J., and Howe, P.D. (2012b). 'See the sport, not the disability: Exploring the Paralympic paradox.' *Qualitative Research in Sport, Exercise and Health*, 4 (2), 189–205.

Richard, R., Joncheray, H., and Dugas, E. (2015). 'Disabled sportswomen and gender construction in powerchair football.' *International Review for the Sociology of Sport*, 52 (1), 61–81.

Shilling, C. (2004). *The body and social theory*. London: Sage.

Silva, C.F., and Howe, P.D. (2012). 'The (in)validity of supercrip representation of Paralympian athletes.' *Journal of Sport and Social Issues*, 36 (2), 174–194.

Smith, B.M., and Perrier, M.J. (2014). 'Disability, sport, and impaired bodies: A critical approach.' In: R. Schinke and K.R. McGannon, eds. *The psychology of sub-culture in sport and physical activity: a critical approach*. London: Psychology Press.

Swain, J., French, S., and Cameron, C. (eds.). (2003). *Controversial issues in a disabling society*. Berkshire: Open University Press.

Tawse, H., Bloom, G.A., Sabiston, C.M., and Reid, G. (2012). 'The role of coaches of wheelchair rugby in the development of athletes with a spinal cord injury.' *Qualitative Research in Sport, Exercise and Health*, 4 (2), 206–225.

Taylor, S.L., Werthner, P., Culver, D., and Callary, B. (2015). 'The importance of reflection for coaches in parasport.' *Reflective Practice*, 16 (2), 269–284.

Thomas, C. (1999). *Female forms: Experiencing and understanding disability*. Oxfordshire: Open University Press.

Thomas, C. (2004). 'Rescuing a social relational understanding of disability.' *Scandinavian Journal of Disability Research*, 6 (1), 22–36.

Thomas, N., and Guett, M. (2014). 'Fragmented, complex and cumbersome: A study of disability sport policy and provision in Europe.' *International Journal of Sport Policy and Politics*, 6 (3), 389–340.

Townsend, R., and Cushion, C. (2018). 'Athlete-centred coaching in disability sport: A critical perspective.' In: S. Pill, ed. *Perspectives on athlete-centred coaching*. London: Routledge, 47–57.

Townsend, R.C., Smith, B., and Cushion, C.J. (2015). 'Disability sports coaching: Towards a critical understanding.' *Sports Coaching Review*, 4 (2), 80–98.

Townsend, R.C., Cushion, C.J., and Smith, B. (2017). 'A social relational analysis of an impairment-specific mode of coach education.' *Qualitative Research in Sport, Exercise and Health*, 10 (3), 346–361.

Townsend, R.C., Huntley, T., Cushion, C.J., and Fitzgerald, H. (2018). 'It's not about disability. I want to win as many medals as possible: The social construction of disability in high-performance coaching.' *International Review for the Sociology of Sport*, 5, 1–17.

Wallerstein, N. (1992). 'Powerlessness, empowerment and heath: Implications for health promotion programs.' *American Journal of Health Promotion*, 6 (3), 197–205.

Wareham, Y., Burkett, B., Innes, P., and Lovell, G.P. (2017). 'Coaching athletes with disability: preconceptions and reality.' *Sport in Society*, 20 (9), 1185–1202.

# 11 Coaching athletes with intellectual disabilities

## Same thing but different?

*Natalie J. Campbell and Jon Stonebridge*

## Introduction

The topic of intellectual disability is arguably one of the least understood, critiqued and researched areas of sports coaching. There is a paucity of practical and accessible resources available to coaches on how to deliver inclusive and integrative sports sessions for people with intellectual disabilities (PwID), there are also insufficient examples in how to develop PwID into elite level athletes. This chapter provides coaches with important population determinants as well as outlining some key clinical and sociological considerations for practitioners when coaching PwID. It also provides illustrative context from the United Kingdom; however, readers are encouraged to explore context within their own country of practice.

## What is an intellectual disability (and what is it not)?

When working with diverse populations, the issue of understanding and using appropriate terminology can be a steep (and meaningful) learning curve for some coaches. In relation to this chapter, coaches might often come across the words 'learning difficulty,' 'learning disability,' 'intellectual disability' and 'cognitive impairment' being used interchangeably – however, it is important to recognise the distinct differences between each term. Consensus amongst experts in medicine, psychology and education has seen a move towards using three separate terms to differentiate the specific needs of an individual with neurological differences – these are 'learning difficulty,' 'cognitive impairment' and 'intellectual disability.'

From here on in, we use the term intellectual disability (ID) and do so in accordance with the definition provided by the World Health Organisational (WHO).[1] Readers are strongly encouraged to explore the differences between the terms 'learning difficulty,' 'cognitive impairment' and 'intellectual disability' in greater depth; however, ID can be understood as:

- an intellectual quotient (IQ) of less than 70
- significantly reduced ability to understand new or complex information

- significantly reduced ability to learn new skills required for independent daily living
- impaired social functioning
- being recognised in early childhood and diagnosed before adulthood (under 18 years)
- lifelong and cannot be cured or overcome with treatment or intervention

Furthermore, it is important to highlight some salient and common misconceptions. ID is not:

*autism spectrum disorder:* Autism is a lifelong, developmental disability that affects how a person communicates with and relates to other people, and how they experience the world around them. It is widely acknowledged as a cognitive impairment (or neurological diversity) as intellect is not commonly diminished by having autism.

*dyslexia/dyscalculia:* These conditions are characterised as a developmental disorder of the brain in childhood, often causing difficulty in learning skills associated with academic progression such as reading, writing and mathematics. Dyslexia and dyscalculia are commonly considered learning difficulties, as individuals may experience difficulty in learning specific associative skills but will not have any reduction in their overall IQ.

*a mental illness, or symptomatic of a mental health problem:* Poor mental health can be developed by anybody at any time in their life and can often be overcome with therapeutic interventions. Mental health is not regarded as an ID, nor a cognitive impairment, nor a learning difficulty.

## The intellectual disability sporting landscape

Increasing practitioner and academic interest in the health and wellbeing of PwID over the past 20 years has resulted in more sporting opportunities than ever for this group, be that through local sports clubs, school activity programmes or nationwide charity initiatives (Einarsson et al., 2015). As with non-ID sport, there are pathways of participation, from recreational play to amateur competition through to elite performance – however, a significant gap in understanding of these pathways is apparent for many coaches. This void in knowledge is duplicitous with regard to both knowing (initially) the existence of the availability of different pathways, and then coaches not knowing how to fully develop individuals once they have selected a sport-specific pathway.

### Participation and recreational play

Participation in sport and PA for PwID in England is overseen by the Royal Mencap Society and Special Olympics Great Britain (SOGB), collectively known as the English Learning Disability Sporting Alliance or the ELDSA (note that the term 'learning disability' is still used due to the historical founding of the Royal Mencap Society in 1946, with 'Mencap' being an amalgamation of the now disused terminology 'mental handicap'[2]). There are eight National Disability Sports Organisations (NDSOs) in England that support the promotion and delivery of disability sport and adapted PA nationwide, of which the ELDSA represent opportunities for PwID. The ELDSA work with National Governing Bodies of sport (NGBs) and County Sport Partnerships (CSPs) to explore opportunities for essential participation growth such as coach education and club development, as well as working with the ID community to offer specialised support in overcoming barriers to participation.

When it comes to competitive sport, the ELDSA has a primary focus on the Special Olympics. The Special Olympic Games are held every four years, with teams from around the globe registering to take part. Importantly, the Special Olympics is not concerned with elite sport and selective processes; rather, it values a competitive experience above winning or sporting excellence (Lantz and Marcellini, 2018). With regard to participation, the ELDSA support numerous multi-sport and PA clubs operating across the United Kingdom delivered by CSPs and NGBs. Many of these clubs are partnered with local Mencap groups, local charities or local special educational needs schools. These sessions predominantly aim to offer fun activities as part of a leisure provision typically focused on increasing daily PA, improving social interaction and enhancing the overall wellbeing of the participants.

### High-performance sports competition

There are two pathways to support PwID into elite sports competition. The first pathway is to compete at the Paralympic Games under the *Intellectual Disability* classification. The eligibility of PwID to represent their country at the Paralympic Games has been a highly contentious issue since a scandal at the Sydney 2000 Paralympic Games saw 10 of the 12 players on the gold medal–winning Spanish basketball team being found guilty of faking their levels of intelligence. Due to this, ID classification was removed from the Paralympic Games. Since Sydney 2000, significant rigorous classification and eligibility procedures for athletes with ID have been developed to ensure the seriousness of high-performance ID sport (Burns, 2015), with three sports debuting the return of ID classification at the London 2012 Paralympic Games – athletics, swimming and table tennis.[3]

A second opportunity for high-performance sport is through a national selection process for PwID to represent their country at the International Federation for Athletes with Intellectual Impairments (INAS) Global Games. These games are held every four years across 18 sports, with an annual calendar boasting sport-specific world and regional championships contributing towards an individual's international rankings. The competitions eligible for international rankings, and subsequently the selection processes for representing Team GB at the INAS Global Games, are orchestrated through the UK Sports Association for People

*Coaching athletes with intellectual disabilities* 145

with Learning Disabilities (UKSA). The critical challenge for sports coaches in this instance is to understand the pathway of ID competition within the NGB and international federation of their particular sport, as not every sport is the same. For example, FIBA (the International Federation of Basketball) endorse INAS and provide support to NGBs in countries that offer high-performance ID as part of their suite of national programmes, i.e. the Fédération Française de Basket-Ball (the NGB of Basketball in France) offer the INAS pathway to ID athletes, whereas Basketball England focus on Special Olympics only. Consequently, a French PwID could represent their country in basketball at INAS competitions (if selected), but this pathway is not available for a British PwID. Conversely, there are international federations that do not support the INAS Games at all, meaning respective NGBs cannot provide high performance pathways even if they wanted to. For example, FISA (the International Federation of Rowing) do not recognise INAS, despite rowing featuring as an INAS sport. The NGB British Rowing, therefore, offer domestic-level participation programmes and competitions for PwID but do not provide an elite pathway. However, in the United States, any PwID wishing to compete for their country in INAS rowing competitions are signposted from the NGB US Rowing to Athletes Without Limits, a charity that facilitates all elite ID sport training, eligibility and competition (for both INAS and the Paralympics).

This brief overview of pathways demonstrates that ID sports pathways can be exceptionally complicated to comprehend. Indeed, the complexity and fragmented nature of pathways of performance for PwID may be hindering the expansion of ID programmes across the country, contributing to identified problems such as under-developed pedagogic resources for coaches as well as limited opportunity for both recreational and performance competition for athletes. There is often a lack of explicit connection between the NGB, SOGB and INAS which serves to enhance the argument that ID is the least supported, strategised and welcomed category of impairment across the sporting landscape in Great Britain. Therefore, coaches are encouraged to actively explore the opportunities and options for participation and elite completion for PwID in their own sport of interest. We suggest, first, to contact the lead disability officer within your NGB, who should be able to provide you with information on the structure, pathways and clubs (or lack thereof) of ID-specific opportunities for participation at recreation and elite level. If this information is not available from your NGB, the next step would be to contact your local CSP and ask about what ID-specific clubs are available in your local area (if any). Following this, exploring the SOGB website will provide coaches with a good understanding of how their sport features within the Special Olympics movement, as well as providing national sport lead contact details. For some sports, this will be the CSP lead whilst for other sports it will be another individual (usually a volunteer) responsible for the overseeing of ID sport within a specific geographical area. For coaches interested in wanting to understand more about the elite pathway opportunities for PwID within their sport, we recommend that you explore the INAS website and contact (in the first instance) the UKSA for further details regarding high-performance ID sport in Great Britain.

## Intellectual disability beyond sport

In addition to being diagnosed with an intellectual disability, a PwID will often experience associated physical, physiological and sensory disabilities (known as comorbidity), meaning it would be dismissive for sports coaches to consider ID in isolation. Practitioners, therefore, are encouraged to work with the 'whole person' to both embrace and embody a holistic coaching philosophy.

Research demonstrates that, overall, PwID will experience poorer indicators of health than their non-ID peers (Cooper et al., 2015; Emerson et al., 2016). Of note, PwID are statistically more likely to have an increased risk of visual impairment and some form of ataxic condition that limits physical movement (Matson and Matson, 2015; Kinnear et al., 2018). This leads to PwID being more likely to be overweight or obese than the general population due to high levels of inactivity coupled with weight-gain side-effects associated with psychotropic medication (Segal et al., 2016). In addition, PwID are at greater risk than the general population of experiencing mental ill-health (Schützwohl et al., 2016), and of experiencing chronic loneliness and social isolation (Wilson et al., 2017). Furthermore, PwID are likely to be diagnosed with associative autism spectrum disorders (Buxbaum et al., 2017), and exhibit increased problem behaviour (defined as socially striking behaviour that causes distress, harm or drawback to the person or to others, e.g. screaming or shouting, aggression towards others) or self-injurious behaviour (Schützwohl et al., 2016). Collectively, these comorbidities will substantially alter the ways in which sport and PA can be experienced by PwID; therefore, the sports coach should be mindful to these differences in health indicators and plan their sessions accordingly. The awareness and recognition of these comorbidities serve to frame some commonalities that the sports coach might experience with their athletes but also present as salient issues that coaches have a duty to be aware of with regard to health promotion and general wellbeing. Examples of how to take positive and deliberate action in applying these initial considerations in practice are provided by Coach Jon Stonebridge in the second half of this chapter.

### Barriers to participation

A socio-political understanding of ID in general is fundamental and coaches are encouraged to develop contextual knowledge of ID specifically within their national sport and PA setting. Data presented in the 2015–2016[4] Sport England Active People Survey reveals that PwID are the second least likely group of people with disabilities to engage with sport and PA. The report indicates that only 14.2% of PwID reported participating in at least one 30-minute session of moderate intensity exercise per week, with only 21.9% participating in any sport of any kind once a month. Worryingly, 78.1% of PwID do not participate in any exercise of any duration at all.

Research undertaken by Van Schijndel-Speet et al. (2014) argues that adults with ID experience the following barriers to activity: (1) health and physiological factors; (2) a lack of self-confidence; (3) a lack of appropriate skills; (4) a lack of support; (5) transportation problems; (6) costs; and (7) a lack of appropriate PA options and materials. Access to participation in sport – regardless of corporeal or neurological ability – is a fundamental human right (Rioux, 2011) and, as such, coaches must recognise that they occupy a central and significant role in abating barriers within their control. Teodorescu and Bota (2014) comment that ID is one of the least understood populations within disability sports coaching, with many mainstream practitioners finding they not only lack confidence in their own professional sporting knowledge when working with this group, but that the perception of PwID is one of *such* 'othering' that many practitioners are fearful of even engaging with PwID to begin with (Hammond, Young and Konjarski, 2014). The evidence of enacted stigma towards PwID from the mainstream sports coaching community is both concerning and problematic, especially as this perception of purposeful 'othering' is often absorbed by family members. Stigmatised treatment faced by PwID can take many forms, from direct discrimination and abuse to the denial of everyday opportunities by loving but over-protective families (Beart, Hardy and Buchan, 2005). Indeed, anecdotal evidence suggests that even when appropriate opportunities to participate in sport and PA are presented, family members are the most effortful barrier to overcome. PwID are aberrantly reliant on a proxy to some degree (teacher, caregiver or family member) to make the conscious decision to introduce sport and PA into their life. With the choice of activity and level of engagement often denied exploration and attention, without question, PwID are one of the most marginalised, disenfranchised and voiceless groups in society (Spassini and Friedman, 2014). Therefore, coaches must be aware of the challenges they face in accessing sport and PA, and even more so the reduced agency afforded to PwID in making their own health-based choices in life (Hatton, 2004).

## Coach Jon

Jon Stonebridge has been a Special Olympics basketball coach for over 10 years and an Intellectual Disability in Sport Trainer for Mencap. The remainder of this chapter is dedicated to providing critical excerpts of Jon's experience of coaching PwID including what he has learnt about himself and his athletes over the past decade. Through these excerpts, salient examples of how Jon practically applies common coaching theory to PwID as well as how he challenges traditional assumed ideologies are highlighted. Furthermore, Jon provides top tips for future coaches about how they can attempt to better embody the professional practice of inclusion in sport, especially when working with PwID. The rest of this chapter covers three areas of coaching that Jon considers to be most pertinent when coaching PwID: (1) first experiences; (2) professional knowledge and pedagogical considerations; and (3) How do you know what you need to know?

## First experiences

### Jon's experience:

*My first experience of coaching PwID was when I was 19 years old coaching at a community basketball programme. A request came from a local Special Needs Education*

148 *Natalie J. Campbell and Jon Stonebridge*

*School for a block of basketball coaching, however none of the coaches came forward to teach the group – not because there were any specific prejudices around PwID (I hope), just that no one felt confident enough to coach them. I had a family friend with ID and although I had no sporting experience, I thought I could give it a go. Naively, I assumed that the 12 participants in my session would be like our family friend. At the first session I quickly realised how wrong I was! There was a vast range of ID within the group – a spectrum of communicative abilities, different levels of ambulatory ability, sedentary to very active individuals – and everything in between. I definitely felt out of my depth.*

*I had planned every minute of the session; however, I soon knew that the drills and skills I wanted to deliver were not going to work and I quickly lost control of the session. There were two reasons for this. Firstly, I was trying to stick to my plan of what works in mainstream school; what I needed to do was adapt my coaching based on the people who were in the sport hall in front of me, rather than push my usual style of coaching. Secondly, I assumed I knew all that I needed to know based on my relationship with one PwID – I had not done any homework on the group to understand the needs of all those taking part.*

### Jon's top tips:

1. *Know your group!* Take time to find out about the varying degrees of ID in your group. However, be sure to make your own decisions about what a participant at your session is capable of achieving. Sometimes parents or personal assistants have limiting beliefs about a PwID – and I am very happy to see these beliefs change over the course of a coaching programme.
2. *What is the purpose of your session?* Fun? Exercise? Skill development? Is the need for an activity that increases fitness, builds teamwork and social confidence more beneficial to your players than motor skill development and technical proficiency in the first instance? If so, cultivate this environment before any high-level pathway coaching is implemented.
3. *Enjoyment first. Always!* This could be the only opportunity your players have to access physical activity and/or interact with people other than their family or personal assistants all week. Any negative emotions from a session might be heightened for a PwID and so ensuring their first few sessions with you are all about enjoyment is key – otherwise they might retreat from sport and PA completely.

In these top tips, Jon provides some meaningful considerations for coaches when working with PwID for the first time.

In the first instance, coaches should be aware that they may (initially at least) find themselves needing to also 'coach' the support network of the PwID, especially if the participant is new to PA in general or new to the sport. Indeed, research argues (Bigby, 2000; Holmbeck et al., 2002; Rimmer et al., 2007; van Ingen et al., 2008; Cunningham et al., 2014) that children with disabilities (physical, sensorial or intellectual) may experience further unintentional yet inhibiting disadvantages in their psycho-sociological growth (compared to

Coaching athletes with intellectual disabilities 149

their peers) if parents limit opportunities of independent development due to an emotional overprotection and/or a perceived lack in the child's ability to thrive, cope and be autonomous. Therefore, increasing the confidence of the parent or personal assistance – as well as the confidence of the participant – is a critical yet fundamental skill for the coach to develop. In addition, coaches should consider the need to balance the competing purposes that may present in their session. As Jones (2007) purports, coaches will often (consciously or not) prioritise the technical and tactical skill progression of their participants before explicitly addressing their required health, psychological and sociological development needs. This, perhaps, is a symptomatic outcome of a 'curriculum of the physical' that often dominates in coach education qualifications. However, the coach should be mindful that this may not be the most appropriate or the most vocalised focus of the session. For example, the health care practitioner of the PwID may have prescribed PA as a means to improve their respiratory system; however, the personal assistant may consider the need for social interaction to take priority over physical activity, yet the PwID may express a desire to learn a particular basketball trick and to have this dictate the session. What should the coach do? This conflict in value and purpose should be discussed (where possible) with your participant as well as the appropriate individuals in their support network to ensure that all individuals agree on the overall objectives set for your practice, and furthermore agree on how these varying priorities can be introduced and included over time.

## Professional knowledge and pedagogical considerations

In the above excerpt, Jon admits that the reluctance of the group to take up the offer to coach basketball to PwID was that they had no relatable experience, despite a number of years' worth collectively as able-bodied players and community coaches. Traditional NGB coach education pathways often produce the dominant ideological discourse that sport-specific knowledge is paramount to delivering a successful coaching session; and so it is not surprising that Jon's colleagues imposed self-limiting beliefs on their ability to coach PwID simply due to a lack of sport-specific experience. However, Jon recognised that despite his lack of professional experience, his rudimentary knowledge of the intellectual disability of one person might be enough to legitimise his volunteering himself as their coach. Côté and Gilbert (2009) intellectualise that sports coaches possess three different types of knowledge: (1) professional knowledge (sport-specific experience); (2) interpersonal knowledge (developing effective coach-athlete relationships); and (3) intrapersonal knowledge (self-reflection and self-awareness skills), with professional knowledge seemingly always privileged. However, as Jon explains later, for him it is the development of interpersonal and intrapersonal knowledge that allowed him to flourish as a Special Olympics coach – placing participant knowledge equal to, or even above, his own professional knowledge. But what happens if a sports coach is invited to work with a group of PwID and they find themselves perceiving to lack both professional and interpersonal

150  *Natalie J. Campbell and Jon Stonebridge*

knowledge? Then having strong intrapersonal knowledge and confidence in your ability to improvise, adapt and reflect are critical aspects of becoming an effective coach for PwID.

There remains (still) a dearth of coach education opportunity within disability sport which has led to a lack of professional training, knowledge and expertise (Cregan, Bloom and Reid, 2007) – especially so in ID sport. Despite there being a small number of workshops available to professionals, these provisions are not recognised qualifications (rather, they are certificates of attendance), are rarely sport-specific, are often grounded in inclusion as opposed to performance, and seldom provide critical pedagogic development and adaptation for PwID. With foundational elements of professional knowledge needed for coaching PwID being chronically ignored by the sports education community, it is exceptionally challenging for coaches to gain any advanced prior learning about the most effective and progressive way to coach PwID whilst simultaneously incorporating current pedagogical theory.

### Constraints-based coaching

A constraints-led approach (CLA) is based on the principles of non-linear pedagogy. Fundamentally, the manipulation of certain constraints to the organism, the environment or the task, challenges the participant to find their own movement solutions to problems presented or goals needed to be achieved. These constraints are understood as the boundaries in which participants can search for such solutions (Renshaw et al., 2016). However, adding constraints to a sport or PA session for PwID needs careful consideration. It could be argued that a PwID enters the sporting and PA environment with evident greater constraints than to their non-ID peers – that of reduced cognitive capacity, impaired perception and noticeable physical differences; and so coaches may need to avoid adding any further organism constraints when exploring skill development. When considering environmental constraints, coaches should be cognizant of potential challenges, distress and consequences of altering previously identified and learnt systems and relationships – for example, deciding to hold the practice outside minutes before it is due to begin could be exceptionally upsetting for some individuals (i.e. a change of routine), whilst for others this decision might also present physiological risks and behavioural challenges (i.e. participants not having appropriate mobility aids, or participants not having suitable knowledge about potential hazards in the outdoor area). Rather, coaches should strive for (at least initially) task constraints that manipulate the choice of training modalities, the goal of the task, or another aspect of the performance which support the participant towards purposeful movement development and outcome.

Progressive coaches would argue that coaching is not commanding; rather, it is about creating an environment where interactions, patterns and skills emerge and evolve. Renshaw et al. (2016) purport CLA to be about designing sessions that meet a broad spectrum of needs and afford movement opportunities based on information that is representative of the game. However, for PwID an element

*Coaching athletes with intellectual disabilities* 151

of command is necessary, with these commands often being delivered through developmentally appropriate instructional cues. The challenge to the coach, therefore, is to explore CLA-based techniques that afford movement without over-complicating the information required to successfully manage the perception-action loop of the participant.

### Teaching games for understanding

The concept of Teaching Games for Understanding (TGfU) was introduced in Bunker and Thorpe's (1982) seminal paper; however, the innovative approach was not widely embraced by the physical education community. Since the late 2000s, new interpretations of TGfU founded on non-linear and holistic developments has seen a revival of the approach within the sports coaching community. This regained support for TGfU has developed its credibility as a contemporary pedagogic method that fosters skill development by situating problem-solving, active learning and decision-making within a dynamic game (Croad and Castro, 2016). In addition, TGfU has a fundamental focus on developing the autonomous learner; therefore, if the aim of the session is for participants to eventually play a game, arguably they can learn *through* the game, which should be achievable for people with mild ID (50–70 IQ). Coaches may assume that the traditional, linear approach to coaching a skill may be preferable for PwID; however, preliminary research shows that providing developmentally appropriate problems for PwID to solve in their daily routine can contribute towards improved global social functioning and reduced signs of distress (Anderson and Kazantzis, 2008; Emond Pelletier, and Joussemet, 2017).

TGfU principally centres on developing modified games based around particular principles of play or tactical problems, with questioning strategies and situated skill learning being key components of the TGfU approach. Initially, the key pedagogical consideration (and the hardest to accomplish) is for the coach to adequately assess and reduce the tactical complexity of the task they are requesting of their ID participants. Cessation of learning within this coaching model may occur during disconnect at the questioning stage of skill development; coaches should be prepared for participants to take longer to learn orders of consequence needed to complete an intention-action gap in a sporting situation. With appropriate instruction and demonstration, most PwID can acquire a skill that is within their physical and intellectual capacity; however, the coaching adaptation will be linked to ensuring that participants understand *why* they are learning a skill, not necessarily *what* skill they are learning (although frequent repetition and reinforcement of skill development will be needed). Fundamentally, coaches need to develop their capacity to ask simple questions that facilitate learning that goes beyond skill acquisition, ensuring that participants are provided with developmentally appropriate time, opportunity and feedback on which to scaffold improvement. Later in the chapter, as one of his top tips, Jon emphasises the benefits of using developmentally appropriate modified games with PwID groups, and this approach is fundamental to TGfU.

## 152 *Natalie J. Campbell and Jon Stonebridge*

Academic literature and practitioner resources available on the adaptation of critical coaching pedagogies are lacking for participants with moderate ID (35–49 IQ), severe ID (20–34 IQ) or profound ID (under 20 IQ), which demonstrates the intellectual ableism of the profession. Coaches are therefore encouraged to reflect upon their own practice when working with more severe ID groups and to share any innovative methods, novel exercises or best practice examples amongst the coaching community to substantially develop this currently deficient area of professional knowledge.

### Jon's experience:

*Finding ID resources particular to your sport may be difficult. My own knowledge has been built up over the last 20+ years of coaching rather than through a particular pedagogic knowledge base on using CLA or TGfU approach for PwID (which would have been really useful!). Drawing from this experience, it is important that a coach can be flexible to meet the needs of the players. The needs will change from group to group, player to player, and sometimes in the course of a session – individualised learning is key and this only comes with getting to know your players over time. This is of course not specific to coaching PwID – this is good coaching practice; but when coaching a PwID it is even more important to know what a player can understand (i.e. applied to TGfU) in terms of coaching instruction and questioning, and what works best for a more enjoyable and constructive session. The real skill, however, is blending the needs of a group of PwID together – this is where a CLA session can become complex and messy. Which is not necessarily a bad thing! A starting point is to pitch your session at the lowest ID capability so that everyone in the group is engaged. Then look at how to challenge those within the higher ID level as you progress slowly to introduce task then environmental constraints and explore the potential for modified games (suited to ability).*

*There are areas of the sport that you may need to work on that you don't expect to. As an example, when working with lower levels of ID in a basketball context, the skill of being able to take the ball from the other team is a hard concept to comprehend. When watching games, you will often see the defensive team just standing by the side of the attacking player who is shooting and will only try and get the ball when it is loose. To coach this tactic, I have to break it down into its simplest form. I have a modified game where I have two groups, with one group stood stationary with a ball on one side of the court. The other group must then run across the court and take the ball from them, then repeat this as I add in some task constraints (i.e. you can only steal with your left hand, or you can only steal the ball when your opponent is bouncing it). This builds throughout the session, so the concept has time to be understood and ends up being incorporated at the end of the game.*

### Jon's top tips:

1.  *You got this!* If you have a coaching qualification you already have the technical and tactical knowledge to work with PwID; you just need to take the first step and get involved. Honestly, have confidence your intrapersonal knowledge and your ability to develop your interpersonal and professional knowledge over time.

## Coaching athletes with intellectual disabilities  153

2.  *Game on!* Make sure at least half of your session is devoted to playing matches. Just because someone has an ID doesn't mean they don't enjoy playing matches as much as anyone else. Importantly, don't presume they are not ready for a game – this could just be that it doesn't fit the picture of what you have in your head of what a game/match should look like! After all, this is the underlying principle behind non-linear pedagogy – TGfU considers that every situation can be made into a game if the coach has a broad enough view of what constitutes a 'game.' The key to this is to develop suitable constraints to make the 'game' suitable for any participant.
3.  *A rule is a rule.* Always stick to the fundamental rules of your sport. Out is out; a foul is a foul. But some modifications can be made, i.e. in basketball you are not allowed to travel with the ball, but if in a lower ability group someone cannot grasp the concept and a takes four steps but there is no disadvantage to the other team you can allow it.
4.  *Keep it simple.* When giving instruction break it down into the simplest chunks you can and always give demonstration and repetition. Don't become disheartened if someone doesn't pick up a skill straight away, it may take longer, or in some cases be prepared for it not to be actualised at all.

## How do you know what you need to know?

Gaining unique knowledge about your participants and providing them with individualised coaching episodes within a group training session is a masterful skill – taking years of engagement, authenticity, patience and reflection (Sheppard, Butler and Griffin, 2017). However, this depth of participant investment and professional practice is perhaps underscored when working with PwID. Notwithstanding the general principles of coaching with regard to providing positive sporting experiences for any participant in a session (regardless of ID or not), coaches who engage in proactive practices before session delivery are likely to substantially reduce the potential for negative, harmful or traumatic experiences for both the participants and the coach.

### Clinical differences

Providing support for PwID involves and requires looking for essential differences, even if those differences are unrelated to a particular disability; indeed, it can be argued that it is both unethical and troublesome to ignore the extent to which these differences might affect a person's capability of purposeful participation in sport and PA (Andric and Wundisch, 2015). Consequentially, to consider PwID under a singular socially stigmatising identity does little to support the sports coach in preparing thoughtful and purposeful practical sessions. Wherever possible, coaches should seek to gain clinically significant information about participants prior to training, allowing them time to adequately prepare for the individual learning and playing requirements of each person – e.g. specific ID diagnoses, degree of ambulatory ability, psychological and behavioural triggers, and contraindications to participation (including physiological, biomechanical, neurological, thermoregulatory and respiratory concerns). For example, due to sensory disorders, some PwID may become distressed by the feeling of sweat on their skin, some may be hypersensitive to certain sport environment smells (e.g. grass), or some may find the sound of a whistle overwhelmingly painful. In prior preparation, coaches can ensure that they provide an athlete-centred experience that is grounded in interpersonal development whilst still being cognizant of individual idiosyncrasies and medical needs. A helpful way to explore this is to create a 'pen profile' depicting all of the individual preferences of participants (either prior to or at the beginning of the first session). Here you might include sections such as 'Independently I can ...', 'With support I can ...' and 'I find it very difficult to ...' You may also benefit from having information regarding methods of communication, type of personal assistance required, mobility needs, considerations concerned with physiology (i.e. thermo-regulation, bathroom breaks and hydration schedules) as well as what the participant does and does not like (i.e. likes to know time frames of exercises; does not like loud noises).

### Communication considerations

The first step in gaining trust and creating a beneficial sporting environment is to ensure that communication is person-first and respectful – talking both to and about your participants in a courteous and professional manner is of paramount importance. Coaches should avoid labelling participants in any derogatory manner; however, it can be prudent for coaches to ask if a participant is comfortable discussing their ID, and if so to ask some important questions. Understanding the participant fully is necessitous, and understanding their disability is a part of that.

It is important that the coaches learn how to identify different emotions that a participant might be feeling during their session (i.e. enjoyment, confusion, distress), perhaps checking in more frequently that they would do a non-ID participant as body language and vocal expression alone can be a misleading representation of how a PwID is feeling (Porter et al., 2001). Furthermore, due to learnt acquiescence, social desirability (Emerson, 2012) and/or to compensate for reduced communication and agency, a PwID may not accurately or easily generate answers regarding self-awareness (e.g. being thirsty) or comprehension of a task (e.g. identifying a target). Therefore, coaches are encouraged to speak with parents and personal assistants where possible to assess perceptions of experience and preferred communication techniques such as hand gestures (i.e. right hand = yes, left hand = no) or the picture-exchange communication system (known as PECS).

### Cues and instruction

Coaches should always strive for polite and positive communication; however, there are a few key methods that coaches can adopt to facilitate learning for PwID:

*Coaching athletes with intellectual disabilities* 155

1. Be clear: Use words that the participant can understand, and for which the participant has a point of reference e.g. 'run in to an area on the court that does not have any of your teammates in it' as opposed to 'find the space.'
2. Be literal: Use practical and accurate language and try not to use metaphors (even if they are part of the sports jargon) as this may be confusing for participants, e.g. 'catching a crab' in rowing or 'drive to the net' in netball.
3. Be concise: Most PwID have a cognitive delay in information processing (especially words) so avoid using long sentences, and multi-part instruction. Instead, give one instruction at a time.
4. Be consistent: Identify a few key words for specific task and environmental cues and ensure these are always used, i.e. in basketball always saying 'basket' instead of interchanging between basket, hoop and net.
5. Be engaged: When making a coaching point, it is important that the PwID is looking at you and can hear you – prompt the person to look at you (if they are comfortable doing so), assign a physical coaching movement/action to this point to remind participants of the point, and (if possible) ask them to repeat the task back to you (as opposed to asking 'do you understand'). However, some PwID prefer not to make eye contact, so it is important to find a method of communication that still lets you know the participant is listening and understands what you are saying.
6. Be mindful: Do not expect the emotions, readiness and behaviours of your participants to be consistent at each training session; be prepared to continuously improvise and adapt your coaching, and to respond accordingly to the needs of each individual.

### Jon's experience:

*It is important to remember that you may be one of the only people that your players have a relationship with outside of their educational or family setting. Building a positive coach-player relationship will not only help them to gain confidence in a sports setting but will translate into their wider social environment. One player comes to mind who the first time I coached their session watched from the corridor as he didn't want to come into the hall – he didn't like places with a lot of people. Session by session through talking, encouragement, solo drills followed by joining the group he was an integral part of the team and took part at the National Games that had 15 teams competing.*

*Talk with the players find out about them, talk to their parents and personal assistants understand why they are there and then challenge what can be achieved. I can remember a parent telling me that their child, who had a moderate intellectual disability coupled with vision impairment, was unable to run. I also remember the look on that parent's face when we had them running, shooting and scoring! [This example of how support-minded parents can actually inhibit progression is addressed earlier in this chapter.]*

*There can be a lot of heightened emotions when PwID play sport, meaning it is important to understand the goals you set your players and the effects this can have. If the goal you are giving to your players is solely focused on winning, the game at the end*

156 Natalie J. Campbell and Jon Stonebridge

of your session will produce a group of individuals who are elated and a group of individuals who are distraught – and these heightened feelings can last for a while. Reading and managing the emotions of all your players will undoubtedly become the greatest skill you'll possess as an ID-specific coach.

### Jon's top tips:

1. *Don't judge.* It is important that if you are new to ID coaching you don't judge what a session or game *should* look like based on what *you* currently think a game should look like. Trust me, your players are often better than you think.
2. *Don't underestimate.* PwID can usually do more than people expect and as a coach it is your role to break the limits that other people often place on them. You have a professional responsibility to reverse such self-limiting beliefs.
3. *Don't overthink it.* Treat each session with the fundamentals that you used at the beginning of your coaching career and you will see success. Positivity, politeness, perseverance and play!
4. *Keep on trying!* As you would with any coaching session, always ensure you reflect upon your own performance, as well as the performance of your players. Ask yourself what worked/did not work, why and what you will do better next time. To start with it will feel like trial and error until you develop your three areas of knowledge (professional, interpersonal, intrapersonal) but – hey – isn't that what most coaching is anyway?

## Conclusion

Most of the principals involved in coaching PwID do not deviate far from those applicable to coaching children or adults in the general population. The foundational elements for good coaching practice that sports coaches already know from general coach education training within their particular sport are equally applicable when coaching people with ID, and it is important to remain aware of the skills you already possess. To use Bowes and Jones' (2006) metaphor of coaches 'working at the edges of chaos' (p. 241), coaches entering the space of ID sport may find themselves overwhelmed by the environmental disorder, the pedagogical misalignment and practical difference of their sessions and the degree of intellectual disability presented to them by their participants.

### Jon's conclusions:

As a coach who works in the ID environment all I can ask is, don't be afraid to get involved. There is often a fear of the unknown and coaches may shy away from getting involved in groups they haven't worked with before. Having read this chapter, you now have some of the knowledge to be able to take your first step into ID coaching, and if you do, it is one that you won't regret. Being involved in sport for PwID has been one of *the most rewarding areas of my life. I have learnt as much from the players as hopefully they have learnt from me. The difference that sport can make in a PwID life on and off the court is astounding. As a coach, you enable your players to gain an identity, improve behaviour and fitness, grow friendship circles, benefit from a structure and provide a safe place to enjoy sport.*

*Coaches of PwID need to be more than people who just turn up to coach a sport. They need a participation focus. The aim of ID sport goes beyond trying to win a game. The focus has to be on making a positive change in the lives of PwID. Coaches have to be a mentor, motivator, volunteer coordinator and friend. Participation will increase and then players can progress further down the competition pathway. Knowing that players that I have worked with are better able to cope with life in part due to the coaching I deliver, is all the reward I need.*

For coaches wishing to further their knowledge in sports coaching for people with ID, we direct them to Hassan, Dowling and McConkey (2014) and their book dedicated to the topic, *Sport, Coaching and Intellectual Disability*.

## Notes

1 Intellectual disability means a significantly reduced ability to understand new or complex information and to learn and apply new skills (impaired intelligence). This results in a reduced ability to cope independently (impaired social functioning), and begins before adulthood, with a lasting effect on development. Disability depends not only on a child's health conditions or impairments but also – and crucially – on the extent to which environmental factors support the child's full participation and inclusion in society. The use of the term intellectual disability in the context of the WHO initiative 'Better health, better lives' includes children with autism who have intellectual impairments. It also encompasses children who have been placed in institutions because of perceived disabilities or family rejection and who consequently acquire developmental delays and psychological problems. [Available at: www.euro.who.int/en/health-topics/noncommunicable-diseases/mental-health/news/news/2010/15/childrens-right-to-family-life/definition-intellectual-disability.]
2 Further information on the political correctness of the term MenCap and why it continues to use 'learning disability' can be accessed at www.independent.co.uk/news/uk/politics/political-correctness-mencap-vows-to-keep-name-despite-row-1534423.html.
3 Events open to PwID in these sport are currently: athletics – long jump, shot put, 1500 m (sport class T/F 20); swimming – 200 m freestyle, 100 m breaststroke, 100 m backstroke (sport class S14); table tennis (sport class T11).
4 Sport England Active People Survey 2015. [Available at: www.activityalliance.org.uk/how-we-help/research/1986-sport-england-active-people-survey-disability-aps10-fact-sheet.]

## References

Anderson, G., and Kazantzis, N. (2008). 'Social problem-solving skills training for adults with mild intellectual disability: A multiple case study.' *Behaviour Change*, 25 (2), 97–108.

Andric, V., and Wundisch, J. (2015). 'Is it bad to be disabled: adjudicating between the mere- difference and the bad-difference views of disability.' *Journal of Ethics and Social Philosophy*, 9, 1.

## 158 *Natalie J. Campbell and Jon Stonebridge*

Beart, S., Hardy, G., and Buchan, L. (2005). 'How people with intellectual disabilities view their social identity: A review of the literature.' *Journal of Applied Research in Intellectual Disabilities*, 18 (1), 47–56.

Bigby, C. (2000). 'Models of parental planning.' In: M. Janicki and E. Ansello, eds. *Community supports for aging adults with lifelong disabilities*. Baltimore, MD: Paul H. Brookes Publishing Co., 81–96.

Bowes, I., and Jones, D. (2006). 'Working at the edge of chaos: Understanding coaching as a complex, interpersonal system.' *The Sport Psychologist*, 20 (2), 235–245.

Bunker, D., and Thorpe, R. (1982). 'A model for the teaching of games in the secondary school.' *Bulletin of Physical Education*, 10, 9–16.

Burns, J. (2015). 'The impact of intellectual disabilities on elite sports performance.' *International Review of Sport and Exercise Psychology*, 8 (1), 251–267.

Buxbaum, J., Cicek, E., Devlin, B., Klei, L., Roeder, K., and De Rubeis, S. (2017). 'Combining autism and ID exome data implicates disruption of neocortical development in both disorders.' *European Neuropsychopharmacology*, 27, S437.

Cooper, S.A., McLean, G., Guthrie, B., McConnachie, A., Mercer, S., Sullivan, F., and Morrison, J. (2015). 'Multiple physical and mental health comorbidity in adults with IDs: Population-based cross-sectional analysis.' *BMC Family Practice*, 16 (1), 110.

Côté, J., and Gilbert, W. (2009). 'An integrative definition of coaching effectiveness and expertise.' *International Journal of Sports Science and Coaching*, 4 (3), 307–323.

Cregan, K., Bloom, G.A., and Reid, G. (2007). 'Career evolution and knowledge of elite coaches of swimmers with a physical disability.' *Research Quarterly for Exercise and Sport*, 4 (4), 339–350.

Croad, A., and Castro, J. (2016). 'Application of game sense approach.' In: Navin, A., ed. *Coaching youth netball: an essential guide for coaches, parents and teachers*. Marlborough: Crowood. pp.54–63.

Cunningham, N.R., Lynch-Jordan, A., Barnett, K., Peugh, J., Sil, S., Goldschneider, K., and Kashikar-Zuck, S. (2014). 'Child pain catastrophizing mediates the relationship between parent responses to pain and disability in youth with functional abdominal pain.' *Journal of Paediatric Gastroenterology and Nutrition*, 59 (6), 732.

Einarsson, I.Ó., Ólafsson, Á., HinriksdÓttir, G., Jóhannsson, E., Daly, D., and ArngrÍmsson, S.Á. (2015). 'Differences in PA among youth with and without intellectual disability.' *Medicine and Science in Sport and Exercise*, 47 (2), 411–418.

Emerson, E. (2012). *Clinical psychology and people with intellectual disabilities* (Vol. 97). Hoboken, NJ: John Wiley & Sons.

Emerson, E., Hatton, C., Baines, S., and Robertson, J. (2016). 'The physical health of British adults with ID: Cross sectional study.' *International Journal for Equity in Health*, 15 (1), 11.

Emond Pelletier, J., and Joussemet, M. (2017). 'The benefits of supporting the autonomy of individuals with mild intellectual disabilities: An experimental study.' *Journal of Applied Research in Intellectual Disabilities*, 30 (5), 830–846.

Hammond, A.M., Young, J.A., and Konjarski, L. (2014). 'Attitudes of Australian swimming coaches towards inclusion of swimmers with an intellectual disability: An exploratory analysis.' *International Journal of Sports Science and Coaching*, 9 (6), 1425–1436.

Hassan, D., Dowling, S., and McConkey, R. (2014). *Sport, coaching and intellectual disability*. London: Routledge.

Hatton, C. (2004). 'Choice.' In: Emerson, E., Hatton, C., Thompson, T., and Parmenter, T., eds. *International handbook of applied research in intellectual disabilities*. Hoboken, NJ: John Wiley & Sons, 335–351.

Holmbeck, G.N., Johnson, S.Z., Wills, K.E., McKernon, W., Rose, B., Erklin, S., and Kemper, T. (2002). 'Observed and perceived parental overprotection in relation to psychosocial adjustment in preadolescents with a physical disability: The mediational role of behavioural autonomy.' *Journal of Consulting and Clinical Psychology*, 70 (1), 96.

Jones, R. (2007). 'Coaching redefined: An everyday pedagogical endeavour.' *Sport, Education and Society*, 12 (2), 159–173.

Kinnear, D., Morrison, J., Allan, L., Henderson, A., Smiley, E., and Cooper, S.A. (2018). 'Prevalence of physical conditions and multimorbidity in a cohort of adults with IDs with and without Down syndrome: Cross-sectional study.' *British Medical Journal*, 8 (2), e018292.

Lantz, E., and Marcellini, A. (2018). 'Sports games for PwID: Institutional analysis of an unusual international configuration.' *Sport in Society*, 21 (4), 635–648.

Matson, J.L., and Matson, M.L. (eds.). (2015). *Comorbid conditions in individuals with IDs.* New York: Springer.

Porter, J., Ouvry, C., Morgan, M., and Downs, C. (2001). 'Interpreting the communication of people with profound and multiple learning difficulties.' *British Journal of Learning Disabilities*, 29 (1), 12–16.

Renshaw, I., Araújo, D., Button, C., Chow, J.Y., Davids, K., and Moy, B. (2016). 'Why the constraints- led approach is not teaching games for understanding: A clarification.' *Physical Education and Sport Pedagogy*, 21 (5), 459–480.

Rimmer, J.H., Rowland, J.L., and Yamaki, K. (2007). 'Obesity and secondary conditions in adolescents with disabilities: Addressing the needs of an underserved population.' *Journal of Adolescent Health*, 41 (3), 224–229.

Rioux, M.H. (2011). 'Disability rights and change in a global perspective.' *Sport in Society*, 14 (9), 1094–1098.

Schützwohl, M., Koch, A., Koslowski, N., Puschner, B., Voß, E., Salize, H.J., Pfennig, A., and Vogel, A. (2016). 'Mental illness, problem behaviour, needs and service use in adults with ID.' *Social Psychiatry and Psychiatric Epidemiology*, 51 (5), 767–776.

Segal, M., Eliasziw, M., Phillips, S., Bandini, L., Curtin, C., Kral, T.V., Sherwood, N., Sikich, L., Stanish, H., and Must, A. (2016). 'ID is associated with increased risk for obesity in a nationally representative sample of US children.' *Disability and Health Journal*, 9 (3), 392–398.

Sheppard, J., Butler, J.I., and Griffin, L.L. (2017). 'Athlete-centred coaching: Extending the possibilities of a holistic and process-oriented model to athlete development.' In: Pill, S. (ed.) *Perspectives on athlete-centred coaching.* London: Routledge, 9–23.

Spassiani, N.A., and Friedman, C. (2014). 'Stigma: Barriers to culture and identity for people with intellectual disability.' *Inclusion*, 2 (4), 329–341.

Teodorescu, S., and Bota, A. (2014). 'Teaching and coaching young people with intellectual disabilities: A challenge for mainstream specialists.' In: *Sport, coaching and intellectual disability*. London: Routledge, 103–119.

van Ingen, D.J., Moore, L.L., and Fuemmeler, J.A. (2008). 'Parental overinvolvement: A qualitative study.' *Journal of Developmental and Physical Disabilities*, 20 (5), 449–465.

van Schijndel-Speet, M., Evenhuis, H.M., van Wijck, R., van Empelen, P., and Echteld, M.A. (2014). 'Facilitators and barriers to PA as perceived by older adults with intellectual disability.' *Mental Retardation*, 52 (3), 175–186.

Wilson, N.J., Jaques, H., Johnson, A., and Brotherton, M.L. (2017). 'From social exclusion to supported inclusion: Adults with ID discuss their lived experiences of a structured social group.' *Journal of Applied Research in IDS*, 30 (5), 847–858.

# 12 The role of physical activity in cancer rehabilitation

*Louisa Beale and Jan Sheward*

## Introduction

Cancer and its treatment cause numerous acute and chronic symptoms and side effects that undermine the health and quality of life of cancer survivors. Being physically active maintains or improves physical function and psychological well-being, reduces the negative impact of several cancer-related side effects, and may also reduce the risk of cancer recurrence and increase the chances of survival.

This chapter will provide an overview of the evidence on physical activity and cancer, as well as offer guidelines for administering activity programmes. It will present the model of CU Fitter™, a cancer-specific exercise programme that runs alongside the Cancer United™ support group, to help people with cancer to lead a more active, happier and healthier life at every stage of their cancer journey, from diagnosis and beyond.

## Background

Cancer survival rates in the United Kingdom have doubled in the last 40 years and 50% of people now survive cancer for more than 10 years (Cancer Research UK, 2018). It is estimated that by 2040 a total of 5.3 million adults in the United Kingdom will be living with or beyond a cancer diagnosis (Maddams et al., 2012), due to a growing and ageing population, early diagnosis and improved treatments for the disease. Surviving cancer often requires treatment for many months or years. The major cancer treatments include surgery, radiation therapy, chemotherapy, hormone or endocrine therapy, biologic or immunotherapy, targeted therapies and stem cell transplantation. While these treatments dramatically improve survival rates, they also produce numerous acute, chronic and late-appearing side effects meaning that cancer survivors may face ongoing poor physical and psychological health that reduces their quality of life (Schmitz et al., 2010). The following list presents many of the adverse effects of cancer and its treatment which extend across physical, cognitive, emotional and social dimensions of life:

- impaired physical function/fitness
- fatigue
- pain

Physical activity in cancer rehabilitation 161

- cardiovascular and pulmonary changes
- reproductive changes (e.g. infertility, early menopause, impaired sexual function)
- changes in body weight and composition
- worsened bone health
- neurological changes (e.g. peripheral neuropathy and cognitive changes)
- impaired immune function, anaemia and lymphedema
- changes in bladder and bowel function
- shoulder disability
- sleep dysfunction
- nausea/vomiting
- breathlessness
- hot flushes
- impaired cognitive function
- anxiety
- stress
- depression
- psychosocial distress
- reduced emotional wellbeing
- poor body image

## Benefits of physical activity

> 'Physical activity is a "wonder drug" in the treatment and recovery of those living with cancer.' (Macmillan, 2012 – Move More Report)

Keeping active can maintain or improve physical function and psychological wellbeing and reduce the negative impact of several cancer-related side effects. Regular physical activity may also reduce the risk of cancer recurrence and increase survival in common cancers such as breast, colorectal and prostate cancer. A systematic review of the available epidemiologic and randomised controlled trial evidence investigating the impact of exercise on (1) cancer mortality and recurrence and (2) adverse effects of cancer and its treatment observed that people who had superior levels of exercise following a diagnosis of cancer had a 28%–44% reduced risk of dying of cancer, a 21%–35% lower risk of cancer recurrence and a 25%–48% reduced risk of all-cause mortality. They also experienced fewer and/or less severe adverse effects from cancer and its treatment than those who did less or no exercise (Cormie et al., 2017).

The message from Macmillan Cancer Support is that physical activity has a potential benefit at every stage of the cancer pathway from pre-treatment through to survivorship or palliative care (Figure 12.1).

The Macmillan evidence review reports that there is emerging evidence that exercising *prior to* cancer surgery or other cancer treatments, often referred to as 'prehabilitation,' improves physical function and helps people to better tolerate treatment and experience fewer complications (Stevinson et al., 2017).

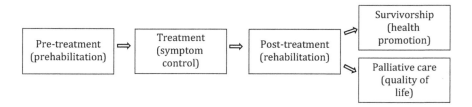

*Figure 12.1* Key stages of the cancer care pathway where physical activity has potential benefit (adapted from Stevinson et al., 2017).

During their cancer treatment, people often lose cardiovascular and muscular fitness, and experience debilitating cancer-related fatigue, pain, and nausea which causes them to reduce their physical activity. Excessive rest then exacerbates loss of physical fitness which may then result in a cycle of accumulating fatigue and reduced physical function (Stevinson et al., 2017). Exercise does not appear to increase cancer-related fatigue in adults, but neither is there conclusive evidence that it benefits cancer-related fatigue (Kelley and Kelley, 2017). A recent consensus statement of international experts finds that a moderate-vigorous intensity exercise programme lasting at least 12 weeks is likely to have the strongest effect at reducing fatigue (Campbell et al., 2019). Furthermore, exercise, and particularly supervised exercise, does improve physical function and quality of life in patients with cancer with different demographic (e.g. age and marital status) and clinical (e.g. disease stage and type of treatment) characteristics during and following treatment (Buffart et al., 2017). Improved physical function and reduction in adverse side effects may allow individuals to tolerate higher dosages of cancer treatment, or to complete their treatment. For example, in women undergoing chemotherapy for breast cancer, aerobic exercise improved self-esteem, aerobic fitness and body composition, while resistance exercise improved self-esteem, body composition, muscular strength and chemotherapy treatment completion rate, with no lymphoedema (swelling caused by deficiency in the lymphatic system) or other adverse events resulting from the exercise programmes (Courneya et al., 2007). Van Waart et al. (2015) also reported that physical activity programmes during adjuvant chemotherapy for breast cancer minimised fitness decline, managed fatigue and symptoms, avoided the need for chemotherapy dose reduction, and facilitated return to work.

The underlying mechanisms of the potential anti-cancer effects of exercise are not yet well understood, but are thought to include regulation of cell growth, e.g. via insulin-like growth factor, gene expression of proteins involved in DNA damage repair, decreased levels of metabolic and sex hormones such as insulin, leptin and oestrogen and modulation of immunity (Thomas et al., 2014). Cancer survivors are at increased risk of developing other chronic diseases such as cardiovascular disease. For instance, in breast cancer, where the five-year survival rate is close to 90%, health outcomes are most impacted by co-morbidities and the adverse effects of cancer treatments (Colzani et al., 2011). As well as mitigating side effects such as reduced physical function and fatigue, physical activity is thought to moderate cardiovascular disease risk factors such as obesity, hypertension and insulin resistance, as well as reducing inflammation and strengthening immune function (Koelwyn et al., 2017).

Even during the last months of their lives, cancer patients may gain significant benefits from remaining physically active. The benefits include maintenance of fitness, functional ability, and independence, reduced fatigue and enhanced wellbeing (Dittus et al., 2017; Lowe et al., 2009). For those diagnosed with progressive, advanced stage cancer, being physically active can help them to feel as if they are slowing the progression of their disease and prolonging their life. For example, in a hospice setting, group exercise offered positive experiences and enhanced quality of life for participants (Turner et al., 2016).

Exercise training programmes have consistently demonstrated effectiveness at reducing anxiety and depressive symptoms and improving health-related quality of life in cancer survivors before and after treatment (Campbell et al., 2019). The positive effect of physical activity on quality of life, which reflects a person's subjective evaluation of their wellbeing and functioning, is multidimensional. A meta-synthesis of 40 published qualitative studies concluded that, in addition to the physical benefits, physical activity improved the psychological, social and spiritual dimensions of quality of life. These themes and sub-themes drawn from the research are summarised in Figure 12.2. The majority of participants were older women, with a diagnosis of breast cancer in almost half of the studies, so the findings may not represent experiences in men, young adults and those with less common types of cancer. Nevertheless, this study adds further detail and insight to the quantitative research evidence that physical activity improves physical,

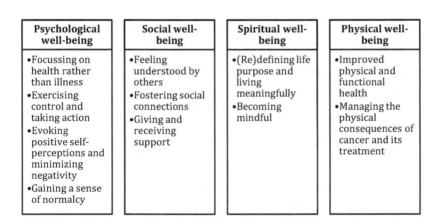

Figure 12.2 Impact of physical activity on dimensions of quality of life in cancer survivors (adapted from Burke et al., 2017).

164 *Louisa Beale and Jan Sheward*

psychological, emotional and social functioning and enhances general life satisfaction in individuals with cancer (Mishra et al., 2012).

## Guidelines for physical activity

It is now clear that physical activity plays a vital role in cancer prevention, management and recovery. There is strong evidence that exercise training is safe before, during and after cancer treatment, and improves the physical and psychological health and quality of life of several cancer survivor groups. Evidence-based physical activity guidelines for cancer populations from the Unites States, Canada, Australia and Europe share the recommendation that cancer survivors should follow the age-appropriate guidelines for health-enhancing physical activity, with specific exercise programming adaptations based on the disease and treatment-related side effects (see guidelines from Macmillan Cancer Support, the British Association of Sport and Exercise Science, the American Cancer Society; American College of Sports Medicine (ACSM), Clinical Oncology Society of Australia (COSA), Canadian Society of Exercise Physiology, Exercise and Sports Science Australia and the National Comprehensive Cancer Network). The UK Department of Health (2019) guidelines for adults recommend 150 minutes per week of moderate intensity activity or 75 minutes of vigorous intensity activity spread across the week, with an additional two days dedicated to strength training, and to avoid sitting for extended periods. Older adults (65+ years) at risk of falls should add balance/coordination exercise twice weekly. Even for individuals undergoing difficult treatments who are unable to meet the guidelines, the recommendations are to avoid inactivity and be as active as abilities and conditions allow.

There is consensus that physical activity should be recommended as part of standard practice in cancer care for all patients, with an acknowledgement that published guidelines for exercise programming offer generic guidance only and that specific activities should be carefully tailored to the individual (COSA, 2018; Stevinson et al., 2017). A framework for cancer exercise guidelines, based on findings of a systematic review of cancer-related exercise specific systematic reviews, has been published by Stout et al. (2017) to help guide exercise prescription and planning for health care providers. This includes guidance on assessment, screening and exercise prescription at cancer diagnosis, during and after treatment. Several organisations advocate the referral of patients to health, exercise or fitness professionals who are trained in the prescription and delivery of exercise (ACSM, 2019; COSA, 2017; Macmillan Cancer Support, 2017). Macmillan Cancer Support (2017) recommend providing a personalised one-on-one behaviour change support to help people living with cancer to become more active or maintain a level of physical activity, but emphasise that this doesn't necessarily require a local, directly delivered activity; with the right support mechanisms in place, signposting can be an effective means of providing a wider range of activity to suit the individual's needs and preferences.

*Physical activity in cancer rehabilitation*    165

Different settings, types and doses of physical activity may impact fitness and health in different ways, but as yet there is little evidence on how the specific contexts and parameters of exercise may influence its effect in individuals with cancer. Physical activity settings reported in the research literature include home, hospital or community-based interventions. Durations typically range from one to twelve months, while types of activity range from structured gym-based aerobic and resistance training, outdoor adventurous physical activities or team challenges, such as climbing a mountain or dragon boat racing, to yoga and tai chi. The dose, in terms of frequency, intensity and time and type (FITT) of activity, also varies considerably and studies to date have not been able to identify any particular FITT factors that moderate the effects of exercise (Buffart et al., 2017). Unsupervised interventions have a larger impact on physical function when weekly energy expenditure is higher (Sweegers et al., 2018). However, supervised physical activity may be better than unsupervised, perhaps due to the expertise, support or attention offered by the exercise instructor, due to a more challenging/effective exercise prescription and/or better adherence (Stout et al, 2017). Group activities can be a good way to foster social connections, undertaking a physical challenge can improve strength and physical fitness, and yoga or tai chi may encourage relaxation and mindfulness (Burke et al., 2017). The most recent ACSM guidelines for health care and fitness professionals include a tentative FITT prescription for some cancer-related health outcomes, including anxiety, depressive symptoms, fatigue, health-related quality of life, lymphoedema and physical function, along with advice about how to implement these prescriptions in practice (Cormie et al., 2018).

The 'optimal' physical activity programme, if there is such a thing, is likely to be dependent on the individual, and the type and stage of cancer and treatment, underlining the importance of tailoring the physical activity advice or programme to suit individual need and being responsive to changes in health, fitness, motivations and goals. Research study interventions tend to prescribe a certain dose or intervention of exercise or physical activity. In the real world, people may prefer to self-select the exercise type and dose and often need behavioural strategies and individualisation in exercise prescriptions to help them adhere to the programme.

## Physical activity levels in individuals with cancer

Despite the importance of being physically active, people tend to be less active after a cancer diagnosis than they were before, and less likely to meet the recommended levels of physical activity than those with no history of cancer (Grimmett et al., 2009, Wang et al., 2015). In 2017, 35.5% of cancer survivors aged 18 years and older reported no physical activity in their leisure time (Centers for Disease Control and Prevention, 2019). The majority of individuals with cancer are insufficiently active and don't participate in the type of high quality exercise programmes that are shown in the literature to elicit health benefits. Of those who start a physical activity programme, only about a quarter remain active after six months (Gomersall et al., 2015).

## Barriers and enablers to physical activity in individuals with cancer

A practitioner supporting people with cancer to become more active will need to understand an individual's barriers to participation, and adopt strategies to overcome these. Barriers may be related to both the physical and psychological effects of cancer and its treatment and to lack of knowledge and support for how to overcome these. During cancer treatment, the most common reported barriers to attendance at exercise sessions were cancer-related, including symptoms and medical appointments (Kirkham et al., 2018). A survey of members of the CU Fitter™ programme, described in more detail later in this chapter, revealed that the physical effects of cancer and treatment was indeed the main barrier to exercise. Half of respondents reported that they had to overcome feeling too unwell, tired or in pain to exercise, and a third had worried about causing physical damage to themselves (Catt et al., 2018). Although there are specific risks for some cancer patients when they exercise, there is consistent evidence that exercise during and after treatment is safe and that adverse events are rare, mild and mainly musculoskeletal injuries, and similar to the events that occur in people without cancer (Cormie et al., 2018; Schmitz et al., 2010; Stevinson et al., 2017). Despite this, there is inadequate support from health practitioners in recommending and facilitating lifestyle change, as reported in a study of colorectal cancer survivors at risk of cardiovascular disease (Maxwell-Smith et al., 2016). Self-consciousness, embarrassment and a negative body image are common issues for individuals with cancer, and many exercise environments may seem intimidating (Catt et al., 2018; Mishra et al., 2012). Lack of confidence or knowledge regarding appropriate physical activity and limited access to targeted programmes and/or facilities where people with cancer can exercise with others in the same situation are further barriers.

Cancer survivors are more likely to start exercising and to sustain this behaviour in the long term in an environment where they feel comfortable and supported. An exercise programme exclusively for individuals with cancer, with the option of group exercise for social support, led by experts who understand their condition can help to overcome many of the barriers to being physically active. Supervised programmes may particularly benefit those who are not sure what activity is best for them or how much they should be doing, those who have tried but never managed to stay active, and those who are anxious about getting injured or becoming unwell. Such programmes can help cancer survivors to develop the skills necessary to maintain a healthier and more active lifestyle in the long term. People with long-term conditions who engage in regular physical activity often feel more able to cope with their condition and, through exercise, feel some level of personal control over their health. Exercise can then become an end in itself and provide a focus, rather than simply being a means to an end (Lowe et al., 2009). By providing an opportunity to do something positive with others who have been through a similar experience, a group-based exercise

*Physical activity in cancer rehabilitation* 167

programme may be valued much more than a traditional support group (Maxwell Smith et al., 2016; Mishra et al., 2012). After treatment, barriers to attendance at an exercise programme are more likely to be life-related (Kirkham et al., 2018), so at this stage the practitioner should consider how exercise can fit around work/ family commitments, e.g. by offering sessions outside normal working hours or support for active travel such as cycling or walking.

## Limitations to the evidence on physical activity and cancer

The majority of research to date has focussed on adults with cancer, and mainly breast cancer and other common cancers such as prostate and colorectal cancers. There are numerous understudied cancer populations, e.g. head and neck, lung and gynaecological cancers, and those with advanced cancer and metastatic disease. It is not known whether the available evidence from the more studied populations will be applicable to individuals with different cancer types/stages where the research evidence is currently limited or lacking. However, it is clear that physical activity has numerous potential benefits for cancer survivors, including management of the side effects of cancer and its treatment, improvements in physical functioning and quality of life, and reduction in risk factors for cardiovascular disease. In the absence of information to suggest that it is risky, it may be more harmful not to recommend it while waiting for further research to be carried out. Having summarised the evidence for the use of physical activity in cancer rehabilitation, it is now appropriate to provide some examples of the way in which it is implemented.

## Example of cancer rehab in practice: Cancer United™ and CU Fitter™

Cancer United™, a registered cancer support charity based in West Sussex, UK, has developed a cancer-specific exercise programme, CU Fitter™, whose mission is to help people with cancer to live a more active, happier and healthier life at every stage of their cancer journey, from diagnosis, via a pathway of guided cancer-specific exercise. An exploratory survey of the CU Fitter™ programme concluded that community grown exercise initiatives such as this bring cancer survivors together, creating their own supportive environment. This, in combination with instructors who are experienced in working with the population and providing an open-ended service, may prove particularly motivating and beneficial (Catt et al., 2018).

Cancer survivor Jan Sheward set up the charity in 2014 to help individuals with cancer to get their lives back on track. For many people, a diagnosis of cancer turns their world upside-down, causes feelings of fear and isolation and makes it hard for them to move forward positively with their lives. Jan realised that there was a need for a specialist service to help people recover through physical activity in a cancer-specific environment.

168  *Louisa Beale and Jan Sheward*

The programme objectives are to:

- help people with cancer to become more physically active
- improve their fitness, health, wellbeing and quality of life
- help them to become more motivated and confident to exercise
- enable and encourage them to become independent in choosing and undertaking safe and effective physical activities

Initially, exercise classes were held alongside weekly Cancer United™ support group meetings in community buildings. People with diverse levels of fitness and exercise experience, with different cancer types and treatments and at varying stages of their cancer journey began to join in, and class sizes grew. It soon became clear that the exercise needed to be more specifically tailored to the individual, and that multiple classes would be needed to cater for the growing number of participants. A disused building was gifted to the charity, money was raised to demolish this and rebuild it and many local businesses and community members donated their time and expertise to complete the project. The CU Fitter™ cancer-specific exercise facility was opened in October 2015 in Angmering, West Sussex. This setting now provides a welcoming, non-threatening environment for exercise. Free transport is offered through the Cancer United™ minibus. The suite of cancer-specific exercise options allows people, under the direction of a cancer trained exercise specialist, to select an activity type and intensity suited to their preferences. They can exercise as part of a group, or alone. Members are welcome to continue exercising with CU Fitter™ for as long as they want to. Long-standing members provide support and advice to new members, acting as role models and buddies.

Classes are delivered by qualified personal trainers who have received additional education in cancer-specific exercise. The trainers first consult with the client to assess their physical and psychological health, individual needs and motivation, before designing an exercise programme or plan tailored to the individual. A range of different group exercise classes are offered, including mobility, flexibility and balance training, and classes to improve muscle strength, bone density and cardiorespiratory fitness. Some classes cater for specific cancer groups (i.e. breast or prostate) or treatment stage (e.g. during chemotherapy). Dance classes, Nordic walking and one-to-one sessions are also available. The dynamic team of CU Fitter™ staff and members routinely come up with fresh ideas for activities, including the recently launched 'Outkick Cancer' walking football and 'Outsing Cancer' choir.

Each person's programme is regularly reviewed and adapted as required, which may involve reducing frequency, intensity and duration during treatment when fatigue is a particular issue, or helping someone prepare for a return to mainstream facilities or sport. CU Fitter™ also offers outreach through 'pop-up' gyms and continues to provide exercise sessions twice weekly in local support group meetings. It is funded mainly through grants, donations and fundraising activities such as the 'Outrun Cancer' annual 5 km walk, jog or run family event. Members also contribute by paying class fees.

*Physical activity in cancer rehabilitation*   169

## CU Fitter™ referral process

Individuals who have had a diagnosis of cancer, are receiving treatment and/ or are in recovery from cancer are eligible for the programme, unless they meet the exclusion criteria in Table 12.1. They may be recommended to join the programme by their clinician, health professional or support group, or may join on their own initiative. Records indicate that majority of participants self-referred after learning about CU Fitter™ from a feature in the media, leaflets distributed in a support group or in the community, or being informed by a friend or other exercise group (Catt et al., 2018). Less than 40% of participants were referred by a healthcare professional, reflecting the limited promotion of physical activity in health care generally and cancer care specifically that has been reported elsewhere. The CU Fitter™ team work hard to establish networks with clinicians and health care professionals and to raise awareness of and promote trust in their programme. Reasons given by participants for joining CU Fitter™ include the following: to improve fitness, to get personalised support from an expert, to exercise with like-minded people who share the experience of having cancer, to get help with the physical and emotional recovery after cancer (Catt et al., 2018).

When a potential participant makes the initial contact with CU Fitter™, usually via a phone call, they will speak to one of the friendly and reassuring staff

*Table 12.1* CU Fitter™ programme exclusion criteria

---

*Cancer-related contraindications*

---

Individuals will NOT be admitted to the programme if they are currently experiencing

- extreme fatigue
- anaemia
- ataxia (loss of coordination and balance)
- extensive skeletal and visceral metastases

An individual *cannot* be referred if they have any of the following conditions/ co-morbidities:

- Recent diagnosis of heart disease, including angina, ischaemic and heart valve disease
- Cardiomyopathy or heart failure
- New/unstable arrhythmias, resting or uncontrolled tachycardia (resting heart rate >100 bpm)
- Symptomatic cerebrovascular disease
- Resting BP > 180/100 mmHg or unstable hypertension or symptomatic hypotension
- Unstable insulin-dependent diabetes
- Acute respiratory disease, including severe or poorly controlled asthma
- Uncontrolled chronic obstructive pulmonary disease
- Severe peripheral vascular disease
- Severe depression or other severe mental illness
- Advanced osteoporosis or osteoarthritis
- Severe back pain
- Acute viral illness

*If any of the above are present, a health professional should be contacted for advice on a more appropriate exercise programme, or the referral should be delayed until symptoms have been corrected.*

---

## 170 *Louisa Beale and Jan Sheward*

who is trained to show empathy, patience and positivity. Individuals who are not ready to start the programme will be invited to a support group. Otherwise, they will be invited for an initial consultation with a specialist exercise instructor.

## Initial consultation

All participants will attend an initial consultation before starting an exercise programme. The consultation allows the instructor to learn about the individual, their cancer and treatment, and how this has affected them, and their past and current medical history. The instructor will assess safety considerations and injury risk, according to the available precautions provided by Macmillan Cancer Care (Stevinson et al., 2017, p. 20) and ACSM (Campbell et al., 2019; p. 2384; Irwin, 2012, pp. 92–95 and pp. 154–157).

The instructor will explain what the programme involves and answer any questions or address any concerns before the individual gives written informed consent to participate in the exercise programme.

Physiological assessment, including measurement of height, weight, resting blood pressure and heart rate and cardiorespiratory fitness and other functional tests if appropriate, will be undertaken and recorded, and the results explained to the participant. Physical activity level and quality of life will also be assessed using validated questionnaires.[1] Physiological, physical activity and quality of life measurements will be repeated at the end of the programme, and 12 months later as part of the programme evaluation process.

The instructor will also discuss with the participant their previous exercise experiences and behaviour, their goals and exercise preferences. The programme recognises that cancer survivors have diverse motivations and barriers to exercise and may have many concerns that impact on the prioritisation of exercise in their lives. It incorporates core behaviour change techniques, including:

- recognising whether or not individuals are open to change
- exploring motivations, enablers and barriers to exercise
- exploring exercise preferences, agreeing goals and developing action plans to help change behaviour
- advising on and arranging social support
- tailoring behaviour change techniques to the individual
- monitoring progress and providing feedback
- developing coping plans to prevent relapse

Once an individual has been identified as suitable to join CU Fitter™, then they can embark on a systematic exercise programme tailored to their needs, some examples of which are explained in the next section.

## CU Fitter™ class examples

Below are some examples of exercise activities that are part of the CU Fitter™ programme. It is not an exhaustive list but offers an insight into the detail of the programme.

*Physical activity in cancer rehabilitation* 171

*Chemosize*: suitable for those undergoing chemotherapy and radiotherapy, these sessions focus on tackling fatigue and stimulating a positive outlook. Suitable for any cancer type and for those who may not have exercised previously.

*Benefits reported by participants (Catt et al., 2018) include: 'there is lots of support and encouragement ... being with people who understand how you feel,' 'help, comfort and understanding. After the first session I was becoming alive again.'*

*Proskick*: designed for men with prostate and testicular cancer but also suitable for those with many other cancer types, this class aims to improve muscle strength and bone density as well as cardiovascular fitness. Exercises are based around boxing gloves and pads, weights, barbells and resistance bands, and encourages peer to peer work in an up-beat environment.

Anti-androgen therapy for prostate cancer causes hot flushes and weakness, loss of muscle strength and bone mineral density. This class aims to create a fun and supportive environment where men can exercise with others who may be dealing with similar symptoms and experiences.

*Benefits reported by participants (Catt et al., 2018) include: 'a professional encouraging instructor in good surroundings,' 'the feeling you're not alone and have a laugh at the banter which goes on.'*

*Fit and Bust*: a programme designed for people with breast cancer who may be undergoing treatment or recovering from surgery and have regained a reasonable range of movement. The class focuses on gaining mobility and building strength, regaining confidence in movements and improving psychological wellbeing and having fun.

Joint and muscle pain, hair loss and hot flushes are common treatment side effects in this group. Participants may wish to remove wigs, if worn, for comfort.

*Benefits reported by participants (Catt et al., 2018) include: 'improved confidence and positive mental attitude,' 'helping me get my life back,' 'a feeling of wellbeing and we have a good laugh as the classes are great fun.'*

Other options include CU Can Yoga, CU Can Pilates, CU Can Run (beginners), Explore the Core, Get up and Booby, Nordic walking, walking football. Details of the current programme can be found on the website, www.cancerunited.org.uk/cancer-exercise.

A survey of people attending the CU Fitter™ exercise programme found that they were more physically active than before their diagnosis, had experienced important fitness and health gains and social support from the programme, adopted healthier eating and stress reducing techniques alongside their exercise programme and intended to maintain or increase their activity in the future (Catt et al., 2018).

## Monitoring and evaluation of CU Fitter™

To monitor change and evaluate the effectiveness of the programme, initial values/baseline measures should be measured and repeated over time (Stout et al., 2017). The CU Fitter™ programme incorporates regular reviewing by the instructor and participant of individual goals, adapting and revising these as appropriate. As part of the evaluation process, measures of fitness, function and quality of life will be repeated at the end of the programme, and after a further 12 months.

The instructor will try to eliminate unnecessary barriers to exercise, e.g. by reinforcing the benefits of exercise frequently and keeping the reasons for NOT exercising to a minimum, while ensuring that key safety issues are identified and addressed. The instructor needs to be aware of reasons for stopping an exercise programme, and when to recommend that a participant should seek advice from a health professional, by referring to the relevant guidelines (Campbell et al., 2019; p. 2384; Irwinl, 2012, pp. 93. 154–157). For example, an exercise programme should be stopped if the individual has an infection or fever, irregular heartbeat, chest, arm or jaw pain, bleeding, unusual sudden muscular weakness, changes in swelling or inflammation, recent and constant severe headaches, cancellation in chemotherapy due to low blood count or severe skin reaction to radiotherapy. Warning signs that an individual should seek advice from health professional include unusual tiredness, dizziness, weakness, unexplained fever or infection, difficulty maintaining weight, leg pain or cramps, unusual joint pain or bruising, sudden onset of nausea during exercise, flare-up of lymphoedema symptoms, or significant changes in coordination, vision or hearing.

## Summary

When coaching/leading physical activity programmes for individuals in cancer recovery, the practitioner needs to know about the type and extent of cancer a person has, the treatments for cancer, the resulting side effects and symptoms and their impact on exercise tolerance, in conjunction with a person's medical history and current health status. It is equally important for the practitioner to understand the psychological responses to having a diagnosis of cancer and how these impact confidence and motivation to exercise. In addition, the practitioner should be familiar with the benefits and risks of physical activity for individuals in cancer recovery and be able to design a safe and effective exercise programme tailored to individual needs.

A large proportion of individuals living with and beyond cancer will derive multiple benefits from well-designed physical activity programmes led by exercise professionals who are knowledgeable about cancer and exercise and experienced in working with this population (Schmitz et al., 2010). Cancer United's™ CU Fitter™ initiative is an inspirational example of how to create an impactful and enjoyable physical activity programme that helps people with cancer to live well.

## Note

1 International Physical Activity Questionnaire (IPAQ) Short Form Last 7 days self-administered format (2002), available at www.ipaq.ki.se; FACT-G Questionnaire Version 4, available at www.facit.org/FACITOrg/Questionnaires.

# References

Buffart, L.M., Kalter, J., Sweegers, M.G., et al. (2017). 'Effects and moderators of exercise on quality of life and physical function in patients with cancer: An individual patient data meta-analysis of 34 RCTs.' *Cancer Treatment Reviews*, 52, 91–104.

Burke, S., Wurz, A., Bradshaw, A., et al. (2017). 'Physical activity and quality of life in cancer survivors: A meta-synthesis of qualitative research.' *Cancers*, 9 (5), 53.

Campbell, K.L., Winters-Stone, K.M., Wiskemann, J., et al. (2019). 'Exercise guidelines for cancer survivors: Consensus statement from International Multidisciplinary Roundtable.' *Medicine and Science in Sports and Exercise*, 51 (11), 2375–2390.

Cancer Research UK. (2018). www.cancerresearchuk.org/.

Catt, S., Sheward, J., Sheward, E., and Harder, H. (2018). 'Cancer survivors' experiences of a community-based cancer-specific exercise programme: Results of an exploratory survey.' *Supportive Care in Cancer*, 26 (9), 3209–3216.

Centers for Disease Control and Prevention. (2019). *National Cancer Institute. Cancer trends progress report.* Center for Health Statistics. National Health Interview Survey. https://progressreport.cancer.gov/after/physical_activity.

Colzani, E., Liljegren, A., Johansson, A.L., et al. (2011). 'Prognosis of patients with breast cancer: Causes of death and effects of time since diagnosis, age, and tumor characteristics.' *Journal of Clinical Oncology*, 29 (30), 4014–4021.

Cormie, P., Zopf, E.M., Zhang, X., and Schmitz, K.H. (2017). 'The impact of exercise on cancer mortality, recurrence, and treatment-related adverse effects.' *Epidemiologic Reviews*, 39 (1), 71–92.

Cormie, P., Atkinson, M., Bucci, L., et al. (2018). 'Clinical oncology society of Australia position statement on exercise in cancer care.' *Medical Journal of Australia*, 209 (4), 184–187.

Courneya, K.S., Segal, R.J., Mackey, J.R., et al. (2007). 'Effects of aerobic and resistance exercise in breast cancer patients receiving adjuvant chemotherapy: A multicenter randomized controlled trial.' *Journal of Clinical Oncology*, 25 (28), 4396–4404.

Department of Health. (2019) *UK physical activity guidelines.* www.gov.uk/government/pub lications/physical-activity-guidelines-uk-chief-medical-officers-report.

Dittus, K.L., Gramling, R.E., and Ades, P.A. (2017). 'Exercise interventions for individuals with advanced cancer: A systematic review.' *Preventive Medicine*, 104, 124–132.

Gomersall, S., Maher, C., English, C., et al. (2015). 'Time regained: When people stop a physical activity program, how does their time use change? A randomised controlled trial.' *PLOS ONE*, 10 (5), 18.

Grimmett, C., Wardle, J., and Steptoe, A. (2009). 'Health behaviours in older cancer survivors in the English Longitudinal Study of Ageing: English Longitudinal Study of Health Ageing.' *European Journal of Cancer*, 45 (12), 2180–2186.

Irwin, M.L. (ed.). (2012). *ACSM's guide to exercise and cancer survivorship.* Leeds: Human Kinetics.

Kelley, G.A., and Kelley, K.S. (2017). 'Exercise and cancer-related fatigue in adults: A systematic review of previous systematic reviews with meta-analyses.' *BMC Cancer*, 17 (1), 693.

Kirkham, A.A., Bonsignore, A., Bland, K.A., et al. (2018). 'Exercise prescription and adherence for breast cancer: One size does not FITT all.' *Medicine and Science in Sports and Exercise*, 50 (2), 177–186.

Koelwyn, G.J., Quail, D.F., Zhang, X., et al. (2017) 'Exercise-dependent regulation of the tumour microenvironment.' *Nature Reviews. Cancer*, 17 (10), 545–549.

Lowe, S., Watanabe, S., and Courneya, K. (2009). 'Physical activity as a supportive care intervention in palliative care patients: A systematic review.' *Journal of Supportive Oncology*, 7 (1), 27–34.

Maddams, J., Utley, M., and Møller, H. (2012). 'Projections of cancer prevalence in the United Kingdom, 2010–2040.' *British Journal of Cancer*, 107 (7), 1195–1202.

Maxwell-Smith, C., Hardcastle, S., Zeps, N., et al. (2016). 'Barriers to physical activity participation in colorectal cancer survivors at high risk of cardiovascular disease.' *Psycho-Oncology*, 26 (6), 808–814.

Mishra, S., Scherer, R., Geigle, P., et al. (2012). 'Exercise interventions on health-related quality of life for cancer survivors.' *Cochrane Database of Systematic Reviews*, 8 (8), CD007566.

National Comprehensive Cancer Network. (2018). *NCCN clinical practice guidelines in oncology – survivorship*. Version 2.2018.

Schmitz, K.H., Courneya, K.S., Matthews, C., et al. (2010). 'American College of Sports Medicine roundtable on exercise guidelines for cancer survivors.' *Medicine & Science in Sport & Exercise*, 42 (7), 1409–1426.

Stevinson, C., Campbell, A., Cavill, N., et al. (2017). *Physical activity and cancer: A concise evidence review*. London: Macmillan Cancer Support.

Stout, L., Baima, J., Swisher A. and Winters-Stone, K. . (2017). 'A systematic review of exercise systematic review in the cancer literature (2005–2017).' *Physical Medicine and Rehabilitation*, 9(S2), S347–S348.

Sweegers, M.G., Altenburg, T.M., Chinapaw, M.J., et al. (2018). 'Which exercise prescriptions improve quality of life and physical function in patients with cancer during and following treatment? A systematic review and meta-analysis of randomised controlled trials.' *British Journal of Sports Medicine*, 52 (8), 505–513.

Thomas, R.J., Holm, M., and Al-Adhami, A. (2014). 'Physical activity after cancer: An evidence review of the international literature.' *British Journal of Medical Practitioners*, 7 (1), a708.

Turner, K., Tookman, A., Bristowe, K., and Maddocks, M. (2016). '"I am actually doing something to keep well. That feels really good": Experiences of exercise within hospice care.' *Progress in Palliative Care*, 24 (4), 204–212.

van Waart, H., Stuiver, M.M., van Harten, W.H., et al. (2015). 'Effect of low-intensity physical activity and moderate-to high-intensity physical exercise during adjuvant chemotherapy on physical fitness, fatigue, and chemotherapy completion rates: Results of the PACES randomized clinical trial.' *Journal of Clinical Oncology*, 33 (17), 1918–1927.

Wang, Z., McLoone, P., and Morrison, D.S. (2015). 'Diet, exercise, obesity, smoking and alcohol consumption in cancer survivors and the general population: A comparative study of 16,282 individuals.' *British Journal of Cancer*, 112 (3), 572–575.

# 13 Decreasing the fear of falling in older adults

## The use of Adapted Utilitarian Judo

*Óscar del Castillo Andrés, Luis Toronjo Hornillo, María Teresa Toronjo Hornillo and María del Carmen Campos Mesa*

### Introduction

The development of programmes aimed at improving the health and quality of life of older adults is a priority for a society that is ageing at an accelerated rate. As indicated by the World Health Organisation itself (WHO, 2018), we are facing a global phenomenon of ageing populations that is caused, among other variables, by a sustained increase in life expectancy. This increase in longevity can lead to an increase in situations of fragility and dependence (Barban et al., 2017); that is, an increase in situations in which people, for reasons related to age, disease or some type of disability, experience a lack or loss of physical or mental autonomy. With regard to the latter, suffering a fall is among the situations that most often strike the older adult population. The WHO (2018) indicates falls as the second major cause of accidental injuries leading to death and considers research and development programmes on this subject a priority.

Regarding the most relevant psychological factors related to the dependence process of the older adult population, Tinetti, Richmond and Powell (1990) see the fear of falling (FOF) as fundamental. These authors define FOF as a person's lack of self-confidence when it comes to avoiding falls while carrying out activities of daily life. In this sense, this syndrome or psychological trauma related to falling leads to a decrease in habitual activities, which in turn leads to a loss of the older adult's functional capacity later on (Myers, Powell, Maki, Holliday, Brawley and Sherk, 1996). FOF increases with age with the onset of diseases and is greater in older adults who have fallen sometime in the last year (Abad and Campos, 2012). This lack of confidence varies from a slight concern about falling to a refusal to do most everyday tasks (Legters, 2002). Given this situation, it is necessary to promote active ageing by adopting a perspective of the life cycle aimed at the improvement of health and the prevention of disease or dependence.

The scientific community and different international organisations, such as World Health Organisation, Health and Environment Alliance, the Royal Society for the Prevention of Accidents (RoSPA) and the Ministry of Health, Consumption and Social Welfare, in Spain, are responding to this demand, with

176 *Andrés, Hornillo, Hornillo and Mesa*

programmes aimed at the maintenance and improvement of physical capacities and qualities in order to prevent falls (Barban et al., 2017). To this physical aspect we must add the development of programmes that work on the psychological factors that most affect the loss of health and life quality of the older adult population, such as the aforementioned FOF. In addition to this fundamentally theoretical approach, there is a need for training and participation of sports coaches who can guarantee the correct understanding, execution and evaluation of these programmes. Working with an adult population requires in-depth knowledge of their needs and characteristics, which are the reason why professionals involved in its implementation, should have specific training and careful specialisation.

The contents of Adapted Utilitarian Judo (JUA) provides a strategy for alleviating problems relating to FOF, both physical and mental, that affect the active ageing of older adults, while improving their health and quality of life. Through JUA (DelCastillo-Andrés, Toronjo Hornillo, Toronjo-Urquiza, Cachón and Campos Mesa, 2018) which is based on the technical contents of traditional Judo (the foundations of Kodokan Judo, created in Japan in 1882 by Master Jigoro Kano), the educational and scientific fields are linked through the practice of sports coaches that work with these special populations. On the one hand, it responds to the global recommendations on physical activity for health made by the WHO (2010) and the American College of Sports Medicine (2011), who recommend that people aged 65 and older perform at least 150 minutes of moderate aerobic physical activity per week, or 75 minutes per week of vigorous aerobic activity, or an equivalent combination of both, in sessions of at least 10 minutes. JUA also responds to the demands of this population with reduced mobility, who must perform physical activities that improve their balance, strength and joint mobility, all this without forgetting the socialising aspects that are so important for the older adult population. On the other hand, JUA works on the psychological aspects related to FOF by teaching different types of falls based on Judo techniques (Taira, Suárez and Montero, 2014) adapted to this population, through collaborative work that allows the older adult to develop and acquire an effective and non-damaging technique of falling. At the same time, they work on orientation and mobility strategies on the ground when the fall has occurred, with the purpose of acting and getting back up in a safe manner. Through this methodology (Campos Mesa, DelCastillo-Andrés, Castañeda Vázquez and Toronjo Hornillo, 2015; Corral, Toronjo-Urquiza, Ruiz and Portillo, 2015), a reduction of the impact on the person is achieved (Pocecco, Gatterer, Ruedl and Burtscher, 2012; Moon and Sosnoff, 2017), which, in addition to reducing the risk of injury in the event of a fall, helps the older adult with their perception of safety in the face of daily tasks and allows them to extend their independence through decreasing the level of FOF.

The JUA interventions have shown to cause a clear decrease of FOF, causing significant improvements in all items analysed by the Falls Efficacy Scale-International (FES-I), both in its domestic and social dimensions, making it of great social interest as a treatment for the reduction of the frailty of older adults (DelCastillo-Andrés et al., 2015).

*Decreasing fear of falling in older adults*   177

This chapter presents the results of the implementation of a JUA programme on FOF for a population of older adults, allowing the demonstration of a useful and supportive tool for sports coaches of special populations. However, it should be noted that putting into practice a 'global fall training programme' for this population is an innovative and delicate subject, both in terms of content and implementation, which is why a key element for the correct development of the programme and the safety of the participants is the professional training of the coaches involved. The opinion of the researchers is that this specific training must be oriented to the areas of health and physical education, and that in addition to a solid academic training and sufficient practical experience with the target population, they must have specific training in the work of safe and protected falls.

## Method

### Sample

Ten women between 65 and 81 years of age participated in the study (with a mean age of $72.7 \pm 8$ years), selected through non-probabilistic-incidental sampling (Sabariego and Bisquerra, 2004), due to their accessibility (sampling for convenience). This sample is classified as healthy and pre-fragile, within the parameters of fragility that are established for the older adult population (García-García et al., 2014). The design is of quasi-experimental nature, with pre-post measurement of the experimental group. The programme complies with the proposals of the Ethics Committee of the Biomedical Research of Andalusia, focused on ensuring the safety of the older adult throughout the execution process.

As inclusion criteria, it was considered necessary for the participants to have an age greater than or equal to 65 years without diagnosed diseases that prevented them from doing exercise. Exclusion criteria were a limitation of doing physical exercise for medical reasons, congestive heart failure, chest pain, dizziness or angina during exercise, and non-controlled high blood pressure (160/100 mmHg).

Regarding the history of falls of the sample (Table 13.1), more than two-thirds of the population reported having suffered a fall, 14% reported having changed their way of life as a result of some fall, and approximately half of the subjects declared to be afraid to fall again.

*Table 13.1* Description of the sample according to fall history and incidents

|       | Has suffered a fall | First fall | Has fallen in previous 6 months | Fall influenced lifestyle | Fear of falling |
|-------|---------------------|------------|---------------------------------|---------------------------|-----------------|
| Yes % | 70                  | 70         | 0                               | 14                        | 60              |
| No %  | 30                  | 30         | 100                             | 86                        | 50              |

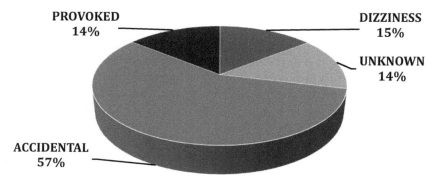

*Figure 13.1* Typology of the falls.

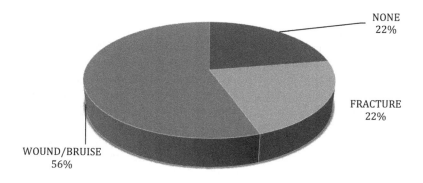

*Figure 13.2* Consequences of the falls.

Regarding the typology (Figure 13.1) and consequences (Figure 13.2) of the falls, for more than half of the sample these appeared to be accidental (in activities with little or no inherent risk), with the most prominent consequences being wounds/bruises (more than half of the subjects) and fractures (above 20%).

## Instruments

The WHO questionnaire for the study of falls in the elderly was used for the functional assessment of the fall (Arriola and Yanguas, 2001). To assess FOF, the 16-item version of the Falls Efficacy Scale-International (FES-I) was applied before (pretest) and after (post-test) the intervention. The FES-I analyses the confidence and ability to avoid a fall while performing the basic activities of daily life (Yardley, Beyer, Hauer, Kempen, Piot-Ziegler and Todd, 2005).

## Procedure

An intervention programme based on Adapted Utilitarian Judo was applied (DelCastillo-Andrés, Toronjo Hornillo, Toronjo-Urquiza, Cachón and Campos Mesa, 2018). The programme was carried out over six weeks with three weekly sessions of 45 minutes each (Table 13.2). All subjects in the sample were informed about the study objectives and agreed to participate in the study with prior informed consent.

To teach ukemis to older adults, we proposed assimilation and assisted assimilation activities (Campos Mesa, DelCastillo-Andrés, Castañeda Vázquez and Toronjo Hornillo, 2015), linked to the necessary security elements that prevent injuries and allow us to automate technical gestures in the most effective way. Two learning sequences were proposed: an autonomous one, assisted with equipment, and another in collaboration with a partner (with or without equipment). As a consequence of this learning process, the older adults were given skills that will allow them to react, protecting themselves and reducing the possible harmful consequences in the event of a fall.

*Note:* in JUA, displacement exercises are performed by elevating the tip of the foot, specifically working on the strength and mobility of the foot and ankle, which serves as a base to train the obstacle avoidance work and maintain or restore balance and stability. During these exercises, the elderly perform

*Table 13.2* Structure and contents of the Adapted Utilitarian Judo lessons

| | | |
|---|---|---|
| Preparation for training | Before starting | Remove jewellery and similar objects, check appropriateness of shoes, put on Judo jacket and belt |
| | Start of the session | Greeting |
| | | Joint mobility and coordination exercises |
| Main phase | Training unit of balance and displacement[1] | Static balance exercises |
| | | Dynamic balance exercises (lower body strength) |
| | | Functional displacement exercises |
| | Fall training unit | Work of progressions and going to the ground |
| | | Work and mobility strategies on the ground |
| | | Recovery of a standing position |
| | | Ukemis |
| | Unit of work of techniques | Judo techniques (adapted) |
| | | Movements of the Judo Kata |
| | | (Nage No Kata, Kime No Kata, and especially Ju No Kata) |
| Post-training | Recovery phase | Moves of Kagami-migaki |
| | | The session is closed with the traditional Japanese good-bye bow |

180 *Andrés, Hornillo, Hornillo and Mesa*

displacements in all directions, at different speeds and looking at different focus points in order to train spatial orientation and awareness.

### Data analysis

A descriptive analysis was carried out through the statistical programme SPSS (V.24.0), presented in terms of frequencies and percentages for the categorical variables, and mean and standard deviation for the numerical variables. The T-test for paired samples was used when analysing the significance of the difference of means, since it is a case study, considering that the differences are significant when $p \leq 0.05$.

## Results

To analyse the evolution of the scores for the pre and post-test of each subject, the cut-off points of the FES-I questionnaire in its 16-item version have been used (Yardley et al., 2005). This questionnaire divides scores in three levels of fear of falling: low (from 16 to 19 points), moderate (from 20 to 27 points) and high (from 28 to 64 points).

Of all the variables analysed through the FES-I, it can be seen in Table 13.3 that the JUA programme has had a significant impact in reducing the fear of the subjects in the following variables: *go up or downstairs, reach up or down for something, walk to answer the phone, walk on a slippery surface, walk in a crowded place, walk on an uneven surface and go up and down a ramp.* They represent the variables that received the highest score in the pretest and therefore are those that caused the greatest fear on the subjects. The JUA programme intervention has therefore been significant for the experimental group, as the table shows ($p = 0.01$).

In Figure 13.3 we can observe the final scores obtained in the FES-I of each of the subjects of the experimental group, before and after the intervention of the JUA program. It shows after the intervention all the subjects reached a low level of fear of falling, except the three that started from a high level of fear (subjects 1, 8 and 10). However, these subjects managed to reduce their fear of falling by 18, 10 and 16 points, respectively.

If we analyse it at the group level (Delbaere, Close, Mikolaizak, Sachdev, Brodaty and Lord, 2010), as shown in Figure 13.3, after the intervention of the JUA programme all subjects are below 20 points, except for the three mentioned above (1, 8 and 10), which have improved in their perception of the fear of falling, to 20 points, reaching the threshold of a low level of fear of falling ($\leq 19$ points), which means that they have gone from a level where the risk of entering a situation of dependency is considered high, to a level that relates to personal autonomy with respect to the FOF.

The results show that there are significant improvements in the individual perception of the fear of falling, these being greater in the subjects with a higher fear of falling at the beginning of the intervention. Some of the older people who

*Decreasing fear of falling in older adults*  181

*Table 13.3* FEES-I pre-post intervention scores and values by variables analysed and complete group

| Variables | Pretest | | Post-test | | t paired samples | |
|---|---|---|---|---|---|---|
| | M | SD | M | SD | t | p |
| Clean the house | 1.00 | 0.00 | 1.00 | 0.00 | – | – |
| Dress or undress | 1.00 | 0.00 | 1.00 | 0.00 | – | – |
| Prepare food | 1.00 | 0.00 | 1.00 | 0.00 | – | – |
| Bath or shower | 1.30 | 0.48 | 1.00 | 0.00 | 1.96 | .08 |
| Do the shopping | 1.20 | 0.42 | 1.00 | 0.00 | 1.50 | .16 |
| Sit down or get up from a chair | 1.00 | 0.00 | 1.00 | 0.00 | 2.23 | – |
| Go up or downstairs | 1.50 | 0.70 | 1.00 | 0.00 | 1.50 | .05* |
| Walk in the neighbourhood (outside) | 1.20 | 0.42 | 1.00 | 0.00 | 6.00 | .16 |
| Reach up or down for something | 2.40 | 0.51 | 1.60 | 0.51 | 2.68 | .00* |
| Walk for answer the phone | 1.80 | 0.91 | 1.10 | 0.31 | 6.00 | .02* |
| Walk on a slippery surface | 3.00 | 0.81 | 1.80 | 0.42 | 1.50 | .00* |
| Visit a friend or relative | 1.20 | 0.42 | 1.00 | 0.00 | 3.25 | .16 |
| Walk in a crowded place | 2.60 | 1.07 | 1.70 | 0.48 | 4.81 | .01* |
| Walk on an uneven surface | 2.50 | 0.97 | 1.30 | 0.48 | 4.00 | .00* |
| Go up and down a ramp | 1.80 | 0.63 | 1.00 | 0.00 | 1.50 | .00* |
| Go out for a social event | 1.20 | 0.42 | 1.00 | 0.00 | 3.25 | .16 |
| Pretest–post-test | 25.70 | 7.91 | 18.30 | 1.94 | 1.96 | .01* |

Note: M = arithmetic average; $DT$ = standard deviation; $t$ = T-student; $p$ = bilateral significance ($*p \le .05$).

have participated in the study have even been able to return to activities of their daily lives that previously were difficult for them because of their fear of falling.

## Discussion and conclusions

In view of the results presented in this chapter, the use of JUA by sports coaches reveals itself to be a potentially useful tool in their daily work on the improvement of health and quality of life of older adults, more specifically, affecting the fear of suffering a fall, a factor that generates a high level of dependence in these subjects.

The results show that the JUA program reduced FOF by more than seven total average points. This data is very encouraging for the prevention of falls since the FES-I score is 18.30 after the intervention, a score indicated as very positive by authors such as Ersoy, MacWalter, Durmus, Altay and Baysal (2009).

The results obtained in our study on FOF are linked to others that propose providing strategies of proprioceptive responses. These responses are based on information coming from the nerve endings of muscles, tendons and joints, which is integrated at the cerebral level, allowing a person to perceive the global

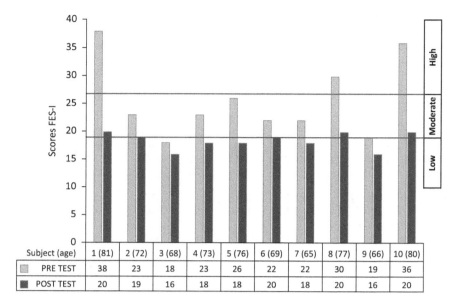

*Figure 13.3* Scores obtained in the FES-I before and after the intervention according to levels of fear of falling.

and segmental position of their body in space, which in turn allows them to offer a motor response through the synchronisation of movements, the speed of execution and the muscular tension performed. Used to this end Tai-Chi has obtained an 11% reduction of FOF in studies such as those by Sattin, Easley, Wolf, Chen and Kutner (2005), data linked to the Activities-Specific Balance Confidence Scale questionnaire.

In the approach proposed by the WHO (2018) to the active ageing of the elderly population, the improvement of dynamic balance has shown positive results in the treatment of FOF, as can be seen in a study by Ersoy, MacWalter, Durmus, Altay and Baysal (2009). JUA contains intensive work on balance, both in its static and dynamic aspects, as authors such as DelCastillo-Andrés, Toronjo Hornillo, Toronjo-Urquiza, Cachón and Campos Mesa (2018) have proposed, showing more positive values than previous studies, since none of them managed to obtain an FES-I index lower than 23 points after treatment. After the JUA intervention, results below 23 points have been obtained in the ten subjects.

On the other hand, there is a direct relationship between the practice of physical activity by older adults and FOF, as has been pointed out by authors such as Kempen, Van Haastregt, McKee, Delbaere and Zijlstra (2009). At this point we must highlight that, thanks to the general physical work done through JUA and its effect on FOF, the subjects were able to perform daily physical activities, such as walking in places with many people or walk on a slippery surface. The latter

FES-I variable received one of the highest scores in our pretest and decreased considerably in the post-test.

Therefore, it is possible to teach the control of falls to older adults using the JUA programme. This programme could be included in the contents of structured physical activity programmes in older people, together with the work on other qualities such as strength, being important for work with older people, as Ishigaki, Ramos, Carvalho and Lunardi (2014) indicate in their work.

We agree with Hagedorn and Holm (2010) when they point out the importance of emphasising that social and recreational programmes are most likely to increase the quality of life of the subjects. In this proposal, the JUA programme works socially and playfully, fostering social interactions among the older adult population. In this way, we are able to obtain our objectives, considering that JUA contributes to the improvement of the quality of life of these people.

One limitation of this study is the sample size, a limitation inherent to a case study. Also, the subjects were not controlled for informal activity, nor were other measurements done such as checking the perceived quality of life or balance, among others, data that could strengthen the influence of the JUA in the FOF. Another limitation is the absence of a control group – a limitation that becomes a future possibility.

To this future possibility, one can add the convenient inclusion of the JUA as an innovative, social and playful programme to the contents of the physical activity programmes, focused on active ageing and on the prevention of frailty in older adults. According to the first data obtained in this study, they are presented as an effective tool when working on both control and reduction of the STAC, for professionals in the fields of older adult (health) care.

In conclusion, the results obtained show that the application of a teaching programme for the control of falls using JUA with older adults can help to reduce the FOF and therefore improve the quality of life of these subjects.

## References

Abad Mateo, M., and Campos Aranda, M. (2012). 'Estudio del síndrome de temor a caerse en personas mayores de 65 años.' 1–177.

Arriola, F.J., and Yanguas, F.J.L. (2001). *Valoración de las Personas Mayores: Evaluar para conocer, conocer para intervenir.* Retrieved from https://dialnet.unirioja.es/servlet/libro?codigo=319432.

Barban, F., Annicchiarico, R., Melideo, M., Federici, A., Lombardi, M.G., Giuli, S., et al. (2017). 'Reducing fall risk with combined motor and cognitive training in elderly fallers.' *Brain Sciences,* 7 (2). doi: 10.3390/brainsci7020019.

Campos Mesa, M.C., DelCastillo-Andrés, O., Vázquez, Castañeda, y Toronjo Hornillo, C., and L. (2015). 'Educajudo: Innovación Educativa y de salud en mayores. Aprendiendo a caerse (Yoko-Ukemi).' *RICCAFD,* 4 (3), 1–10. Retrieved from https://idus.us.es/xmlui/bitstream/handle/11441/63673/Educajudo_Innovacion_educativa_y_de_salud_en_mayores_Aprendiendo_a_caerse_Yoko_Ukemi.pdf?sequence=1.

Corral, J.A., Toronjo-Urquiza, T.R.P., and P.J.L. (2015). 'Educajudo como innovación educativa y de salud para personas mayores: Aprendiendo a caerse (Ushiro-Ukemi).'

## 184 *Andrés, Hornillo, Hornillo and Mesa*

In: *Longevidad Y Salud Innovación En La Actividad física*. Malaga (España), 87 Retrieved fromwww.upo.es/aula-mayores/export/sites/aula_abierta_mayores/documentos/2014-1 5/actas_congreso.pdf.

DelCastillo-Andrés, O., Toronjo-Hornillo, L., Castañeda, C., Chacón-Borrego, F., Corral, J.A., González-Campos, G., Portillo, L., Toronjo, T., and Campos-Mesa, M.C. (2015). 'Evaluación del temor a caer tras la aplicación de un programa de Judo Utilitario.' In: *IX Congreso Internacional de la Asociación Española de Ciencias del Deporte*, 465, April, Toled.

Delbaere, K., Close, J., Mikolaizak, S., Sachdev, P, Brodaty, H. and Lord, S. (2010) 'The Falls Efficacy Scale International (FES-I). A comprehensive longitudinal validation study'. *Age and Ageing*, 39 (2), 210–216,

DelCastillo-Andrés, Ó., Toronjo-Hornillo, L., Toronjo-Urquiza, M., Cachón Zagalaz, J., and Campos-Mesa, M. (2018). 'Adapted utilitarian judo: The adaptation of a traditional martial art as a program for the improvement of the quality of life in older adult populations.' *Societies*, 8 (3), 57. doi: 10.3390/soc8030057.

Ersoy, Y., MacWalter, R.S., Durmus, B., Altay, Z.E., and Baysal, O. (2009). 'Predictive effects of different clinical balance measures and the fear of falling on falls in postmenopausal women aged 50 years and over.' *Gerontology*, 55 (6), 660–665.

Garcia-Garcia, F.J., Carcaillon, L. Alfaro, A. and Larrion, J.L. (2014) 'A new operational definition of frailty: The Frailty Trait Scale', *Journal of the American Medical Directors Association*, 15 (5), 371–382.

Hagedorn, D.K., and Holm, E. (2010). 'Effects of traditional physical training and visual computer feedback training in frail elderly patients: A randomized intervention study.' *European Journal of Physical and Rehabilitation Medicine*, 46 (2), 159–168.

Ishigaki, E.Y., Ramos, L.G., Carvalho, E.S., and Lunardi, A.C. (2014). 'Effectiveness of muscle strengthening and description of protocols for preventing falls in the elderly: A systematic review.' *Brazilian Journal of Physical Therapy*, 18 (2), 111–118.

Kalina, R.M., and Mosler, D. (2017). 'Risk of injuries caused by fall of people differing in age, sex, health and motor experience'. In: T. Ahram, ed. *Advances in human factors in sports, injury prevention and outdoor recreation, AHFE 2017:. Advances in intelligent systems and computing, vol. 603*. Cham: Springer, 84–88. doi: 10.1007/978-3-319-60822-8_8.

Kempen, G.I., van Haastregt, J.C., McKee, K.J., Delbaere, K., and Zijlstra, G.R. (2009). 'Socio-demographic, health-related and psychosocial correlates of fear of falling and avoidance of activity in community-living older persons who avoid activity due to fear of falling.' *BMC Public Health*, 9 (1), 170.

Legters, K. (2002) 'Fear of falling', *Physical Therapy*, 82 (3), 264–272.

Moon, Y., and Sosnoff, J.J. (2017). 'Safe landing strategies during a fall: Systematic review and meta-analysis.' *Archives of Physical Medicine and Rehabilitation*, 98 (4), 783–794. doi: 10.1016/j.apmr.2016.08.460.

Myers, A.M., Powell, L.E., Maki, B.E., Holliday, P.J., Brawley, L.R., and Sherk, W. (1996). 'Psychological indicators of balance confidence: Relationship to actual and perceived abilities.' *The Journals of Gerontology – Series A: Biological Sciences and Medical Sciences*, 51A (1), M37–M43. doi: 10.1093/gerona/51A.1.M37.

Pocecco, E., Gatterer, H., Ruedl, G., and Burtscher, M. (2012). 'Specific exercise testing in judo athletes.' *Archives of Budo*, 8 (3), 133–139. doi: 10.12659/AOB.883246.

Sabariego, M., and Bisquerra, R. (2004). *El proceso de investigación*. Retrieved from https://dialnet.unirioja.es/servlet/articulo?codigo=1090804.

Sattin, R.W., Easley, K.A., Wolf, S.L., Chen, Y., and Kutner, M.H. (2005). 'Reduction in fear of falling through intense Tai chi exercise training in older, transitionally frail adults.' *Journal of the American Geriatrics Society*, 53 (7), 1168–1178.

Taira, S., Suárez, J.J., and Montero, M. (2014). *La esencia del judo*. Madrid: Satori.

Tinetti, M.E., Richman, D., and Powell, L. (1990). 'Falls efficacy as a measure of fear of falling.' *Journal of Gerontology*, 45 (6), 239–243. doi: 10.1093/geronj/45.6.P239.

WHO. (2018). 'Fact sheets.' Retrieved from www.who.int/es/news-room/fact-sheets/det ail/falls.

Yardley, L., Beyer, N., Hauer, K., Kempen, G., Piot-Ziegler, C., and Todd, C. (2005). 'Development and initial validation of the Falls Efficacy Scale-International (FES-I).' *Age and Ageing*, 34 (6), 614–619. doi: 10.1093/ageing/afi196.

## Glossary

**Accidental injuries:**   Although in this work the term 'accidental injuries' is used, since it is the term commonly used with respect to falls that occur in at-risk populations, the expression that is suggested as more appropriate is that of 'unintentional injuries.' The second term avoids the burden associated to the word 'accident' as an 'inevitable' event, which implies the idea that we cannot do anything to prevent them.

**Dynamic balance exercises:**   Exercises made to strengthen the balance using dynamic situations. In these exercises the objective is to improve the strength and body position as well as the reactions to imbalances and feelings of instability through the movement of the body and the change of weight distribution.

**Dependence:**   Permanent physical state in which people require the attention of another or other people or important aids to perform basic activities of daily life due to age, illness or disability and linked to the lack or loss of physical, mental, intellectual or sensory autonomy.

**Falls Efficacy Scale-International:**   Instrument that measures the fear of suffering a fall by the older adult, regardless of whether they are physically active. The scale is based on Bandura's theory of self-efficacy (1977), which measures the level of security with which older people perform different basic activities of daily life.

**Fear of Falling:**   Consequence or psychological trauma that results in a decrease in daily activities and a subsequent loss of the functional capacity of the older adult.

**Fragility:**   Clinical-biological syndrome characterised by a decrease in the resistance and physiological reserves of the older adult in stressful situations, as a result of the cumulative wear of physiological systems, causing greater risk of suffering adverse health effects such as falls, disability, hospitalisation, institutionalisation and death.

**Functional displacement exercises:**   In order to maintain the independence and adequacy of the implementation of the BADL, the ability of the older adult to carry out autonomous movements in safety conditions must be taken into account, which implies the change of weight distribution when walking, as well as the modification of the body position and its centre of gravity. For this reason, the inclusion of dynamism and variety in the directions, ways

186 *Andrés, Hornillo, Hornillo and Mesa*

of moving and rhythms, in which movement is practised is essential, so the basic displacements of Judo are used.

**Ju No Kata:** It is a sequence of Judo techniques, which is translated as 'Form of Flexibility.' It is composed of 15 techniques, divided into three groups, in which the application of flexibility to oppose force is taught. It was created by Jigoro Kano in 1887.

**Kagami-migaki:** Its translation from Japanese is 'Polish the mirror.' This movement is part of another Judo Kata, and is performed as part of the functional warm-up, to work on the improvement of coordination, joint mobility of the upper body, bilateralism, concentration, breathing and postural control. It is a movement that starts from an upright posture and with the feet parallel and separated to the width of the shoulders. With the elbows slightly open and the hands together with both palms facing forward, raise the hands in front of the chest and continue upwards, drawing a large circle outward with both hands simultaneously, until they are again in the starting position.

**Kata:** The translation from Japanese is 'shape,' and they are movements grouped in a traditional way that contain the essence of Judo techniques.

**Kime No Kata:** It is the group of movements that contains the traditional personal defence techniques of Judo.

**Nage No Kata:** It is the group of movements that contains the techniques of the fundamental throws of Judo. It consists of 15 throws that are divided into five groups.

**Older adults:** The United Nations considers the population over 60 years of age to be older adults. However, in most developed countries this age is considered to be 65.

**Ukemis:** Break-falling techniques. In Judo, learning how to fall properly is very important so as not to hurt yourself and to be able to progress. In all sessions a part of falls is introduced as part of the warm-up. The break-falling techniques include backwards, to the sides, forward and forward rolling.

**Static balance exercises:** Exercises that have the objective of strengthening the balance from static positions. The main trained elements are strength, body position and knowledge of the sensations that precede the imbalances and instability.

# 14 Physical activity and ageing
## Keep moving!

*Peter Watt and Janus Gudlaugsson*

## Introduction

Promoting healthy lifestyles across a lifespan for all members of a population is an aim for most countries. For the elderly, there are a greater number of factors that need to be considered when compared with children or younger adults. During ageing a high proportion of people will experience physical changes and reduced activity capacity. Common conditions in older age include sensory deficits, musculoskeletal problems, respiratory diseases, diabetes, depression and dementia. Elderly people are more likely to experience several complex health states that occur only later in life, geriatric syndromes – the consequences of multiple underlying factors. Geriatric syndromes are strong predictors of death and may be mitigated by improved health care, including physical activity. This chapter contains information concerning the main issues that affect barriers to, engagement with and adherence to physical activity in the elderly. Examples of interventions to improve activity and health outcomes will be provided with evidence of their effectiveness.

## Background

The world's elderly population is increasing; for example England's number of 80- to 90-year-olds is expected to rise by 50% between 1995 and 2050 (Biley, 2002). Advances in immunisation, hygiene and food supply have led to increased life expectancy in the world, for example, in Japan the elderly population has increased fourfold from 5.7% in 1960 to 23.1% in 2010 (Arai et al., 2012). In addition, the very elderly (aged 75 years and older), often more frail, exceeded 10% of that nation's population in 2008. Post-employment retirement years offer opportunities and new aims to achieve this longevity. To appreciate an ageing population for their value and experience, societies should create conditions where the elderly may enjoy a healthy life, through social participation and contribution (Arai et al., 2012). Evidence will be provided in this chapter from studies related to promoting exercise with the elderly across the world.

Many nations show an increasing elderly population. For example, Iceland, in 1990, had 10% of its population aged 65 years and older, and in 2018 this rose to 13% and predicted to increase to 25% by 2060 (Statistics Iceland, 2015). Alongside demographic changes, disability and associated morbidity have

188    *Peter Watt and Janus Gudlaugsson*

increased shifting health care burden to chronic diseases (e.g. cardiovascular disease and cancer), the dominant causes of disability and mortality in the elderly (Hoffman et al., 1996; Fries et al., 2011). Chronic non-communicable diseases cause 86% of all deaths in the EU and 65% worldwide, and it is expected that the number of elderly persons with functional limitations and disability will increase due to the growing number of very old individuals (WHO, 2015 and 2018).

Health promotion interventions may provide effective solutions to address the issues. Older adults use healthcare services regularly; their physicians represent key social influence, information and direction and should offer opportunities for primary prevention, such as promoting an active lifestyle (van der Bij et al., 2002). This is an effective approach and measured changes in physical activity (PA) and short-term changes occur to health care costs when adults initiated a physically active lifestyle (Martinson et al 2003). Increased PA imparts benefits across the lifespan and affects financial aspects of health promotion programmes, and, when implemented, whether aimed at improving nutrition and/or increasing PA, they have shown significant savings in terms of reduced absenteeism and medical costs (van Dongen et al., 2011).

The health benefits of PA are clear, but there are barriers to engaging in PA, especially among older people and those who are less likely to meet public health goals for sustained activity. Enabling older people to start and adhere to regular exercise poses particular challenges. Many barriers for activity are attitudinal and concern psychological components, such as confidence, perceived exercise enjoyment and satisfaction in PA intervention programmes specifically designed for this age group (Ory et al., 2002). If not addressed, loss of independence occurs at many levels; mobility-related impairment, especially in the lower extremity, is the most critical factor for the elderly and is predictive of future hospitalisation and disability in non-disabled individuals (Penninx et al., 2000; Ross et al., 2013). Independent older individuals may be able to carry out many everyday tasks successfully, but not always in a safe manner, often unable to respond when losing balance, leading to a fall (Rantanen, 2003). Many older individuals consider the capacity to carry out activities of daily living safely (i.e. functional independence) to be of greater concern than prevention of disease (Paterson et al., 2004). Moreover, the health-related quality of life and life expectancy of individuals who live in a dependent state, e.g. full-time care home, are greatly reduced (Paterson and Warburton, 2010). It is clear that even the weakest members of an older population can respond favourably to exercise and PA; fitness remains essential in older age for an independent lifestyle (Chodzko-Zajko et al., 2009). Understanding the role of PA and fitness in altering ageing-related changes in health and function has important public health implications, especially for meeting the needs of the growing population of older adults.

## Ageing and the benefits of regular physical activity

Physical activity is any movement that substantially increases energy expenditure. This includes leisure-time PA, exercise, sport, transportation, occupational

## Physical activity and ageing 189

work and chores. Exercise, a subset of PA, is planned PA, structured, repetitive and purposive to improve or maintain one or more components of physical fitness as an objective (Garber et al., 2011). The goals of an exercise programme are likely to be different for elderly adults compared with younger adults. In the elderly, PA is about maintaining activity and health, whereas in the young it may be more likely to achieve goals such as maximum or near-maximum capacity in terms of endurance, strength and power, flexibility and agility (Cunningham et al., 2013).

Despite the importance of exercise for healthy ageing more than 50% of those 65 to 74 years old and almost 66% of those over the age of 75 years reported no leisure-time PA. Inactivity is more likely as a person ages and inactivity increases more in high-income countries (Hallal et al., 2012).

In a study of PA patterns and sedentary behaviour in older Icelandic adults, it was found that 74.5% of their non-sleeping time was sedentary and 21.3% was low-light activity (Arnadottir et al., 2013). Most older adults do not meet general recommendations for PA (Nelson et al., 2007). The American College of Sports Medicine (ACSM) Position Stand, 'Exercise and Physical Activity for Older Adults,' provided a strong starting point regarding the evidence for benefits of regular exercise training and PA for older adults (Chodzko-Zajko et al., 2009). There is also a growing body of evidence for the prescription of exercise and physical activity for older adults with chronic diseases and disabilities (Nelson et al., 2007).

### Endurance training

Aerobic training, or cardiorespiratory endurance training (ET), helps resist fatigue and leads to better central and peripheral blood flow. It is often measured as the maximal oxygen consumption or $VO_{2max}$, which may help set suitable exercise programmes (Spina et al., 1997). ET programmes set at an intensity of $\geq 60\%$ of pre-training $VO_{2max}$, for three days a week or more, lasting 16 weeks or more, significantly increase $VO_{2max}$ in healthy middle-aged and older adults; improvements in $VO_{2max}$ are observed with longer training periods (20 to 30 weeks) (Huang et al 2005). In healthy subjects older than 75 years of age, ET has also shown to be effective in increases of $VO_{2max}$, but the magnitude of improvement was significantly less in participants older than 75 (Malbut et al., 2002).

ET also affects metabolic factors to improve glyceamic control and diabetes risk and reduce atherogenic lipids (low-density lipoproteins, LDL) from circulation (Katsanos, 2006; Sillanpaa et al., 2009). The scale of effect on metabolic control depends on the training intensity; moderate- and high-intensity ETs increase glucose metabolism in the muscles of older people, but higher-intensity endurance programmes result in greater improvements in whole-body insulin action (DiPietro et al., 2006).

Three months or more of moderate-intensity ET, at $\sim 60\%$ of $VO_{2max}$, induced cardiovascular adaptations in healthy older adults, which may be seen at rest and in response to acute dynamic exercise, consistently lowering heart

190 *Peter Watt and Janus Gudlaugsson*

rate at rest (Huang et al., 2005). During submaximal exercises, smaller rises of systolic, diastolic and mean blood pressures during submaximal exercise improved vasodilator and $O_2$ uptake capacities of trained muscle groups and cardioprotective effects (Wray et al., 2006). These include reductions in atherogenic (blocked arteries) risk factors, artery stiffness, improved endothelial and baroreflex function (vessel flow) and increased vagal tone (autonomic nervous system) (Okazaki et al., 2005).

For weight management, overweight older adults may reduce total body fat after moderate-intensity ET ($\geq$ 60% of $VO_{2max}$), without dietary modification. Average losses of 0.4 to 3.2 kg of fat (1–4% of total body weight) were positively related to the number of exercise sessions (Kay et al., 2006; Greendale et al., 2000).

### Resistance training

Resistance training (RT) increases strength, power and muscular endurance. Muscle power is the product of force and velocity whilst strength is a measure of maximum force. RT in older people increases one repetition maximum (1RM) or 3RM performance by 25% to greater than 100% (Ochala et al., 2005; Carmeli et al., 2000).

Functional gains are better measured as power, relevant for day-to-day activities, than strength in older adults (Foldvari et al., 2000). Age-related loss of muscle power occurs at a greater rate than the loss of strength, most likely due to a disproportionate reduction in the size of faster-contracting Type II muscle fibres (Skelton et al, 1995; Klein et al., 2003). Substantial increases in power may still occur after RT in older adults; higher-velocity training protocols have led to gains in power that are comparable or greater than gains in maximum strength (Fielding et al., 2002; Newton et al., 2002).

Moderate- or high-intensity RT may decrease total body fat mass (FM), by 1.6–3.4%, and there may be sex-specific effects: elderly women lost 12% of intra-abdominal adipose tissue (IAAT) and 6% of subcutaneous adipose tissue (SAT) after 25 weeks of moderate-intensity (65–80% of 1RM) (Treuth et al., 1995).

### Physical performance and ageing

Balance is important when stationary or moving for older adults' activities and daily living. Older people have an increased risk of falling, especially frail older adults with a previous fall history (Spirduso et al., 2005). Higher levels of PA, particularly walking, leads to a 30–50% reduction in the risk of osteoporotic fractures (Gillespie et al., 2003). Lower body strength training and walking over difficult or uneven terrain improves balance and are recommended as a part of an exercise training intervention to reduce falls (Booth et al., 1994; Gillespie et al., 2003). Older individuals at the highest risk of falls benefit more from an individually tailored exercise training programme within a larger, multifactorial falls-prevention intervention (Day et al 2002). Training programmes of strength, flexibility, walking and balance all reduce the risk of injurious and non-injurious falls (Tinetti et al., 1994; Norton et al., 2001).

### Physical activity and quality of life

Quality of life (QoL) describes satisfaction with multiple aspects of life and is measured using self-report inventories, for example Satisfaction with Life-Scale (Diener, 1984; Pavot et al., 1991). PA is positively associated with many, but not all, domains of QoL. Significant increases in self-efficacy and improvements in health-related QoL are most likely to occur and benefits for social function, such as adjusting to changing roles and responsibilities associated with growing older (Phillips et al., 2012). A major benefit of PA is empowerment to undertake a more active role in society, providing opportunities to widen social networks; stimulate new friendships; and acquire positive new roles in retirement.

### Nutrition

Nutrition is intimately linked to ageing and PA and is a core element for effective outcomes for the elderly population. Energy expenditure is the amount of fuel (calories/Joules) used to live and be physically active. To prevent weight gain, energy intake should be balanced to energy expended (Roberts and Dallal, 2005). Total and resting energy requirements decrease progressively with age, largely due to decreases in PA and reduced muscle mass, so fewer calories are needed to maintain weight (Pannemans and Westerterp, 1994). Physical inactivity lowers energy requirements directly, by reducing energy expenditure and a decline in basal metabolic rate due to loss of lean mass. The loss of lean mass, muscle in particular, with gains of total body fat and visceral fat content continue into late life, is termed sarcopenia and has consequences for function mobility and metabolic requirements and responses (Evans, 2004). Information provided should be based on national or international public health guidance for older individuals, i.e. WHO, including the importance of fruit and vegetable consumption, wholegrain bread and other cereal rich in fibre, dairy products containing low quantities of fat, cod-liver oil or other vitamin D product and water, foodstuff proportions, fish, meat, salt consumption, oils, saturated and unsaturated fats. Care should be taken in recommending increased consumption of supplements without sufficient evidence of inadequacies or effectiveness of the regime from randomised controlled studies. Recent reviews concluded that combining exercise with oral nutritional supplements or increased protein intake (to around 1.2 g protein/kg per day) may provide some additional improvements to muscle strength but there were no effects on measures of physical function, nutritional status or morbidity in nutritionally vulnerable older adults (Wright and Baldwin, 2018). Recent evidence suggests that there is little benefit of increasing protein intake above recommended levels for bone health in healthy adults (Darling et al., 2019). Likewise, extra protein alone does not seem to be warranted for treatment of sarcopenia or muscle weakness (Millward, 2014).

## PA and older adults: Effective intervention evidence

To be effective exercise training programmes should be based on evidence from good, reproducible studies to provide planned programmes and measures for individuals, groups or populations to change, improve or increase their PA producing positive health outcomes. Intervention programmes aim to increase PA or focus on physiological changes to fitness, strength or quality of life as a consequence of participation. The changes lead to health improvements, reduced risk of developing coronary heart disease, improved mood or quality of life (see figure 14.1 adapted from Bouchard et al., 2012).

As a starting point, walking is effective for encouraging PA; however, strength training is also important and requires either specialist facilities or creative use of household items and local facilities (van der Bij et al., 2002). The most effective interventions are multilevel, with community support, individually tailored programmes addressing balance, gait and falls risks.

A summary of evidence-based guidelines for PA in older adults was produced in the ACSM Position Stand 'Exercise and Physical Activity for Older Adults' (Chodzko-Zajko et al., 2009). An intervention of 150 minutes of walking and complementary strengthening, stretching and balance exercises per week reduced risks of major mobility impairment and improved chair-rise ability, standing balance and walking speed compared to a control group (Pahor et al., 2006). Other studies investigating multi-component exercise training have found positive results on functional and mobility outcomes relative to people not involved in the PA intervention (Shumway-Cook et al., 2007; Nelson et al., 2004), and a systematic review of 29 randomised clinical trials found high adherence to the intervention and that facility-alone strategies were less effective than those home-based or supervised home-based interventions (King et al., 1998).

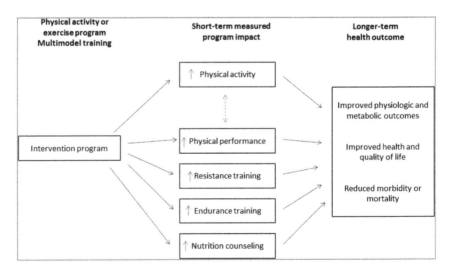

*Figure 14.1* Range of outcomes of an intervention program, including both the behaviour of being physically active and more physiologic outcomes.

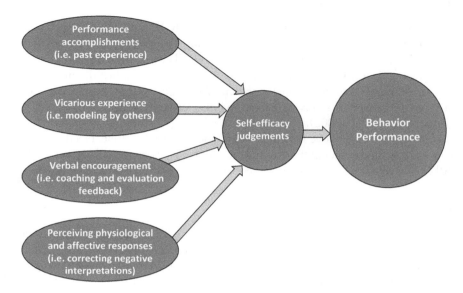

*Figure 14.2* Behaviour performance, adapted from Bandura (2004).

Vand der Bij et al. (2002) also evaluated the effect of education or counselling interventions in promoting PA; all reported short-term (five months to one year) significant increases in PA. Counselling may provide for better engagement in PA; improved participation rates may be achieved when incorporated in short-term PA interventions; however, long-term studies have not shown greater adherence. More effective approaches for maintaining exercise participation are necessary (Taylor et al., 2004). Self-efficacy is an important determinant of PA behaviour and peer support, especially for individuals who are uncertain of their ability, may help engagement (Bandura, 2004).

### Evidence from an applied study

A national implementation of a multimodal training counselling intervention was provided to elderly volunteers in Iceland. Measured outcomes were relevant to real-life situations, such as walking, strength and mobility, independence and quality of life.

The intervention provided:

- Six months intervention in the form of endurance, strength classes and advisory information on health issues (e.g. nutrition)
- Information about the issues of PA in older age
- Ideas for sustainable, long-term training plans to meet international recommendations for PA

## The intervention programme

The intervention programme took place with daily ET and twice-a-week RT, supported by at least six lectures over the six-month intervention, two or three on nutrition and four on healthy ageing, ET, RT and how to train. It was designed to increase PA and affect physiological measures of fitness and health. Such exercise programmes may be the major source of vigorous activity for participants, and such programmes motivate people to consider being generally more active (Tudor-Locke et al., 2002).

The aim was to improve health, physical function, quality of life, blood pressure and lipid profiles, reducing the risk of coronary heart disease (Guðlaugsson et al., 2012). The following sections describe each discipline of the training intervention.

## Endurance training

Aerobic exercise training consisted of daily walking, swimming, cycling or other activity that challenged the cardiovascular system to increase breathing and heart rate. The duration of the training session was increased progressively as this promotes the supercompensation and adaptation to a progressive exercise programme (Bompa and Haff, 2009).

Heart rate was monitored to help target each individual's work during the training sessions. In week one participants trained for 20 minutes at each session, seven days a week on a 400-metre running track. The duration was increased with two recovery weeks at weeks 9 and 18. The average walking duration per day, over the programme, was 34 minutes. An instructor was present for all sessions for the first and final eight weeks but only once per week in weeks 9 to 18. Other sessions were self-administered, following the training intervention plan from the programme. Participants were instructed in how to use the Karvonen formula to find target heart rate (Karvonen and Vourimaa, 1988).

Calculation:

$$\text{Target heart rate} = (220 - \text{age}) - \text{resting heart rate}$$
$$\times \text{intensity required} + \text{resting heart rate}$$

Example: age 60, resting heart rate 76 bpm, for 50% intensity.

$$220 - 60 = 160$$

$$160 - 76 = 84 \left(\text{heart rate reserve} - \text{HRR}\right)$$

$$50\% \text{ of } 84 = 42.$$

Target heart rate $= 76 + 42 = 118$ bpm during exercise.

Exercise intensity was set at 50–60% for the first eight weeks, then increased to 60% for 10 weeks and 70% for the final eight weeks.

## Resistance training

RT occurred twice a week, separated by two days using circuit series strength equipment. Participants were trained to use equipment by one or more health instructors for the first three to four months. RT comprised 8 to 12 exercises for all major muscle groups; load was based on performance in initial sessions focusing on resistance–endurance training for the first three months, shifting to strength-power for the final three months.

Exercises included leg press, leg extensions and calf raises, bench press, chest cross, shoulder press, pull downs, biceps curls and triceps extensions. There were also exercises for abdominal muscles and the back. For the first two weeks the training programme consisted of two sets of ten repetitions (2 × 10) at 50% of one-repetition maximum (1RM). Every two weeks the load was increased by two repetitions at each station. In the 13th week the repetitions increased to 18 in two sets. After six weeks, two weeks of no exercise were included. The aim of the first 13 weeks was to accustom the participants to new exercises and techniques, to educate them about the importance of sessions and prepare them for power training. For the power training programme intensity was increased from 2 × 10 RM in the 14th week to 4 × 6 RM by the 24th week. The participants took a one-and-a-half-minute rest between each set. The 9th and 18th weeks included no resistance training and 20 minutes of ET every day.

## Lectures and nutrition counselling

The exercise training intervention programme was supported by seven lectures covering healthy ageing, ET, RT, how to exercise, and three lectures on nutrition. The lectures provided information on the frequency of the ET and RT, when group training occurred, the duration of the training and the intensity setting of the training. Subsequent lectures considered the benefits of regular ET and its effect on preventing health problems. Emphasis was placed on daily walking and guidance on appropriate intensity, frequency and duration of ET. For RT, issues such as safe lifting and the importance of strength and power for effectiveness were emphasised. Further content targeted the ageing process and how to optimise successful ageing, regular effective PA and quality of life for frail and elderly people.

## Results from the training intervention

- Older adults improved functional performance, increased strength and endurance after the intervention.
- Short physical performance battery tests, six-minute walk test and 8 foot up and go test scores improved after the intervention.
- BMI decreased; lean body mass increased over the intervention time period and was sustained at 12 months after the start of the intervention.
- Blood triglycerides and blood pressure decreased from the initial measures.

## 196 Peter Watt and Janus Gudlaugsson

- Quality of life improved over the six-month intervention.
- The group maintained the improvements over 12 months afterwards, without further intervention from practitioners.

## Summary of recommendations for PA in older adults

The planning and individualised delivery of holistic approaches, with input and involvement of participants, are likely to lead to better outcomes, engagement and adherence. All participants should be aware of the aims of the project, given the opportunity to discuss individual issues and any special aims. The philosophy for implementation should take into account behaviour change, supporting structures and materials, self-efficacy and outcome expectations. The continuous supply of information and rationale to exercise type and intensity relative to participant needs are also key factors in successful interventions for the long-term health of older adults.

## References

Arai, H., Ouchi, Y., Yokode, M., Ito, H., Uematsu, H., Eto, F., Oshima, S., Ota, K., Saito, Y., Sasaki, Y., Tsubota, K., Fukuyama, H., Honda, Y., Iguchi, A., Toba, K., Hosoi, T., and Kita, Ti. (2012). 'Toward the realization of a better aged society: Messages from gerontology and geriatrics.' *Geriatrics and Gerontology International*, 12 (1), 16–22.

Bandura, A. (2004). 'Health promotion by social cognitive means.' *Health Education and Behaviour*, 31 (2), 143–164.

Biley, A. (2002) 'National service framework for older people: promoting health.' *British Journal of Nursing*, 11 (7), 121–130.

Bompa, T., and Haff, G. (2009). *Periodization and methodology of training*. Vol. 3. Champaign, IL: Human Kinetics.

Booth, F.W., Weeden, S.H., and Tseng, B.S. (1994). 'Effect of aging on human skeletal muscle and motor function.' *Medicine and Science in Sports and Exercise*, 26 (5), 556–560.

Bouchard, C., Blair, S.N., and Haskell, W.L. (2012). *Physical activity and health*. Champaign, IL: Human Kinetics.

Carmeli, E., Reznick, A.Z., Coleman, R., and Carmeli, V. (2000). 'Muscle strength and mass of lower extremities in relation to functional abilities in elderly adults.' *Gerontology*, 46 (5), 249–257.

Chodzko-Zajko, W.J., Proctor, D.N., Fiatarone Singh, M.A., Minson, C., Nigg, C., Salam, G., and Skinner, J.S. (2009). 'American College of Sports Medicine position stand: Exercise and physical activity for older adults.' *Medicine and Science in Sports and Exercise*, 41 (7), 1510–1530.

Cunningham, M.A., Carroll, D.D., Carlson, S.A., and Fulton, J. (2013). 'Awareness and knowledge of the 2008 physical activity guidelines for Americans.' *Journal of Physical Activity and Health*, 11 (4), 693–698.

Darling, A., Manders, R., Sahni, S., Zhu, K., Hewitt, C., Prince, R., Millward, D., and Lanham-New, S. (2019). 'Dietary protein and bone health across the life-course: An updated systematic review and meta-analysis over 40 years.' *Osteoporosis International*, 30 (4), 741–761. doi: 10.1007/s00198-019-04933-8.

Day, L., Fildes, B., Gordon, I., Fitzharris, M., Flamer, H., and Lord, S. (2002). 'Randomised factorial trial of falls prevention among older people living in their own homes.' *British Medical Journal*, 325 (7356), 128.

Diener, E. (1984). 'Subjective well-being.' *Psychological Bulletin*, 95 (3), 542–575.

DiPietro, L., Dziura, J., Yeckel, C., and Neufer, P. (2006). 'Exercise and improved insulin sensitivity in older women: Evidence of the enduring benefits of higher intensity training.' *Journal of Applied Physiology*, 100 (1), 142–149.

Evans, W. (2004). 'Protein nutrition, exercise and aging.' *Journal of the American College of Nutrition*, 23 (6 Suppl), 601S–609S.

Fielding, R., LeBrasseur, N., Cuoco, A., Bean, J., Mizer, K., and Fiatarone Singh, M. (2002). 'High-velocity resistance training increases skeletal muscle peak power in older women.' *Journal of American Geriatrics Society*, 50 (4), 655–662.

Foldvari, M., Clark, M., Laviolette, L., Bernstein, M., Kaliton, D., Castaneda, C., Pu, C., Hausdorf, J., Fielding, R., and Singh, M. (2000). 'Association of muscle power with functional status in community-dwelling elderly women.' *The Journals of Gerontology:. Series A, Biological Sciences and Medical Sciences*, 55 (4), 192–199.

Fries, J., Bruce, B., and Chakravarty, E. (2011). 'Compression of morbidity 1980–2011: A focused review of paradigms and progress.' *Journal of Ageing Research*, Article, 56, 34–44. 261702.

Garber, C., Blissmer, B., Deschenes, M., Franklin, B., Lamonte, M., Lee, I., Nieman, D., and Swain, D. (2011). 'American College of Sports Medicine position stand: Quantity and quality of exercise for developing and maintaining cardiorespiratory, musculoskeletal, and neuromotor fitness in apparently healthy adults: Guidance for prescribing exercise.' *Medicine and Science in Sports and Exercise*, 43 (7), 1334–1359.

Gillespie, L., Gillespie, W., Robertson, M., Lamb, S., Cumming, R., and Rowe, B. (2003). 'Interventions for preventing falls in elderly people.' *Cochrane Database of Systematic Reviews*, 4, CD000340.

Greendale, G., Salem, G., Young, J., Damesyn, M., Marion, M., Wang, M., and Reuben, D. (2000). 'A randomized trial of weighted vest use in ambulatory older adults: Strength, performance, and quality of life outcomes.' *Journal of American Geriatrics Society*, 48 (3), 305–311.

Guðlaugsson, J., Guðnason, V., Aspelund, T., Siggeirsdottir, K., Olafsdottir, A., Jonsson, P., Arngrimsson, S., Harris, T., and Johannsson, E. (2012). 'Effects of a 6-month multimodal training intervention on retention of functional fitness in older adults: A randomized-controlled cross-over design.' *International Journal of Behavioural Nutrition and Physical Activity*, 9 (1), 107.

Hallal, P., Andersen, L., Bull, F., Guthold, R., Haskell, W., and Ekelund, U. (2012). 'Global physical activity levels: Surveillance progress, pitfalls, and prospects.' *Lancet*, 380 (9838), 247–257.

Hoffman, C., Rice, D., and Sung, H. (1996). 'Persons with chronic conditions: Their prevalence and costs.' *JAMA*, 276 (18), 1473–1479.

Huang, G., Gibson, C., Tran, Z., and Osness, W. (2005). 'Controlled endurance exercise training and VO2max changes in older adults: A meta-analysis.' *Preventative Cardiology*, 8 (4), 217–225.

Huang, G., Shi, X., Davis-Brezette, J., and Osness, W. (2005). 'Resting heart rate changes after endurance training in older adults: A meta-analysis.' *Medicine and Science in Sports and Exercise*, 37 (8), 1381–1386.

Karvonen, J., and Vuorimaa, T. (1988). 'Heart rate and exercise intensity during sports activities: Practical application.' *Sports Medicine*, 5 (5), 303–311.

Katsanos, C. (2006). 'Prescribing aerobic exercise for the regulation of postprandial lipid metabolism: Current research and recommendations.' *Sports Medicine*, 36 (7), 547–560.

Kay, S., and Fiatarone Singh, M. (2006). 'The influence of physical activity on abdominal fat: A systematic review of the literature.' *Obesity Reviews*, 7 (2), 183–200.

King, A., Rejeski, W., and Buchner, D. (1998). 'Physical activity interventions targeting older adults: A critical review and recommendations.' *American Journal of Preventative Medicine*, 15 (4), 316–333.

Klein, C., Marsh, G., Petrella, R., and Rice, C. (2003). 'Muscle fiber number in the biceps brachii muscle of young and old men.' *Muscle and Nerve*, 28 (1), 62–68.

Malbut, K., Dinan, S., and Young, A. (2002). 'Aerobic training in the oldest old': The effect of 24 weeks of training.' *Age and Ageing*, 31 (4), 255–260.

Martinson, B., Crain, A., Pronk, N., O'Connor, P., and Maciosek, M. (2003). 'Changes in physical activity and short-term changes in health care charges: A prospective cohort study of older adults.' *Preventative Medicine*, 37 (4), 319–326.

Millward, D.J. (2014). 'Protein requirements and aging.' *American Journal of Clinical Nutrition*, 100 (4), 1210–1212.

Nelson, M., Layne, J., Bernstein, M., Nuernberger, A., Castaneda, C., Kaliton, D., Hausdorff, J., Judge, J., Buchner, D., Roubenoff, R., and Fiatarone Singh, M. (2004). 'The effects of multidimensional home-based exercise on functional performance in elderly people.' *The Journals of Gerontology. Series A, Biological Sciences and Medical Sciences*, 59 (2), 154–160.

Nelson, M., Rejeski, W., Blair, S., Duncan, P., Judge, J., King, A., Macera, C., and Castaneda-Sceppa, C. (2007). 'Physical activity and public health in older adults: Recommendation from the American College of Sports Medicine and the American Heart Association.' *Medicine and Science in Sports and Exercise*, 39 (8), 1435–1445.

Newton, R., Hakkinen, K., Hakkinen, A., McCormick, M., Volek, J., and Kraemer, W. (2002). 'Mixed-methods resistance training increases power and strength of young and older men.' *Medicine and Science in Sports and Exercise*, 34 (8), 1367–1375.

Norton, R., Galgali, G., Campbell, A., Reid, I., Robinson, E., Butler, M., and Gray, H. (2001). 'Is physical activity protective against hip fracture in frail older people?' *Age and Ageing*, 30 (3), 262–264.

Ochala, J., Lambertz, D., Van Hoecke, J., and Pousson, M. (2005). 'Effect of strength training on musculotendinous stiffness in elderly individuals.' *European Journal of Applied Physiology*, 94 (1–2), 126–133.

Okazaki, K., Iwasaki, K., Prasad, A., Palmer, M., Martini, E., Fu, Q., Arbab-Zadeh, A., Zhang, R., and Levine, B. (2005). 'Dose-response relationship of endurance training for autonomic circulatory control in healthy seniors.' *Journal of Applied Physiology*, 99 (3), 1041–1049.

Ory, M., Jordan, P., and Bazzarre, T. (2002). 'The Behavior Change Consortium: Setting the stage for a new century of health behavior-change research.' *Health Education Research*, 17 (5), 500–511.

Pahor, M., Blair, S., Espeland, M., Fielding, R., Gill, T., Guralnik, J., Hadley, E., King, A., Kritchevsky, S., Maraldi, C., Miller, M., Newman, A., Rejeski, W., Romashkan, S., and Studenski, S. (2006). 'Effects of a physical activity intervention on measures of physical performance: Results of the lifestyle interventions and independence for Elders Pilot (LIFE-P) study.' *The Journals of Gerontology. Series A*, 61 (11), 1157–1165.

Pannemans, D., and Westerterp, K. (1994). 'Energy expenditure, physical activity and basal metabolic rate of elderly subjects.' *British Journal of Nutrition*, 73 (4), 571–581.

Paterson, D., Govindasamy, D., Vidmar, M., Cunningham, D., and Koval, J. (2004). 'Longitudinal study of determinants of dependence in an elderly population.' *Journal of American Geriatrics Society*, 52 (10), 1632–1638.

Paterson, D., and Warburton, D. (2010). 'Physical activity and functional limitations in older adults: A systematic review related to Canada's Physical Activity Guidelines.' *International Journal of Behavioural Nutrition and Physical Activity*, 7, 38.

Pavot, W., Diener, E., Colvin, C., and Sandvik, E. (1991). 'Further validation of the Satisfaction with Life Scale: Evidence for the cross-method convergence of well-being measures.' *Journal of Personality Assessment*, 57 (1), 149–161.

Penninx, B., Ferrucci, L., Leveille, S., Rantanen, T., Pahor, M., and Guralnik, J. (2000). 'Lower extremity performance in nondisabled older persons as a predictor of subsequent hospitalization.' *The Journals of Gerontology. Series A, Biological Sciences and Medical Sciences*, 55 (11):M691–697.

Phillips, S., Wojcicki, T., and McAuley, E. (2012). 'Physical activity and quality of life in older adults: An 18-month panel analysis.' *Quality of Life Research*, 22 (7), 1647–1654.

Rantanen, T. (2003). 'Muscle strength, disability and mortality.' *Scandinavian Journal of Medicine and Science in Sports*, 13 (1), 3–8.

Roberts, S., and Dallal, G. (2005). 'Energy requirements and aging.' *Public Health Nutrition*, 8 (7A), 1028–1036.

Ross, L., Schmidt, E., and Ball, K. (2013). 'Interventions to maintain mobility: What works?' *Accident Analysis and Prevention*, 61, 167–196.

Shumway-Cook, A., Silver, I., LeMier, M., York, S., Cummings, P., and Koepsell, T. (2007). 'Effectiveness of a community-based multifactorial intervention on falls and fall risk factors in community-living older adults: A randomized, controlled trial.' *The Journals of Gerontology. Series A, Biological Sciences and Medical Sciences*, 62 (12), 1420–1427.

Sillanpaa, E., Hakkinen, A., Punnonen, K., Hakkinen, K., and Laaksonen, D. (2009). 'Effects of strength and endurance training on metabolic risk factors in healthy 40–65-year-old men.' *Scandinavian Journal of Medicine and Science in Sports*, 19 (6), 885–895.

Skelton, D., Young, A., Greig, C., and Malbut, K. (1995). 'Effects of resistance training on strength, power, and selected functional abilities of women aged 75 and older.' *Journal of American Geriatrics Society*, 43 (10), 1081–1087.

Spina, R., Turner, M., and Ehsani, A. (1997). 'Exercise training enhances cardiac function in response to an afterload stress in older men.' *American Journal of Physiology*, 272 (2 Pt 2), 995–1000.

Spirduso, W., Francis, K., and MacRae, P. (2005). *Physical dimensions of aging*. Champaign, IL: Human Kinetics.

Statistics Iceland. (2015). 'Census figures.' www.statice.is/Statistics/Population.

Taylor, A., Cable, N., Faulkner, G., Hillsdon, M., Narici, M., and Van Der Bij, A. (2004). 'Physical activity and older adults: A review of health benefits and the effectiveness of interventions.' *Journal of Sport Sciences*, 22 (8), 703–725.

Tinetti, M., Baker, D., McAvay, G., Claus, E., Garrett, P., Gottschalk, M., Koch, M., Trainor, K.., and Horwitz, R. (1994). 'A multifactorial intervention to reduce the risk of falling among elderly people living in the community.' *The New England Journal of Medicine*, 331 (13), 821–827.

Treuth, M., Hunter, G., Weinsier, R., and Kell, S. (1995). 'Energy expenditure and substrate utilization in older women after strength training: 24-h calorimeter results.' *Journal of Applied Physiology*, 78 (6), 2140–2146.

Tudor-Locke, C., Jones, R., Myers, A., Paterson, D., and Ecclestone, N. (2002). 'Contribution of structured exercise class participation and informal walking for exercise to daily physical activity in community-dwelling older adults.' *Research Quarterly for Exercise and Sport*, 73 (3), 350–356.

van der Bij, A., Laurant, M., and Wensing, M. (2002). 'Effectiveness of physical activity interventions for older adults: A review.' *American Journal of Preventative Medicine*, 22 (2), 120–133.

van Dongen, J., Proper, K., van Wier, M., van der Beek, A., Bongers, P., van Mechelen, W., and van Tulder, M. (2011). 'Systematic review on the financial return of worksite health promotion programmes aimed at improving nutrition and/or increasing physical activity.' *Obesity Reviews*, 12 (12), 1031–1049.

WHO. (2015). *World report on ageing and health*. ISBN 978 92 4 069479 8 (epub).

WHO. (2018). www.who.int/news-room/fact-sheets/detail/ageing-and-health.

Wray, D., Uberoi, A., Lawrenson, L., and Richardson, R. (2006). 'Evidence of preserved endothelial function and vascular plasticity with age.' *American Journal of Physiology. Heart and Circulatory Physiology*, 290 (3):H1271–1277.

Wright, J., and Baldwin, C. (2018). 'Oral nutritional support with or without exercise in the management of malnutrition in nutritionally vulnerable older people: A systematic review and meta-analysis.' *Clinical Nutrition*, 37 (6 Pt A), 1879–1891.

# Concluding thoughts and future considerations

*James Wallis and John Lambert*

This book has presented diverse examples of interventions and case studies, all of which demonstrate the centrality of the person within the coaching process. Each chapter communicates many of the considerations and challenges to coaches and significant others involved in the design and delivery of sport or physical activity programmes for populations with specific needs. Our concluding thoughts attempt to draw together, for the benefit of coaches and the profession as a whole, some of the recurring themes that resonate throughout the text. In doing so our intention is to focus on the transferability of knowledge across different contexts and to offer some recommendations for future practice that we hope readers will recognise as key to future planning and delivery. The final section takes a broader macro-view of issues for the future direction of coach education in evolving to meet the demands of coaches working across diverse contexts and to ultimately suggest ways that it might better meet the performance, health and physical activity needs of *all* participants.

## Considerations for coaches

We have been fortunate to gather contributors to this book from such an array of different backgrounds and who have coached, led and researched a diverse range of populations in varying settings. It is hoped that our readers, be they coaches, coaching students or other interested parties from the world of coaching, have learned important lessons from each chapter and been guided by the know-how of each author. There are some common threads that run through the book which are worth reflecting upon at this stage.

It is clear that every coach needs a working knowledge of the group of people that they are working with. Whilst it is obvious that nobody should attempt to run a session with, for instance, a cancer rehabilitation group without prior information on each recipient, it is not always apparent to coaches that they need to gain knowledge of the population that they are working with. For example, up and down the land there are enthusiastic 'amateur' coaches running sessions for children with scant knowledge of the appropriate motivational climate that they should be creating or the pedagogical approach that is suitable for that group of children.

Another recurring theme across each chapter was the empathy that each author has for the recipients of their work and the need to relate to individual members of the group. In other words, to understand what it would be like 'to be in their shoes.' The applied psychologists Deci and Ryan (2000), in their research on Self-Determination Theory (SDT), discuss 'relatedness' as one of the key determinants of intrinsic motivation in humans. The importance of 'interacting with, connecting to and experience caring' is apparent in all chapters in this book, and the most effective coaches at all levels have this relatedness in abundance.

To some extent, it is understandable that inexperienced coaches may get obsessed with structure and 'content' knowledge as they may feel more secure in a controlling situation, but they need to be guided to take the next step to where they begin to identify the discrete needs of each individual and of the group as a whole; whether it be a young child in need of reassurance, an elderly person requiring words of encouragement or a group of adult refugees who seek a welcoming smile.

Coaches need to develop in an environment of 'emotional safety' with a supportive mentor so that they feel able to take risks, seek advice and gain constructive feedback. They need to understand how challenging it may be working with certain groups and that mistakes are likely to be made. The editors speak from experience, having implemented a values-based coaching methodology through translator/co-coaches with children who could only speak Arabic and Hebrew during a sport for peaceful co-existence projects in Israel. Apart from the significant political, cultural and social barriers between the Arab and Jewish children, there were language barriers to overcome. In that difficult context we needed to show resilience, patience, adaptability and humility, all valuable qualities for every coach.

Our experience on the 'Football for Peace' project demonstrated the necessity of engaging with agencies that have greater experience with and knowledge of the population that the coach is working with. In this case it was local coaches, administrators, youth workers and parents who offered some useful insights into individuals and the group as a whole. For example, the coaches from the United Kingdom were taught key Hebrew and Arabic phrases that would help them connect directly with the children as the sharing of language provides an important cultural bond in that context. The majority of chapters in this text have stressed the importance of gaining an understanding of the specific population from agencies working within or outside the coaching setting.

A shift from a coach-/sport-centred to a person-centred perspective was an important move, particularly in a sport for development setting (Lambert, 2013). As we gradually empowered the children and local coaches, they bought into the aims of the project to a far greater extent. Equity and inclusion, respect and responsibility were central values to the project. The young participants were given responsibility for organising the team selection and substitutions in a fair way and to referee their own games. This strategy gave them an opportunity to demonstrate all of the core values. This coaching method has synergy with Deci

*Concluding thoughts, future considerations* 203

and Ryan's notion of 'autonomy-support,' that is another key factor in developing intrinsic motivation in people.

Coaches are often highly regarded by participants and can be very influential. It is imperative that the coach models those values that they wish to cultivate within their particular situation (Lambert, 2013). We were working at 30°C heat in Israel, and one of the local coaches was offered water, but he refused unless it was also available to all of his players. If a coach places emphasis on equity and inclusion, it is advisable to try and give equal attention to each individual in the group and be seen to be fair to everyone. People learn not only from what coaches say but also from what they do.

This brings us on to our final and most important consideration for coaches, and another theme running through the book. There is a responsibility for coaches to create a positive learning environment for *all* participants and that the *only* way of achieving that is to adopt a 'developmental' approach to coaching that values each participant equally irrespective of sporting ability. Rather than merely focussing on winning and sport outcomes, we have a duty to offer support to everyone by praising prosocial behaviour, hard work, application and improvement. Developing 'perceived competence' in people is the third element of SDT and the advancement of intrinsic motivation. As Beedy (1997, p. 4) puts it 'your performers may forget what you say but they will never forget how you make them feel.'

## Considerations for coaching

It is undeniable that sport holds a position of high importance in contemporary society; its value and contribution goes way beyond measures of performance, vicarious entertainment and income generation. It is universally accepted as being a power for good through its contributions to multiple dimensions of health, community building, social integration, empowerment, reconciliation and harmonious co-existence. Widening opportunity to engage and achieve success in sport are often key agenda items for national and international bodies. For example, article 1 of the United Nations' International Charter asserts that 'the practice of physical education, physical activity and sport is a fundamental right for all' (UNESCO, 2015, p. 2), which includes inclusive, adapted and safe opportunities for 'all human beings' (UNESCO, 2015, p. 2). A recurring theme to this and many other policies, strategies and position statements are suitability, appropriateness and applicability of content for the positive engagement of diverse groups. Coaching is the vehicle through which many people experience sport and physical activity. Its objectives are often simple and clear, but its processes too often miss the key feature of speaking directly to participants.

To succeed in this respect, coaching must work harder to emerge from its White male power base in relation to organisational structure of coaching and the design of policy and practice. As Kamphoff and Gill (2015) contend, it is presently not acceptable to expect anyone who is not White and male to 'fit in' to sport systems. By and large, coaches often do not reflect the population that they are working with in terms of gender, ethnicity and class. One core principle of positive coach-participant relationships is that recipients of coaching must feel related to their surroundings, the activity, the coach and the context. They must feel a sense of belonging in their environment and kinship with their coach (Lafreniere et al., 2011). This text has cited multiple cases where positive coach-participant interaction is nurtured by commonality, mutual understanding and shared agendas.

The understanding and consideration of such non-sport features of the coaching environment may have a significant impact on the success of sport programmes (Hartmann, 2003). It is important to recognise the subtle but powerful components that enhance and sustain engagement which go beyond sport-specific content; factors such as the personal qualities of the leader (Nash & Sproule, 2009), positive inter-personal relationships (Sandford et al., 2006), suitable levels of autonomy (Felton & Jowett, 2013) and meeting the participation motives of distinct groups (Lee et al., 2013). If the benefits of sport are to be realised it is no longer sufficient to offer sport participation without deliberation on the *site* of participation. Indeed, without consideration of these situational factors and the application of a sound, evidence-based pedagogic approach, sport settings may actually be counter-productive to achieving desired goals. Coaching that is poorly framed and delivered could be worse than no coaching at all.

The nature of coaching research is a further consideration that can be drawn out of this text. We have presented multiple case studies of applied practice, some of which have been based on the research activity of the authors. Certain coaching populations are well researched, having been the subject of interest for many decades, others less so. It is natural that societal and demographic shifts provide relatively 'new' and fertile areas of interest for academics which have the potential to contribute to knowledge and application. Of growing concern to coaches and academics alike is the accessibility and relevance of coaching research to the applied domain (Lyle, 2018). Well reported in coaching literature is the so-called 'theory-practice gap' (Bush et al., 2013) and, in addition, the time-lag between research findings and application to practice (Farrow et al., 2008). Notwithstanding the production of research for research's sake and to meet institutional or contractual targets, a central purpose of sport coaching research must be to enhance the evidence-base that informs practising coaches currently carrying out their work. It is hardly surprising that coaches ignore or reject research that is laden with jargon and inaccessible language. One consequence of this is that there is disengagement between theory and practice, with the latter remaining fixed, traditional and failing to evolve in keeping with the needs of diverse groups. Bridging the 'gap' requires joint investment from all involved in coaching, whether in academia, policy or practice domains. For academics this could mean increased use of action research, context-specific case studies and investigations using naturalistic settings as possible good starting points to more practitioner compatible research (Lyle, 2018). The following sections will address the issue of how coaches and coach educators can engage with evidence-based practice and move their work forwards.

## Considerations for coach education

Sufficiently well-informed coach education which is open to keeping pace with new knowledge, and, in turn, can improve the quality of coaching interventions and participant outcomes must surely be the 'holy grail' for all with interest in the field. This new vision for coach education is likely to be undermined by the continued dominance of technical and tactical knowledge in accredited coaching courses and, thus, eventually in practice. This book has highlighted the absolute centrality of people, populations and context to successful coaching practice, and it is hoped that the messages will get through to stakeholders with responsibility for the design, delivery and accreditation of coach education. However, this is only likely if there is a collective effort from all sides of the 'gap' to unify research, education and practice.

Maintaining the *status quo* in coach education is not an option given the expanding policy, health and performance expectations on the sport and exercise industries (Ross et al., 2018). A fundamental rethink on the structure and content of National Governing Body (NGB) coach education programmes is required. Maintaining the existing state of affairs as far as academic coaching literature is concerned would be similarly futile for the long-term future of coaching. There have been calls for 'academic translations' (Lyle, 2018) and 'knowledge products' (Holt, 2016) which would offer applied versions of academic papers that can be easily understood in practice. Many of the contributors to this text are 'academic practitioners' who are able to merge theory and practice and hold positions in both domains. Regardless of affiliation to a particular sport, public or academic body, individuals with insight and experience who are current practitioners hold the key to finally bridging the 'gap.' This may require current NGB coach education departments to review the knowledge, experience and CPD status of their existing workforce and to reflect on the knowledge needed and actions required to bring it up to date. Those with responsibility for the education of future coaches should not sustain the influence of socialisation and acculturation which allows coach status to be determined by virtue of longevity in the field, social networking or having earned respect through distinguished sport performance.

Attempts to professionalise coaching have previously made an insignificant impact in this regard. It remains to be seen whether the Chartered Institute for the Management of Sport and Physical Activity (CIMSPA) professional standards add sufficient weight to the argument for change and unite stakeholders across knowledge *creation, education* and *action.* The drafting of specific standards aligned to context, people and populations is a strong starting point that must now be backed up with pressure on sports bodies and employers to recognise any shortfall in competence and knowledge of their workforce.

In England at least, there are bold statements of intent for the future of coaching (for example, Coaching in an Active Nation, Sport England 2016), where recognising the changing face of sport and physical activity and responding to participant needs are core themes. Contemporary coaching (and therefore coach education) needs a fully educated workforce that understands the importance of context to coaching methodology. A reconceptualisation of 'elite' coaching away from merely an alignment to being a coach of elite athletes, along with the redesign of pathways to elite coach status may be good starting points, for example, being considered an elite coach of primary-aged children, an elite coach of participants with learning disabilities, an elite sport for development coach working in divided societies or an elite grass-roots coach extend beyond the traditional viewpoint of the 'elite' label. To gain the knowledge required to acquire such status would require multiple coach education pathways that are not levelled purely on the basis of increasing depth of sport-specific content, content which is often of secondary importance to the knowledge needs of most coaches. Re-construction of the current single, linear, technocratic coach education 'levels' is long overdue as in many cases it is an antiquated approach which too often results in highly certified coaches operating in spheres where they have little understanding of people or context. Only then may we close the 'gap' and be more confident that future coaches will be open-minded and have a more robust set of approaches suitable to the environment that they operate in and the needs of the participants. They will then be equipped to coach the person in the activity, not merely impose the activity on the person.

## References

Beedy, J.P. (1997). *Sports plus: Positive learning using sports*. Hamilton: Project Adventure.

Bush, A., Silk, M., Andrews, D., and Lauder, H. (2013). *Sports coaching research: Context, consequences and consciousness*. London: Routledge.

Deci, E.L., and Ryan, R.M. (2000). 'The 'what' and 'why' of goal pursuits: Human needs and sel-determination of behaviour.' *Psychological Inquiry*, 11 (4), 227–268.

Farrow, D., Baker, J., and McMahon, C. (2008). *Developing sports expertise: Researchers and coaches put theory into practice*. London: Routledge.

Felton, L., and Jowett, S. (2013). '"What do coaches do" and "how do they relate": Their effects on athletes' psychological needs and functioning.' *Scandinavian Journal of Medicine and Science in Sports*, 23 (2), 130–139.

Hartmann, D. (2003). 'Theorising sport as social intervention: A view from the grassroots.' *Quest*, 55 (2), 118–140.

Holt, N.L. (2016). *Positive youth development through sport*. London: Routledge.

Kamphoff, C., and Gill, D. (2015). 'Issues of exclusion and discrimination in the coaching profession.' In: Gilbert, W., Denison, J., and Potrac, P., eds. *Routledge handbook of sports coaching*. London: Routledge, 52–66.

Lafreniere, M.K., Jowett, S., Vallerand, R.J., and Carbonneau, N. (2011). 'Passion for coaching and the quality of the coach-athlete relationship: The mediating role of coaching behaviours.' *Psychology of Sport and Exercise*, 12 (2), 144–152.

Lambert, J. (2013). 'How can we teach values through sport? Teaching values through sport in divided societies.' In: Whitehead, J., Telfer, H., and Lambert, J., eds. *Values in youth sport and physical education*. London: Routledge, 152–165.

Lee, M., Whitehead, J., and Balchin, N. (2013). 'Which sport values are most important to young people?' In: Whitehead, J., Telfer, H., and Lambert, J., eds. *Values in youth sport and physical education*. London: Routledge. 49-65.

Lyle, J. (2018). 'The transferability of sport coaching research: A critical commentary.' *Quest*, 70, 1–19.

Nash, C., and Sproule, J. (2009). 'Career development of expert coaches.' *International Journal of Sports Science and Coaching*, 4 (1), 121–138.

Ross, E., Gupta, L., and Sanders, L. (2018). 'When research leads to learning, but not action in high performance sport.' *Progress in Brain Research*, 240, 201–217.

Sandford, R., Armour, K., and Warmington, P. (2006). 'Re-engaging disaffected youth through physical activity programmes.' *British Educational Research Journal*, 32, 251–271.

United Nations Educational, Scientific and Cultural Organisation. (2015). *International charter of physical education, physical activity and sport*. Paris: UNESCO.

# Index

Note: page references in **bold** indicate tables; *italics* indicate figures.

Adapted Utilitarian Judo (JUA) for older adults 176–183, **177**, *178*, **179**, **181**, *182*, 185–186
ageing and physical activity 187–196; background 187–188; benefits of 188–191; endurance training 189–190, 194; intervention programme *192*, 192–196; nutrition 191, 195; physical performance 190–191; quality of life 191; recommendations 196; resistance training 190, 195; *see also* older adults and fear of falling
agencies, engagement with 202
Aggerholm, K. 49
Altay, Z. E. 182
Anderson, E. 126
Andrés, O.C. 49
Athanases, S. Z. 126
athlete-centred approach in disability coaching 131, 132–135
athletic motor skill competencies (AMSC) 31, 32
Atkinson, W. 65
autism spectrum disorder 143, 146
autonomy-support concept 203

ball projection machines 15–16
BAME (black, Asian and minority ethnic) coach recruitment 100–111; advertisements 103–104; applications 104–105; appointments 107–108; interviews 105–107; programmes and initiatives 102–103
banter 49–51, 122, 126, *126*
basketball, intellectual disability coaching 145, 147–156
Baysal, O. 182

Beedy, J. P. 203
belonging 118–119, 204
bias 116; racial 101, 109
Blackett, A. 7
BMX Freestyle coach education programme (case study) 60–70
Bota, A. 147
Bourdieu, P. 60, 64–69
boxing 47, 49, 54, 55–56
Bradbury, S. 101
Brazilian jiu jitsu (BJJ) 53
Bridge, M. W. 30
Brighton Table Tennis Club 87, 93, 95
bullying and the LGBT community 116–117
Bunker, D. 5, 151

Cachón Zagalaz, J. 182
Campos Mesa, M. C. 182
cancer rehabilitation, physical activity in 160–172; background 160–161; barriers and enablers to 166–167; benefits of 161–164, *162*, *163*; Cancer United™, CU Fitter™ exercise programme 166, 167–172, **169**; guidelines for 164–165; levels of 165; limitations 167
Carlsson, H. 49
Cassidy, T. 52, 54
Caudwell, J. 122
Chartered Institute for the Management of Sport and Physical Activity (CIMSPA) 2; professional standards 205
children and youth 24–34; Composite Youth Development Model (CYDM) 31, 32; Developmental Model of Sport Participation (DMSP) 29–30; developmental models overview 28–29;

## 210   Index

Long-Term Athlete Development (LTAD) model 28–29, 31; physical foundations 24–26; physical training 27; positive physical development 30–31; practice applications and recommendations 31–34, **33**; primary school education 26; Youth Physical Development Model (YPDM) 31, 32

Chow, J.-Y. 13

clock face game (cricket) 14

coach education programmes 6–7; BMX Freestyle (case study) 60–70; disability sport coaching 137–139; disadvantaged communities 61–64; future considerations for 205–206

coaches and coaching: contexts 1–3; future considerations for 201–204; *see also* environments, coaching

Coalter, F. 87

Cockman, M. 39

Comar, T. A. 126

combat sports *see* women in combat sports

community development through sport 86–88; *see also* disadvantaged communities

Composite Youth Development Model (CYDM) 31, 32

constraints-led approach (CLA) 17–19

content knowledge 1, 7, 202

Côté, J. 2, 7, 29, 149

cricket 133, 135; Rainbow Coaching System (RCS) in 11–12, *12*, 16–17; youth performance examples 14, 16–17, 18–19, 20

cultural awareness 95, 110

Cushion, C. 7, 137, 139

Deci, E. L. 202–203

DelCastillo-Andrés,O. 182

deliberate practice approach 9, 29

DePalma, R. 119

developmental approach 203

Developmental Model of Sport Participation (DMSP) 29–30

disability sport coaching 3, 131–139; athlete-centred approach 131, 132–135; coach education 137–139; empowerment discourse in 132–135; medical-model perspective 134–135; recommendations 139; social relational model 136–137, 139n1; *see also* intellectual disability coaching

disadvantaged communities 60–70; key messages for development in 69–70;

non-linear pedagogy 60, 62–64, 70; sociological framework of Bourdieu (habitus, field, social capital) 64–69; source coach education programme 61–64; sport for development programme 60–61

discrimination: in BAME coach recruitment 101; against LGBT youth 115–120; against women 47–48, 49

diversity 2–3, 114, 203–204

Durmus, B. 182

dyslexia/dyscalculia 143

early specialisation approach 9–10

ecological approaches 5, 13, 15, 17

elite performance 29, 206

emotional sensitivity 88–89

empathy 92, 170, 202

empowerment in disability sport coaching 132–135

English Football League (EFL), BAME coach recruitment 102–111

English Learning Disability Sporting Alliance (ELDSA) 144

environments, coaching 15, 18, 19, 202, 204; creating inclusive 85–88, 90–91, 94–96; *see also* safe spaces

equity 51, 113–115, 121, 123, 124, 136, 202–203

Ericsson, K.A. 9

Ersoy, Y. 182

female combat athletes *see* women in combat sports

field (sociological concept) 65, 67–69

Fitzgerald, H. 136–137

Fletcher, R. 65

football 39, 42–43, 85–86, 94–96; BAME coach recruitment 100–111

Football 4 Peace (F4P) International 202; F4P *vs.* homophobia (F4PvH) campaign (case study) 121–122; 'Off-pitch Manual' 93

former athletes as coaches 6, 7

Fraser-Thomas, J. 29

fun 32

Gallahue, D. 25

games 14, 92–93, 95, 124; teaching games for understanding (TGfU) 151–153

gender inequalities 49–50, 87; *see also* women in combat sports

German sports clubs, volunteer work with refugees within (case study) 72–83

## Index 211

Gilbert, W. 2, 7, 149
Gill, D. 203
Goodway, J. 25
Gordon, S. 114
Gould, D. 94–95
Green, K. 3
Green, M. 61
Guérandel, C. 54
Gullich, A. 30
Gunter, K. 27

habitus 65–66
Hagedorn, D. K. 183
heteronormative culture 118–119
hockey 30
holistic coaching 10
Holm, E. 183
Howe, P. D. 133
Huizinga, J. 90
humour in combat sport environments 49–51

immersive training environments 15
inclusion 2, 202–203; female combat athletes 47, 51, 54; LGBT youth 114–115, 118–125; participants with disabilities 136–138; participants with intellectual disabilities 150; refugees 88
information and movement coupling 15–17
intellectual disability coaching 142–157; associated disabilities 146–147; barriers to participation 146–147; clinical differences among participants 153–154; coach Jon Stonebridge (in practice examples) 147–156; communication considerations 154; constraints-led approach (CLA) 150–151; cues and instruction 154–155; defining intellectual disability 142–143, 157n1; intellectual disability beyond sport 146–147; knowledge acquisition in 153–156; participation pathways (recreational, high-performance) 143–145; professional knowledge and pedagogy 149–153; teaching games for understanding (TGfU) 151–153
International Federation for Athletes with Intellectual Impairments (INAS) Global Games 144–145
interpersonal knowledge 7, 149–150, 152, 154, 156
Ishiko, T. 27

Jennett, M. 119
Jones, R. 149
Jones, R.L. 7
judo 47

Kamphoff, C. 203
Kato, S. 27
Khan, N. 92
kickboxing 47, 50–51
Kohe, G.Z. 3

Lafferty, Y. 54
language use: BMX Freestyle coach education programme (case study) 67–68; in female combat sport environments 49–51; with LGBT youth 125–127, *126*; with refugees 92
Lave, J. 119
Lawson, H. A. 6–7
Lee, M. 38–45
LGBT (lesbian, gay, bisexual, and transgender) youth 113–127; bullying 116–117; discrimination against 115–120; Football 4 Peace International, F4P *vs.* homophobia (F4PvH) campaign (case study) 121–122; language 125–127, *126*; role of teachers, coaches and peers 119–120; safe spaces 122–125
Little League Baseball 28
Lloyd, R. S. 31–32
Long-Term Athlete Development (LTAD) model 28–29, 31
long-term sport programmes 94
Lopes, V. P. 25

MacWalter, R. S. 182
Martens, R. 28
Martin, J. 3
McCormack, M. 125–126
McDonough, P. M. 65
McKay, J. 54
Mennsesson, C. 54
mental health of LGBT youth 117–118
mental illness 143, 146
mentoring 202
Meuser, M. 75
Moody, J. M. 31
motor skill competence 25–26, 30–32
movement competence 31–32
Murray, D. 96

Nagel, U. 75
Nathan, S. 96

## 212  Index

National Disability Sports Organisations (NDSOs) 144
National Strength and Conditioning Association (NSCA) 27
Navarro, Z. 65
Newell, K. M. 17
Nichols, K. 49
Noble, G. 65
non-linear pedagogy 11, 60, 62–64, 70; in youth performance coaching 10, 13, 18, 20

obesity 24–25
older adults and fear of falling 175–183, **177**, *178*, 190; Adapted Utilitarian Judo (JUA) programme 176–183, **179**, **181**, *182*, 185–186; key terms 185–186; *see also* ageing and physical activity
outcomes, education, LGBT youth 117–118
Ozmun, L. 25

parasport *see* disability sport coaching
participants, knowledge and needs of 3, 7, 88, 95, 153–154, 196, 201, 202
people with intellectual disabilities (PwID) *see* intellectual disability coaching
perceived competence 203
perception and action coupling 15–17
person-centred perspective 202–203
Peters, D.M. 3
Petocz, P. 114
physical foundations for children and youth 24–26
physical inactivity 24–26
play-based activity 29
political correctness 50–51
Powell, L. 175
power relations 87, 89, 131, 134–137; *see also* empowerment
Powis, B. 133, 135
primary school education 26
professional knowledge 7, 149–153
professional standards 2, 205
Purdue, D. E. J. 133

Rainbow Coaching System (RCS) 11–13, *12*, 16–17
recruitment processes 7; of BAME coaches 100–111
refugee engagement through sport 85–97; and community development 86–88;

emotional sensitivity in coaching 88–89, 91; positive social interaction 88, 92–95; trauma-informed approach 87, 88, 89–92, 94
Reid, A. 114
Renshaw, I. 62–63, 150
reproductive coaching 8
resistance training in youth populations 27, 32
respect 49, 50, 52, 68, 88, 93, 95, 123–124, 154, 202
Rhinehart, R. 66
Richmond, D. 175
role models for LGBT youth 119, 120, 122, 124–125, 127
Ronglan, L.T. 49
rowing 145
Royal Mencap Society 143–144
Ryan, R. M. 202, 203

safe spaces 85, 91–92, 96, 202; LGBT youth advocacy 122–125
scheduling 94
Schijndel-Speet, Van 146–147
Schulenkorf, N. 93, 123
Schwartz, S. 39
self 119
Self-Determination Theory (SDT) 202–203
self-esteem 90, 96
sexism 49
sexuality, assumptions about female combat athletes 51–54
Situated Learning theory 119
'6-ball challenge' (cricket) 14
skateboarding coach education programme (case study) 60–70
Skinner, J. 65
Smith, A. 3, 26
soccer *see* football
social capital 65, 68–69
social divisions 92–93
social interaction, positive 88, 92–95
social relational model in disability sport coaching 136–137, 139n1
socialisation of coaches 6–7
Spaaij, R. 123
Spacey, G. 122
Special Olympics Great Britain (SOGB) 143–145
specialisation, early 29–31
Spectrum of Teaching Styles 8
Sport England, Coaching Plan for England (2017–2021) 2

Sport for Development (SfD) 61, 69, 86–96, 202–203
sport values of young people 38–45; identifying 39–40, **40**; implications for coaches and significant others 42–45; relative importance of 40–41, *42*; sport-specific scenarios 42–44
squats 31–32
stereotype threat 50
stereotyping: BAME coaches 101, 109; women in combat sports 49–50, 52, 54–57
Stone, C. 90, 91, 93, 94
Stout, L. 164
Sugden, J. 96
Syed, M. 9
table tennis 87, 93, 95

Tai-Chi 182
Tawse, H. 134
teaching games for understanding (TGfU) 5; in intellectual disability coaching 151–153
technocratic coaching 8–9
tennis 39, 43–44
Teodorescu, S. 147
Thomas, C. 137
Thorpe, R. 5, 151
three-cone rotation game (cricket) 14
Tinetti, M. E. 175
Tomlinson, A. 64
Toms, M.R. 30
Toronjo, T. 182
Toronjo-Hornillo, L. 182
Toronjo-Urquiza, M. 182
Townsend, R. 133, 134, 135, 137, 138, 139
trauma-informed approach 87, 88, 89–92, 94
trust 94–95, 124

values, sport *see* sport values of young people
Van Waart, H. 162
Vand der Bij, A. 193
voluntary work with refugees within sport clubs (case study) 72–83; changes within

sport clubs 76–77; context 73–75; difficulties 77–78; new members and volunteers/'socially committed volunteers' 78–79, 81–82; recommendations 79–82; sports club members 75–76

Wacquant, L. 66
Watkins, M. 65
Wenger, E. 119
Whelan, L. 3
Whitehead, Jean 45
Whitley, M. 94–95
women in combat sports 47–57; language and humour in sport environment 49–51; sexuality, assumptions about 51–54; stereotyping as outsiders and intruders 49, 54–57
workplaces, coaching 7, 101, 109, 110

Yap, A. 55
young people *see* children and youth; sport values of young people; youth performance
youth performance 5–21; background and context 5; (re)connecting performer and environment 13–14; constraints-led approach (CLA)/manipulating constraints 17–19; coupling perception and action (information and movement) 15–17; deliberate practice approach 9; early specialisation approach 9–10; examples in cricket 14, 16–17, 18–19, 20; non-linear pedagogy 11, 13; progressive approaches to developing 10–13; Rainbow Coaching System (RCS) 11–13, *12*, 16–17; reproductive coaching 8; stability and instability balancing 19–20; technocratic coaching 8–9; traditional approaches 5–7; traditional approaches and their limitations 8–10, 13
Youth Physical Development Model (YPDM) 31, 32
Youth Sport Value Questionnaire (YSVQ) 41